Essential Test Tips Video from Trivium Test Prep

Dear Customer,

Thank you for purchasing from Trivium Test Prep! Whether you're looking to join the military, get into college, or advance your career, we're honored to be a part of your journey.

To show our appreciation (and to help you relieve a little of that test-prep stress), we're offering a **FREE CSET *Essential Test Tips* Video** by Trivium Test Prep. Our video includes 35 test preparation strategies that will help keep you calm and collected before and during your big exam. All we ask is that you email us your feedback and describe your experience with our product. Amazing, awful, or just so-so: we want to hear what you have to say!

To receive your **FREE *CSET Essential Test Tips* Video**, please email us at 5star@triviumtestprep.com. Include "Free 5 Star" in the subject line and the following information in your email:

1. The title of the product you purchased.
2. Your rating from 1 – 5 (with 5 being the best).
3. Your feedback about the product, including how our materials helped you meet your goals and ways in which we can improve our products.
4. Your full name and shipping address so we can send your **FREE *CSET Essential Test Tips* Video**.

If you have any questions or concerns please feel free to contact us directly at 5star@triviumtestprep.com.

Thank you, and good luck with your studies!

CSET Multiple Subject Test Prep
2 Practice Exams and CSET Study Guide for California

Eric Canizales

Copyright ©2023 Trivium Test Prep

ISBN-13: 9781637983546

ALL RIGHTS RESERVED. By purchase of this book, you have been licensed on copy for personal use only. No part of this work may be reproduced, redistributed, or used in any form or by any means without prior written permission of the publisher and copyright owner. Trivium Test Prep; Accepted, Inc.; Cirrus Test Prep; and Ascencia Test Prep are all imprints of Trivium Test Prep, LLC.

Federal Motor Carrier Safety Administration (FMCSA) and Department of Transportation (DOT) were not involved in the creation or production of this product, is not in any way affiliated with Trivium Test Prep, and does not sponsor or endorse this product.

Image(s) used under license from Shutterstock.com

Table of Contents

Introduction i
What is the CSET? i
What's on the CSET English exam? i
How is the CSET Multiple Subjects exam scored? iv
How is the CSET Multiple Subjects exam administered? iv
About Cirrus Test Prep iv

1. Reading, Language, and Literature 1
Foundations of Language 1
English Language Development and Acquisition 5
English Language Development and Acquisition for Non-Native Speakers 6
Literacy Development 13
Fluency 14
Assessment 17
Conventions of Language 22
Literature and Informational Texts 29
Reading Literature and Informational Texts 34
Writing 37
Research 42
Non-Written Communication 46
Answer Key 50

2. History and Social Science 52
World History 52
United States History 73
Early California History 88
From the Gold Rush to the Present 94
Other Social Studies Topics 101
Answer Key 116

3. Science 119
Physical Science 119
Life Science 130
Earth and Space Science 148
Science Skills and Processes 156
Answer Key 160

4. Math 162
Number Sense 162
Algebraic Thinking 171
Geometry and Measurement 185
Math in Research 196
Answer Key 204

5. Physical Education and Human Development 208
Basic Movement Skills 208
Exercise Physiology 209
Health 211
Physical Education and Social Development 212
Answer Key 214

6. Visual and Performing Arts 215
Dance 215
Music 216
Theatre 220
Visual Arts 221
Answer Key 224

Practice Test #1 225
Subtest I: Reading, Language, and Literature 225
Subtest II: History and Social Science 231
Subtest III: Science 235
Subtest IV: Mathematics 241
Subtest V: Physical Education 249
Subtest VI: Human Development 252
Subtest VII: Visual and Performing Arts 254

Practice Test #1 Answer Key 257
Subtest I: Reading, Language, and Literature 257
Subtest II: History and Social Science 259
Subtest III: Science 261
Subtest IV: Mathematics 263
Subtest V: Physical Education 267
Subtest VI: Human Development 268
Subtest VII: Visual and Performing Arts 269

Online Resources 271

Online Resources

Trivium includes online resources with the purchase of this study guide to help you fully prepare for the exam.

Practice Tests

In addition to the practice test included in this book, we also offer an online exam. Since many exams today are computer based, practicing your test-taking skills on the computer is a great way to prepare.

Review Questions

Need more practice? Our review questions use a variety of formats to help you memorize key terms and concepts.

Flash Cards

Trivium's flash cards allow you to review important terms easily on your computer or smartphone.

Cheat Sheets

Review the core skills you need to master the exam with easy-to-read Cheat Sheets.

From Stress to Success

Watch "From Stress to Success," a brief but insightful YouTube video that offers the tips, tricks, and secrets experts use to score higher on the exam.

Reviews

Leave a review, send us helpful feedback, or sign up for Trivium promotions—including free books!

Access these materials at:

cirrustestprep.com/cset-multiple-online-resources

Introduction

Congratulations on choosing to take the CSET Multiple Subjects exam! By purchasing this book, you've taken the first step toward becoming a teacher in California.

This guide will provide you with a detailed overview of the CSET Multiple Subjects exam, so you will know exactly what to expect on test day. We'll take you through all of the concepts covered on the test and give you the opportunity to evaluate your knowledge with practice questions. Even if it's been a while since you last took a major test, don't worry; we'll make sure you're more than ready!

What is the CSET?

The California Subject Examinations for Teachers: Multiple Subjects exam is a criterion-referenced test used to assess the subject-matter expertise of prospective elementary or special education teachers.

What's on the CSET English exam?

The exam contains both multiple-choice and constructed-response questions. It is broken into four subtests:

Subtest I: Reading, Language, and Literature; History and Social Science

Reading, Language, and Literature

There are 26 multiple choice questions covering the following subtopics:

- Language Structure and Linguistics
- Language Development and Acquisition
- Literacy
- Assessment
- Conventions of Language
- Writing Strategies
- Writing Applications
- Non-Written Communication
- Research to Build and Present Knowledge
- Reading Literature
- Reading Informational Text
- Text Complexity

There are 2 short, constructed-response questions (answers of 100 – 200-words).

History and Social Science

There are 26 multiple-choice questions covering the following subtopics:

- Ancient Civilizations
- Medieval and Early Modern Times
- The United States: Early Exploration, Colonial Era, and the War for Independence
- The United States: The Development of the Constitution and the Early Republic
- The United States: Civil War and Reconstruction
- The United States: The Rise of Industrial America
- California: The Pre-Columbian Period through the Gold Rush
- California: Economic, Political and Cultural Development Since the 1850s

There are 2 short, constructed-response questions (answers of 100 – 200 words).

Subtest II: Science and Mathematics

Science

There are 26 multiple-choice questions covering the following subtopics:

- Structure and Properties of Matter
- Principles of Motion and Energy
- Structure of Living Organisms and Their Function (Cell biology)
- Living and Nonliving Components in Environments (Ecology)
- Life Cycle, Reproduction, and Evolution (Genetics and Evolution)
- The Solar System and the Universe (Astronomy)
- The Structure and Composition of the Earth (Geology)
- The Earth's Atmosphere (Meteorology)
- The Earth's Water (oceanography)

There are 2 short, constructed-response questions (answers of 100 – 200-words).

Mathematics

There are 26 multiple-choice questions covering the following subtopics:

- Numbers, Relationships Among Numbers, and Number Systems
- Computational Tools, Procedures, and Strategies
- Patterns and Functional Relationships
- Linear and Quadratic Equations and Inequalities
- Two-and-Three Dimensional Geometric Objects
- Representational Systems, Including Concrete Models, Drawings, and Coordinate Geometry
- Techniques, Tools, and Formulas for Determining Measurements
- Collection, Organization, and Representation of Data

- Inferences, Predictions, and Arguments Based on Data
- Basic Notions of Chance and Probability

There are 2 short, constructed-response questions (answers of 100 – 200 words).

Subtest III: Physical Education, Human Development, and Visual and Performing Arts

<u>Physical Education</u>

There are 13 multiple-choice questions covering the following subtopics:

- Basic Movement Skills
- Exercise Physiology: Health and Physical Fitness
- Movement Forms: Content Areas
- Physical Growth and Development
- Self-Image
- Social Aspects of Physical Education
- Cultural and Historical Aspects of Movement Forms

There is 1 short, constructed-response question (answer of 100 – 200 words).

<u>Human Development</u>

There are 13 multiple-choice questions covering the following subtopics:

- Cognitive Development
- Social Development
- Physical Development
- Influences on Development

There is 1 short, constructed-response question (answer of 100-200 words)

<u>Visual and Performing Arts</u>

There are 13 multiple-choice questions covering the following subtopics:

- Dance: Movement
- Dance: Technical Skills
- Dance: Analysis
- Music: Elements of Music
- Music: Musical Ideas and Connections
- Music: Selecting Music
- Theatre: Creating a Story
- Theatre: Improvisation and Design
- Theatre: Contextual Analysis
- Visual Art: Tools, Materials, and Techniques

- Visual Arts: Connections and Value
- Visual Arts: Purposes

There is 1 short, constructed-response question (answer of 100 – 200 words).

How is the CSET Multiple Subjects exam scored?

Multiple-choice items are scored by a machine, and constructed-response items are scored by at least two California educators. Constructed-response items are scored on a scale of 1 – 3 using a holistic rubric based on alignment to purpose, subject matter knowledge, and support.

Raw scores are first calculated, and then scores are transformed to scaled scores from 100 – 300. An overall score of 220 is the passing score for each subtest. Scores per subtest are valid for up to ten years. Once each subtest is passed, examinees do not need to take that subtest again in the event that portions of the exam must be retaken because all parts were not passed. Results are released within five weeks of the test date.

How is the CSET Multiple Subjects exam administered?

The CSET is a computer-based exam available at testing centers and through online proctoring during certain testing windows. A basic four-function, on-screen calculator is provided for Subtest II. Examinees are given 3 hours to complete Subtest I, 3 hours to complete Subtest II, and 2 hours and 15 minutes to complete Subtest III. If all tests are taken together, 5 uninterrupted hours of testing time are provided.

About Cirrus Test Prep

Cirrus Test Prep study guides are designed by current and former educators and are tailored to meet your needs as an incoming educator. Our guides offer all of the resources necessary to help you pass teacher certification tests across the nation.

Cirrus clouds are graceful, wispy clouds characterized by their high altitude. Just like cirrus clouds, Cirrus Test Prep's goal is to help educators "aim high" when it comes to obtaining their teacher certifications and entering the classroom. We're pleased you've chosen Cirrus to be a part of your professional journey!

1. Reading, Language, and Literature

Foundations of Language

Human Language

Human language varies among cultures throughout the world, but all languages share some similarities:

- All languages are learned by human babies at roughly the same time, regardless of location.
- All languages also have basic rules or—**grammar**—that specifies how words should be put together:
    - Languages from anywhere in the world have a way for people to communicate when in time an action occurs.
    - The ways in which this time is indicated—through verb conjugation, word endings, or separate words that indicate when an action occurs—vary widely.
- All languages also have formal and casual, or slang forms as well as various dialects and accents:
    - Dialects and accents may be particular to a certain geographic location or group in a society.
    - In contrast to a dialect is an **idiolect**, which is a particular language form or structure used solely by one individual.

Furthermore, all languages are rooted in the context of their use. **Pragmatics** is the study of language within its context. Language can also be studied in terms of

- **phonology** (the organization of sounds);
- **morphology** (the study of words and their parts);
- **syntax** (how words combine to form groups like phrases, clauses, and sentences); and
- **semantics** (the study of what words mean or to what they refer).

Practice Question

1) Which statement describes how all languages are similar?
   A. They use verb conjugation.
   B. They are learned at roughly the same time.
   C. They are spoken in a single accent.
   D. They use words to show when an action occurs.

Morphology

As noted, morphology is the study of words and word parts, known as **morphemes**. Morphemes come in various types, as described in Table 1.1.

Table 1.1. Types of Morphemes		
Type	Definition	Examples
Free morphemes	• words used on their own	*help, go, big*
Bound morphemes	• those which must be added to another morpheme	*-ly, -ing, un-*
Derivational morphemes	• affixes (prefixes and suffixes) that, when added to another word, create a new word • essential building blocks of the English language • added to base words in English or **roots**, often derived from Latin or Greek	prefixes: *un-, re-, pre-* suffixes: *-able, -ive, -ion*
Inflectional morphemes	• denote a plural or tense but do not make an entirely new word or change the word to a new part of speech	*-s, -ed, -ing*

Related to morphology is **etymology**, the study of the history or origin of words. It often focuses on tracing the root word back to its origin and meaning.

> **Did You Know?**
>
> English words that come from French or German words often originated from Latin words. The great majority of English words therefore have true Greek or Latin origins.

With roots and affixes, or derivational morphemes, new words are formed. For example, *cent* is a Latin root meaning "one hundred." **Affixes** are added to words or roots to change their meanings. For example, the prefix *per-* can be added to *cent* to make the word *percent*, effectively changing the meaning to "one part in a hundred." Likewise, the suffix *–ury* can be added to *cent* to make the word *century*, effectively changing the meaning to "a period of one hundred years."

Table 1.2. Common Roots and Affixes

Root	Definition	Example
ast(er)	star	asteroid, astronomy
audi	hear	audience, audible
auto	self	automatic, autograph
bene	good	beneficent, benign
bio	life	biology, biorhythm
cap	take	capture
ced	yield	secede
chrono	time	chronometer, chronic
corp	body	corporeal
crac/crat	rule	autocrat
demo	people	democracy
dict	say	dictionary, dictation
duc	lead/make	ductile, produce
gen	give birth	generation, genetics
geo	Earth	geography, geometry
grad	step	graduate
graph	write	graphical, autograph
ject	throw	eject
jur/jus	law	justice, jurisdiction
log or logue	thought	logic, logarithm

Table 1.2. Common Roots and Affixes

Root	Definition	Example
luc	light	lucidity
man	hand	manual
mand	order	remand
mis	send	transmission
mono	one	monotone
omni	all	omnivore
path	feel	pathology
phil	love	philanthropy
phon	sound	phonograph
port	carry	export
qui	rest	quiet
scrib or script	write	scribe, transcript
sense or sent	feel	sentiment
tele	far away	telephone
terr	the earth	terrace
uni	single	unicode
vac	empty	vacant
vid	see	video
vis	see	vision

Practice Questions

2) Use roots and affixes to determine the meaning of the underlined word:

Monograph most nearly means

A. a mathematical concept.
B. a written study of a single subject.
C. an illness caused by a virus.
D. a boring piece of art.

3) Use roots and affixes to determine the meaning of the underlined word:
My sister is a polyglot and comfortably travels all over the world.

A. a person who speaks many language
B. a person who loves to travel
C. a person who is extremely intelligent
D. a person who is unafraid of new places

English Language Development and Acquisition

Language acquisition is the process through which humans develop the ability to understand and create words and sentences to communicate. Many experts believe that children have an innate ability to acquire **oral language** from their environments. Even before babies can speak, they cry and coo in reaction to environmental stimuli or to communicate their needs. They recognize basic variants in the speech patterns of those around them, such as **articulation**, defined as the distinct sounds of speech; they can also identify contrasts when exposed to new languages. With this awareness, cooing and crying quickly turn into **babbling**, the first stage of language acquisition. This stage generally lasts from six months to around twelve months. In this stage, infants make a variety of sounds but may begin to focus on sounds for which they receive positive reinforcement. For example, babbles such as *baba* and *yaya* tend to garner praise and excitement from parents, so these may be repeated until the coveted *mama* or *dada* is produced.

> **Did You Know?**
>
> Ninety-five percent of all babbling by babies throughout the world is composed of only twelve consonants: *p, b, t, d, k, g, m, n, s, h, w, j.*

At around one year old (varying from child to child), children start using first words, usually nouns. During this single-word stage, or **holophrastic stage**, these solitary words are generally used to express entire ideas. For example, "Toy!" may mean "Give me the toy." After a few months, this shifts to two-word utterances such as "Mommy go" or "David bad." The **two-word stage** may last through early toddlerhood but generally gives rise to the **telegraphic phase** of oral language development at around age two and a half. In this stage, speech patterns become more advanced, though sometimes prepositions, articles, and other short words are missing. Telegraphic speech includes phrases such as "See plane go!" and "There go teacher." This stage persists until children are mostly fluent in the home language, generally at age three or four.

Practice Question

4) A young child utters "go" to ask to go to the playground. In which stage of language development is this child?
   A. babbling
   B. two-word stage
   C. telegraphic phase
   D. holophrastic stage

English Language Development and Acquisition for Non-Native Speakers

Not all students learn English as their first language, and some may have **limited English proficiency**, which is a limited ability to read, speak, write, or understand English because it is not one's primary language.

Since early childhood is when students best learn new languages, many schools have programs designed to develop **dual language learners**, which are defined as those who are learning two languages simultaneously. This may take the form of a language immersion program where young children who speak English are placed in an environment where another language is spoken for part or most of the day. These programs are generally made up of students with a monolingual English background and students with some proficiency in a second language, with the goal of having students develop both languages through classroom instruction and social interaction with their peers.

Dual language programs can also take another form where students who speak only English at home are placed in a completely immersive environment to quickly become proficient in a second language. These programs have become very popular in many large cities as the need for a workforce that is fluent in more than one language continues to grow.

Children whose home languages are not English will be dual language learners in most typical, majority-English education programs. These young children, who are still developing skills in their home languages as part of the natural arc of child development, will also be developing skills in a second language. Teachers working with dual language learners must promote English language skills while supporting the ongoing development of the children's home languages. This **bilingualism**, or the ability to fluently speak two languages, is a huge benefit to the child and should therefore be nurtured. Children who develop two or more languages simultaneously have been found to have advantages in social-emotional development, early language and literacy, and overall cognitive development.

These students should also be encouraged to pursue **biliteracy**, or the ability to proficiently read and write in two languages. While language immersion programs will likely offer this component explicitly, all teachers can encourage students and families to read and write in both English and their home languages as appropriate so as to develop these proficiencies. Some districts and schools offer classroom curriculum resources in languages other than English to encourage this, and many educational publishers and technology companies offer resources in commonly spoken second languages, such as Spanish. Above all, when there are students who are learning English, teachers should not push them to discard or stop developing their heritage languages.

Children who are learning two languages may engage in **code-switching**, or alternating between two languages or dialects. It occurs most often in children when they begin a sentence in one language but complete it in another. This is a somewhat remarkable thing, and it shows that these children are maintaining grammatical rules in both languages. Code-switching is natural, normal, and expected, and it is no cause for concern. Rather than chiding students for code-switching, teachers should use these opportunities to expand students' vocabulary and knowledge in both languages, dependent, of course, on the teacher's proficiency in the children's native languages. Constantly correcting students for code-switching undermines their overall development and does not validate their need to communicate.

Students in the primary grades who have already developed fluency in their home languages but who have limited English proficiency are not considered dual language learners but rather **English language learners (ELLs)**, which are defined as students who need specialized instruction in English and other academic subject areas due to a lack of English proficiency. Instruction for these students will also vary considerably based on the program; however, most research suggests that best practices include helping students obtain English proficiency quickly while providing appropriate support and differentiation so that students can continue learning across content areas. It is important for teachers, especially of young students who may feel nervous in a new environment at first, to make English language learners feel comfortable in the classroom. Teachers can do that through strategies such as using visuals and predictable routines and by not forcing students to speak until they are ready.

> **Helpful Hint**
>
> Interlanguage effects can be thought of as rules that may or may not always be true and that may have been learned when trying to acquire a second language. For example, many people learning Spanish are taught that nouns ending in –*o* are masculine and nouns ending in –*a* are feminine. While a helpful rule, there are exceptions. For example, the word *el mapa* is a masculine noun that ends with –*a*.

Some students will go through a **silent period** where they may not speak much, and this is normal when learning a new language. Students may also be reluctant to practice newly acquired English language skills for fear of making mistakes, so teachers should make sure the classroom is a safe space where all attempts to use the new language are validated and praised.

The acquisition of a second language should not always be viewed as a linear progression. When students acquire a second language, they also develop what is known as an **interlanguage**, or a system of rules for the use of the new language. Interlanguage can be based on the rules of the student's first language or the rules of both the first and new languages. It can even be based on features of neither language. **Interlanguage effects** can therefore sometimes work against second-language development if based on erroneous assumptions or nonexistent patterns.

Five **stages of language acquisition** have been identified for students learning a second language (see Table 1.3.). These stages are defined as preproduction, early production, speech emergence, intermediate fluency, and advanced fluency and correlate to five **levels of language proficiency:**

- L1 (entering)
- L2 (beginning)
- L3 (developing)
- L4 (expanding)
- L5 (bridging)

Table 1.3. Stages of Second-Language Acquisition	
Stage	Characteristics
Preproduction	Preproduction is also known as the silent period. Though these learners may have close to 500 words in their receptive vocabularies, they refrain from speaking but will listen and may copy words down. They can respond to visual cues (i.e., pictures and gestures) and communicate their comprehension; however, students will sometimes just repeat what they have heard—a process known as parroting. Parroting aids students in adding to their receptive vocabularies, but it should not be mistaken for producing language.
Early production	In this stage, learners have achieved 1,000-word receptive and active vocabularies. They now produce single-word and two- to three-word phrases and can respond to questions and statements. Many learners in this stage enjoy engaging in musical games or word plays that help them memorize language chunks that they can use later.
Speech emergence	English language learners have a vocabulary of about 3,000 words by the time they reach this stage of second-language acquisition. They are able to chunk simple words and phrases into sentences that may or may not be grammatically correct. They respond to modeling of correct responses better than direct correction. At this stage, learners are also more likely to participate in conversations with native speakers since they are gaining confidence in their language skills. These learners can understand simple readings when reinforced by graphics or pictures and can complete some content work with support.
Intermediate fluency	By the intermediate fluency stage, second-language learners have acquired a vocabulary of about 6,000 words. They are able to speak in more complex sentences and catch and correct many of their errors. They are also willing to ask questions to clarify what they do not understand. Learners at

Table 1.3. Stages of Second-Language Acquisition

Stage	Characteristics
	this stage may sound fluent, but they have large gaps in their vocabulary as well as in their grammatical and syntactical understanding of the language. They are often comfortable speaking in group conversations that avoid heavy academic language.
Advanced Fluency	Second-language learners who reach advanced fluency have achieved cognitive language proficiency in their learned language. They demonstrate near-native ability and use complex, multi phrase, and clause sentences to convey their ideas. Though accents are still detectable and idiomatic expressions are sometimes used incorrectly, the language learner has essentially become fluent.

Practice Question

5) Marlin enjoys participating in class discussions with his peers and even initiates them occasionally. Though he sometimes makes errors in his speech, he is able to self-correct and often repeats the correct phrasing back to himself. In which stage of second-language acquisition might Marlin be?
   A. preproduction
   B. early production
   C. speech emergence
   D. intermediate fluency

Language Structure and Literacy Foundations

Humans learn language in predictable patterns that often combine speaking, reading, and writing. Such language development typically begins with an understanding of sounds.

Phonological Awareness is an understanding of how sounds, syllables, words, and word parts can be orally manipulated to break apart words, make new words, and create rhymes. It is an important foundational skill for learning to read and literacy development. **Phonemic awareness** is a type of phonological awareness that focuses on the sounds in a language. It is an understanding of how each small unit of sound, or **phoneme**, forms the language by creating differences in the meanings of words.

For example, the phonemes /m/ and /s/ determine the difference in meaning between the words *mat* and *sat*.

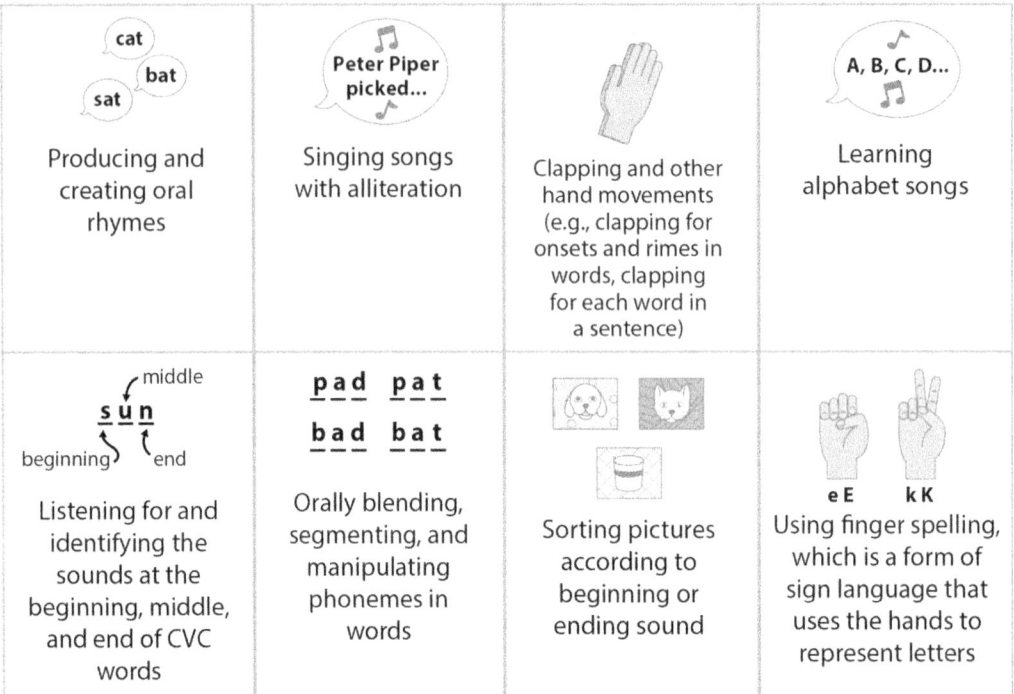

Figure 1.1. Phonological Awareness Strategies

There are forty-four different phonemes in the English language. These include letter combinations such as consonant diagraphs (e.g., /sh/) and vowel diphthongs (e.g., /oi/) where the letters work together to produce one sound. Teachers build phonemic awareness in their students by using a variety of techniques, such as phoneme blending, phoneme segmentation, phoneme substitution, and phoneme deletion.

Phoneme blending is combining phonemes to make a word; for example, /m/ /a/ /t/ combines to form *mat*. **Phoneme segmentation** is separating phonemes into words. For example, separating the sounds in the word *mat* isolates the phonemes /m/ /a/ /t/.

Building phonemic awareness in students is the latter part of a developmental sequence that contributes to a strong foundation in phonological awareness. Prior to focusing on phonemic awareness, teachers build phonological awareness with exercises that task students with orally manipulating the phonological units of spoken **syllables**. These phonological units are defined as onsets and rimes and can be blended, substituted, segmented, and deleted just like phonemes. The **onset** of a syllable is the beginning consonant or consonant blend. The **rime** includes the syllable's vowel and its remaining consonants. For example, in the word *block*, the consonant blend /bl/ is the onset, and the remainder of the word –*ock* is the rime.

The **alphabetic principle** presumes an understanding that words are made up of written letters or symbols that represent spoken sounds. In order to procced with more advanced reading concepts, children must first have a firm grasp of letter sounds.

Once students have a solid foundation in phonological awareness, they are ready to begin phonics instruction. **Phonics** is the study of the relationship between the spoken sounds in words and the printed letters that correspond to those sounds, or **letter-sound correspondence**, sometimes referred to as **sound-symbol correspondence**. In explicit phonics instruction, letters and their corresponding sounds are first taught in isolation, then blended into words, and finally applied to decodable text.

> **Helpful Hint**
> Remember that onsets are the first part of the word, or the first "button" readers see— the "ON" button. Rimes are the parts of the word that rhyme such as c-*at*, h-*at*, b-*at*, and so on.

Phonics instruction draws on the strategy of **decoding**, or the ability to pronounce the sounds of written words orally and glean meaning. Because of its focus on the specific sound structures of words, phonics instruction tends to involve more explicit, direct instruction and is not without critics, who believe it overemphasizes the mechanics of reading while sacrificing the enjoyment. However, most classrooms today employ a combination approach that balances inquiry-based student learning, allowing for the open exploration of high-interest literacy games and activities, with more direct instruction when necessary.

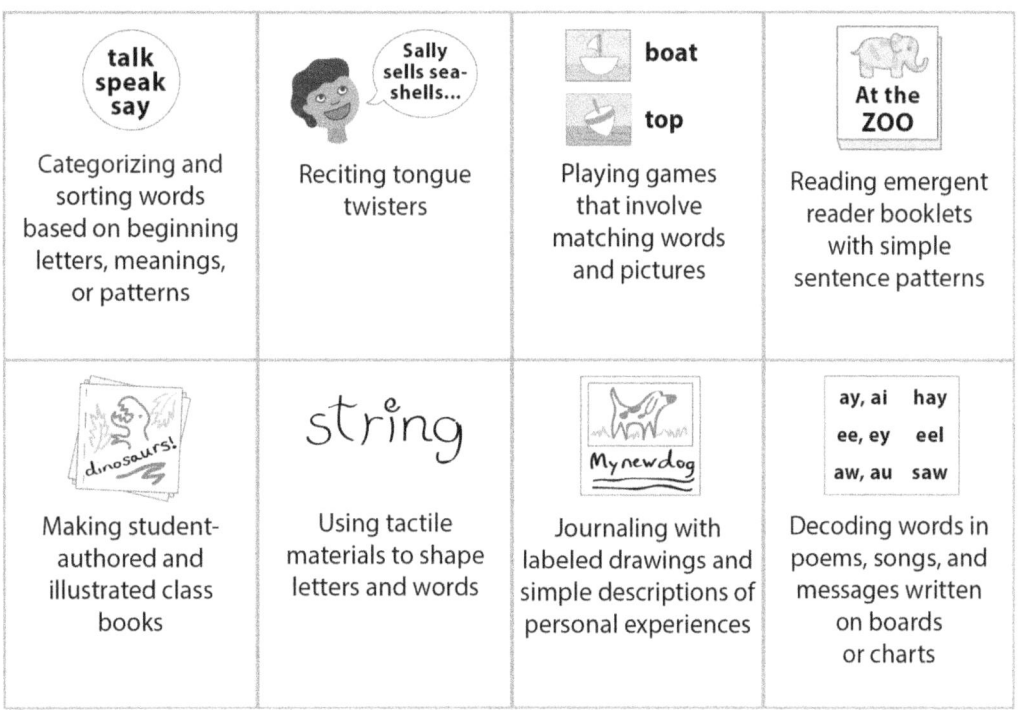

Figure 1.2. Phonics Strategies

Some words are decodable, meaning they follow basic principles of phonics. These words can typically be sounded out effectively if basic structural deviations, like long vowel sounds with a word ending in –*e*, and various digraphs, where two letters make a single sound such, as /th/ and /ay/, are mastered.

However, there are some words that deviate from basic sound structures and cannot be sounded out. These words must be presented to students with great frequency so that they can simply be memorized. These words must become **sight words**, or words that require no decoding because they are instantly recognized and read automatically. It is recommended that some high-frequency decodable words, such as *and* and *get*, also be memorized by sight so as to increase reading rate and fluency.

Initially, the most common sounds for each letter and **high-frequency** letter-sound correspondences, or those that occur most often in the English language, are introduced. In order to assist students beginning to read simple VC (vowel-consonant), VCC (vowel-consonant-consonant), CVCC (consonant-vowel-consonant-consonant), and CVC (consonant-vowel-consonant) words early on, a few short vowel sounds are introduced as well. Letters with names that bear a strong relationship to their sounds are introduced before letters that do not. For example, the sound of the letter *s* can be heard at the end of its name.

Phonics instruction progresses from simple to more complex letter-sound correspondences and sounds/spellings (or the spellings of words based on letter-sound correspondences). Short-vowel sound spellings are introduced before long-vowel sound/spellings, and letters that are similar in appearance (e.g., *b* and *d*) or sound (e.g., /m/ and /n/) are taught separately along the instructional continuum. As students move through kindergarten and the primary grades, they progress from decoding two- or three-phoneme words with letters representing their most common sounds to longer words and more complex sound/spelling patterns.

Table 1.4. Phoneme Chart

Phoneme	Example	Phoneme	Example	Phoneme	Example
Consonants		**Vowels**		**R-Controlled Vowels**	
/b/	bat	/a/	lap	/ã/	hair
/d/	dog	/ā/	late	/ä/	art
/f/	fish	/e/	bet	/û/	dirt
/g/	goat	/ē/	see	/ô/	draw
/h/	hat	/i/	hit	/ēə/	rear
/j/	jump	/ī/	ride	/üə/	sure
/k/	kick	/o/	hop	**Diagrams/Digraphs**	
/l/	laugh	/ō/	rope	/zh/	measure
/m/	milk	/oo/	look	/ch/	chick
/n/	no	/u/	cut	/sh/	shout
/p/	pot	/ū/	cute	/th/	think
/r/	rat	/y//ü/	you	/ng/	bring
/s/	sit	/oi/	oil		

Table 1.4. Phoneme Chart

Phoneme	Example	Phoneme	Example	Phoneme	Example
Consonants		*Vowels*		*R-Controlled Vowels*	
/t/	toss	/ow/	how		
/v/	vote	/ə/ (schwa)	syringe		
/w/	walk				
/y/	yak				
/z/	zoo				

Practice Question

6) A teacher says, "hat" and instructs students to produce the sounds they hear in the word. Which strategy is the teacher using to build phoneme awareness?
   A. phoneme blending
   B. phoneme deletion
   C. phoneme segmentation
   D. phoneme substitution

Literacy Development

Stages of Literacy Development

To achieve full **literacy**, or the ability to read and write, children often go through stages. Before children sound out words, they are in an **emergent literacy** stage, typically lasting from preschool to early kindergarten. During the emergent literacy phase, children are able to recognize **environmental print**, or words in their surroundings, such as "STOP" on a red stop sign. They may also know the letters and even some letter sounds. Children then develop **alphabetic fluency**, where they begin to apply phonics skills, decode basic words, and even read word-by-word orally. This is the learning-to-read stage; it often takes place in late kindergarten and lasts through first grade.

In the third stage of literacy development, often referred to as the **transitional stage**, students are less reliant on adult help for unknown words and instead begin to apply strategies on their own. In this stage, children begin to comprehend the whole text instead of reading word-by-word. This stage often occurs during second grade.

After the transitional stage, students enter the **intermediate stage**, which marks the movement from learning to read to reading to learn. Many experts believe students must be reading to learn by the end of third grade to have the best opportunity for learning in the years that follow. In the intermediate stage, students begin to read longer texts, learn vocabulary, and consider perspectives in the texts they encounter.

In the last stage of literacy learning, **advanced reading**, students are fully fluent and read and write a variety of complex texts. The advanced reading stage may vary but often emerges between the ages of eleven and fourteen.

Practice Question

7) When should students ideally begin reading to learn instead of learning to read?
   A. first grade
   B. second grade
   C. third grade
   D. fourth grade

Fluency

Fluency refers to the rate, accuracy, and expression of a piece when read. Fluency is an important measure of a student's reading development; lack of fluency will hamper overall comprehension as well as enjoyment of reading. Reading **rate** is a measure of speed and is generally calculated in words per minute. **Accuracy**, or the correct decoding of words, is generally entwined with rate when measuring fluency, as reading quickly but incorrectly is not desirable.

While fluency is not limited to oral reading, it is virtually impossible to assess fluency during silent reading, and most educators rely on frequent oral reading assessments to help determine student progress. While several standard measures exist, one of the most researched is the Hasbrouck-Tindal oral reading fluency chart. This chart is designed to measure progress over the course of the school year and from grade to grade by comparing students in percentiles with their peers on a scale of words read correctly per minute. It is important to remember that all students will develop fluency on different timelines, and assessments of fluency are most accurate when they are developmentally appropriate and when they are not presented as high-stakes testing situations.

In addition to rate and accuracy, **prosody**, or the overall liveliness and expressiveness of reading, is also a skill to nurture in students. Prosody may involve appropriate pauses and various changes in pitch and intonation based on punctuation and the overall meaning of the piece. Developing prosody in students should involve a combination of modeling by teachers—as they read stories, passages, and even directions aloud—and giving students plenty of opportunities for oral reading practice.

Helpful Hint

There are various software applications that allow teachers to record and track students' oral reading progress. While this technology cannot replace frequent live listening to students reading, it can augment it and speaks to the importance of oral reading in gauging students' overall

Educators may find it challenging to find time for oral reading assessment in the classroom as they balance multiple priorities; however, teachers must make time to listen to all students read aloud with regularity, regardless of grade level. While examining written work and performance on independent or group practice activities may give some indication of a student's overall development, to get the fullest picture, teachers must gather as much data as possible. Assessing student fluency through oral reading is seminal to an overall understanding of a particular student's learning situation.

Fluency is highly correlated with comprehension because students who struggle to read and decode individual words will have difficulty comprehending entire sentences and paragraphs. Additionally, students who read at a very slow rate may have trouble recalling what they have read. It is well worth the time investment to listen to students read aloud as much as possible.

Practice Question

8) A second-grade teacher notices that his students often read in monotone during oral reading practice. Which strategy would BEST help his students develop prosody?
    A. setting aside timed oral reading each day
    B. modeling an appropriate reading rate
    C. using ability grouping for silent reading
    D. having students act out a play from a script

Vocabulary Development

While fluency is essential for reading to learn, students also need vocabulary knowledge to comprehend what they read. Children learn vocabulary in a variety of ways, including repeated exposure in speech and print and through explicit instruction.

Students will be exposed to a wide variety of vocabulary in a literacy-rich classroom, and teachers can further aid vocabulary acquisition through incorporating new words and new meanings into the daily routine. Some vocabulary acquisition will involve learning **content-specific words** that require students to first understand the vocabulary of the subject before applying the knowledge. Consider that even a kindergarten student must master dozens of basic math terms before applying them. For example, the terms *triangle*, *hexagon*, and *rectangle* must all be learned intrinsically before a student can separate or sort items by shape. Additionally, third graders must learn terms like *habitat*, *natural resource*, *metric system*, and *variable* to be able to apply them to science and math assignments.

Student vocabulary must also grow to include the various homonyms, or **multiple-meaning words**, that exist in the English language. The word *interest*, for example, might mean one thing as it applies to a math unit on saving money and another when used in a freewriting assignment on a topic of *interest*.

As students progress in vocabulary development, they will also begin to consider the difference between the **denotative**, or literal meaning of a word, and its **connotative**, or more subtle meaning. For example, the word *take* literally means to reach for and obtain something, but the word's connotation is different from the word *snatch*, which, though it has a similar denotative meaning, implies a more negative action. Connotative meanings may be challenging for English language learners to glean at first, so they may need scaffolding and supports in lessons aimed at word connotations.

Practice Question

9) Which word has a potential negative connotation?
    A. skim
    B. read
    C. immerse
    D. study

Spelling Development

Students typically begin to write and spell simple words as they are developing other language skills, such as speaking, listening, and reading; however, it is important to view spelling as part of a developmental continuum and to not overemphasize correct spelling too early when preschool students are still forming mock letters or letter strings. A standard **continuum of spelling** (see Table

1.5.) can be referenced to tailor spelling instruction appropriate to grade level while always keeping in mind the differing developmental levels within a classroom.

Table 1.5. The Continuum of Spelling	
By the end of first grade, most students should be able to correctly spell short words with . . .	<ul><li>short vowel sounds with a consonant-verb-consonant (*cat*, *dog*, *pin*) pattern [CVC];</li><li>vowel-consonant pattern (*up*, *egg*) and [VC];</li><li>simple consonant-vowel pattern (*go*, *no*) [CV]; and</li></ul> consonant blends and digraphs in simple and high-frequency words (*chat*, *that*) [CCVC].
By the end of second grade, most students should be spelling words with . . .	<ul><li>final consonant blends (*rant*, *fast*, *bend*, *link*) [CVCC];</li><li>regular long vowel patterns (*ride*, *tube*) [CVC];</li><li>double consonant endings (*lick*, *fuss*);</li><li>more complex long vowel patterns (*suit*, *fail*); and</li></ul> *r*-controlled vowels (*near*, *bear*, *hair*, *are*).
By the end of third grade, most students should be able to spell words with . . .	<ul><li>non-*r*-controlled but other consonants that influence vowels (*stall*, *draw*);</li><li>diphthongs (*coil*, *soon*, *enjoy*, *wow*);</li><li>soft *g*'s and *c*'s (*dice*, *hedge*);</li><li>short vowel patterns (*head*, *sought*);</li><li>silent consonants (*tomb*, *known*, *gnaw*, *wrote*);</li><li>advanced digraphs and blends (*phase*, *character*, *whose*);</li><li>contractions;</li><li>two-syllable words;</li><li>compound words;</li><li>words with suffixes that show number or degree (*fastest*, *foxes*); and</li></ul> special spelling rules such as doubling the final letter on CVC words when adding certain suffixes (*napping*, *saddest*).

Explicit spelling instruction will generally begin with simple consonant-vowel-consonant (CVC) patterns and progress as students learn new phonics structures. Practice with **homophones**, or words that have the same pronunciation but different spellings and meanings, should begin in third grade—or sooner—for some students. Common homophones include *there/their/they're*, *to/two/too*, and so on. It is important to point out to students that software applications that might detect spelling errors in other words often fail to pick up on spelling errors with homophones, so students should be extra vigilant when editing and revising writing that contains these words.

> **Did You Know?**
>
> Diphthongs are sounds created by two vowels together, such as in the word *oil*.

Knowledge of spelling rules or patterns is also important. Some of these are **position-based patterns**, such as the following:

- The letter *i* comes before the letter *e* (except when a long sound is present).
- When there is a vowel blend (e.g., /ee/ea/ai/oa), the sound made is typically a long vowel sound based on the first letter.
- When there is a vowel-consonant-e pattern (e.g., *take* or *rate*), the vowel is usually long.

Other spelling rules are based on suffixes:

- Drop a silent *e* before adding any suffix that begins with a vowel (e.g., give/giving).
- Keep the *e* when the suffix starts with a consonant (e.g.,. use/useful).
- Drop the *y* when adding a suffix (e.g., baby/babies).

Other common spelling rules can be learned and taught with word families, such as words that end in *-ion* (vacation, station, decision) or words that end in *-ck*, such as luck, duck, and struck.

Practice Question

10) Which word has a CVC pattern?
    A. gap
    B. onto
    C. drink
    D. and

Assessment

Assessment of Developing Literacy

Students who are not yet fluent readers will need specific assessment techniques to ensure they are mastering foundational skills that form the building blocks of later reading instruction. Since concepts of print are the first stage of reading development, these skills must be mastered thoroughly. Most of the time, these assessments are informal and might include any of the following:

- asking students to point to the parts of a book (e.g., title, front cover, back)
- presenting students with a book and observing as they interact with it
- asking students to point to a word, sentence, or picture

As students progress to developing phonetic awareness or overall phonemic awareness, assessment is also conducted in a highly interactive manner. Students might be asked to clap out sounds or words, think of rhyming words, repeat words or sounds, and so on.

Once students begin to work on letter recognition and sound-symbol knowledge, a letter chart or letter-sound chart can be used as an assessment tool. Students can cross off each letter or letter sound once it is mastered. The same assessment method with a chart or list can be used for sight words (often with a Dolch word list), consonant blends, digraphs, diphthongs, and other challenging sounds.

There is an important distinction between children's ability to sing the alphabet song or point to and say letters or sounds in order (which many master quite early) and the different (though related) skill of letter and letter-sound recognition in isolation. For this reason, it is a good idea to always assess phonics skills in different contexts. For example, students can be asked to point to certain letters or sounds (/b/, /ch/, /i/) in a book or story. This type of **embedded phonics** assessment ensures that students can transfer knowledge and apply it in connected texts.

In addition to more structured assessment methods, such as charts and lists, phonics skills can be assessed through any number of hands-on activities. Students can play with letter/sound cards or magnets and form or dissect words. Students can match up cards with different rimes and onsets or different target consonant or vowel sounds.

In assessing decoding, or the ability to sound out a word and glean meaning, an oral assessment approach continues to be the gold standard. There are many assessment tools designed specifically to aid in assessing such skills, including the popular **Quick Phonics Screener**, which assesses a student's ability to read a variety of sounds and words.

When assessing decoding skills, it is important to note student strengths and weaknesses; however, teachers must also develop a general idea of the student's overall approach and "word-attack skills," or methods of decoding unfamiliar words. Attention to how students approach any oral reading task can provide significant information on strategies they are already using, as well as those they do not use but might find beneficial. Though the age of the student certainly comes into play, sometimes older students still mastering decoding might be able to verbalize the way they approach such challenging words. Questions posed to the student about strategy or method can also yield valuable information.

In addition to these methods, there are also several published assessment instruments for pre-readers and emerging readers:

- Letter knowledge and phonemic awareness can be assessed using the **Dynamic Indicators of Basic Early Literacy Skills (DIBELS)** and the **Early Reading Diagnostic Assessment (ERDA)**.
- The **Comprehensive Test of Phonological Processing (CTOPP)** and **Phonological Awareness Test (PAT)** can also be used as instruments to assess phonemic awareness.
- Other instruments that assess early reading skills include the **Texas Primary Reading Inventory (TPRI)**, **Test of Word Reading Efficiency (TOWRE)**, and even the kindergarten version of the **Iowa Test of Basic Skills (ITSB)**.

Regardless of the assessment instruments used, assessing emerging readers can be challenging since young children often find assessment scenarios intimidating. Any single assessment is only as useful as the portion of the full picture that it provides. The fullest picture of a student's pre-reading development can best be gleaned through observation and input from both parents and teachers. Portfolios, observational records, checklists, and other informal assessment methods can provide much insight into the development of emergent readers.

Practice Question

11) A kindergarten teacher who wants to assess student mastery of phoneme blending would MOST likely
   A. ask students to add affixes to various root words.
   B. have students match up cards with onsets and rimes and say each word.
   C. ask students to remove a letter from a word, add a new one, and read the new word.
   D. have students point to items in the classroom that begin with a certain letter sound.

Assessment of Literacy

Assessing each student in an individual oral context is best but certainly not always possible. This can make assessing reading skills and **metacognitive reading strategies**, or the thought process behind reading, a challenge. Further, it is often hard to fully assess any one student's individual thought process. With these caveats, assessing reading skills and strategies with an eye for gaps that might be addressed through intervention is an important task.

Word-attack skills, or the strategies students use to make sense of word, can be assessed through observation and oral reading. Teachers should take note of what happens when students encounter words they do not know. Do they immediately ask for help? Skip over the word? Reread the word? Slow down? Speed up? Assessing word-attack skills relies on observing students as they read aloud but also on the assessment of underlying skills that lead to a strong word-attack tool kit. Do students make use of all text features and graphic elements? Do they sound out the word or make inferences based on roots and affixes? Do they use context clues?

> **Helpful Hint**
>
> Asking comprehension questions after listening to students read is a simple, effective way to monitor oral comprehension.

The assessment of vocabulary typically happens in the context of breadth (the number of words one knows) or depth (the ability to use the vocabulary in varied and nuanced ways). It also happens in the context of an isolated assessment (a vocabulary test) or as an embedded assessment as an adjunct to another assessment, such as one of reading comprehension or oral fluency.

Such assessments can also be context-independent: "What does the word *contortion* mean?" or context-dependent: "What does the word *contort* mean in the following sentence?" Educators should consider what "bank" they will draw vocabulary from in order to assess students. Typically, teachers who assess vocabulary students will need to comprehend the language of classroom instruction, the textbook, and any literature the class will read. Reference materials, such as the *EDL Core Vocabularies*, define "target" words per grade level. Published standardized vocabulary instruments, such as the classic **Peabody Picture Vocabulary Test (PPT)**, which requires no reading or writing, can also be used to assess individual students.

Assessing oral fluency is generally done by assessing reading accuracy, prosody, and automaticity. This can be tracked in numerous ways. Teachers may keep **running records** that track accuracy, self-correction, and the use of fix-up strategies and word attack skills. Running records use forms so that teachers can mark errors, self-corrections, and how students use cues to make meaning of texts. These forms are filled out as the student reads the same text the teacher has.

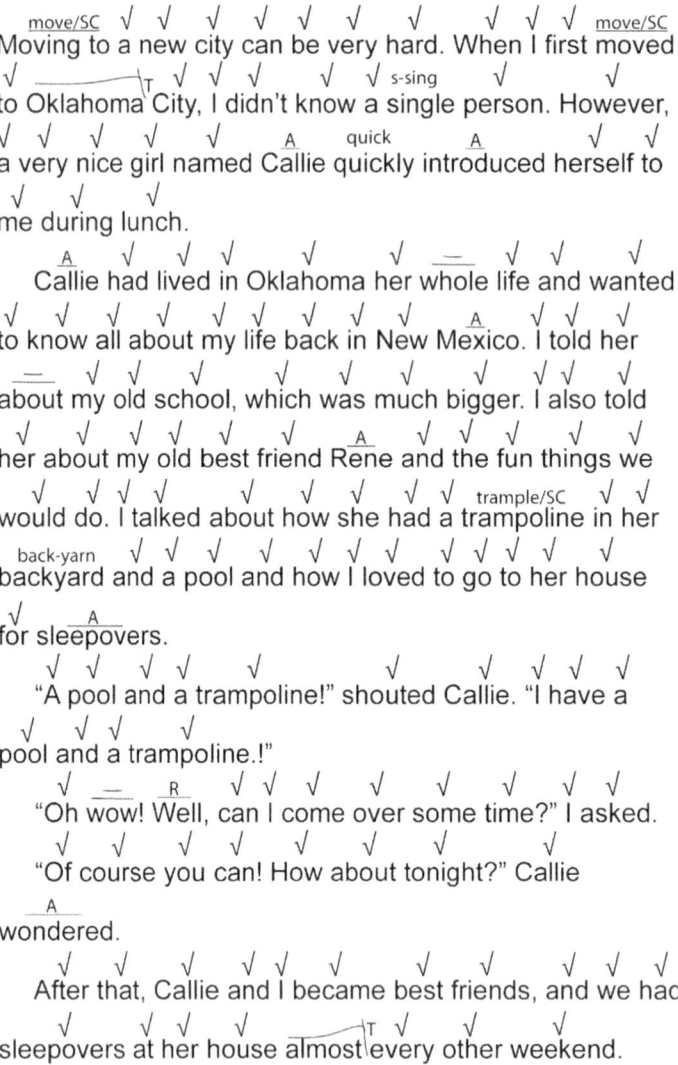

Figure 1.3. Running Record

Students can also be measured for oral reading skills using various fluency norms charts that indicate the average number of words read correctly per minute per grade. While several standard measures exist, one of the most researched is the **Hasbrouck-Tindal oral reading fluency chart**. As described in the "Literacy Development" section, this chart (see Table 1.6.) measures progress over the course of the school year and from grade to grade. It compares students in percentiles with their peers on a scale of the number of words read correctly per minute.

Table 1.6. Hasbrouck-Tindal Oral Reading Fluency Chart

Grade	Words Correct Per Minute (50th percentile)		
	Fall	Winter	Spring
1	---	29	60
2	50	84	100
3	83	97	112
4	94	120	133
5	121	133	146
6	132	145	146

Comprehension while reading silently can be assessed through cloze exercises. In these exercises, words are removed from the text and students must fill them in. There are other written exercises aimed at determining level of comprehension. Some students might struggle to answer written questions; therefore, a full assessment of silent reading comprehension should include an oral component as well.

One of the most common assessments is the **Informal Reading Inventory (IRI)**. There are multiple versions created by various entities. One of the more popular versions is **Pearson's Qualitative Reading Inventory (QRI)**. These assessments include oral reading of word lists that assess the accuracy of word identification. The QRI also contains passages and questions that assess both oral and silent reading comprehension. Standardized norm-referenced test batteries, such as the Iowa Test of Basic Skills and Stanford Achievement Test, as well as several criterion-referenced tests such as the Partnership for Assessment of Readiness for College and Careers (PARCC), also test reading comprehension.

As in all types of reading assessment, comprehension assessment does not require a lengthy formal written test. Simply asking students to recount or retell a story they have read or to recall the most important or interesting parts of a text can provide valuable data. Furthermore, self-assessment should be ongoing and explicitly taught to all readers to monitor comprehension. As students self-assess, they can apply fix-up or fix-it-up strategies as needed when comprehension breaks down.

Writing assessments often take the form of students actually composing written pieces, such as stories, poems, or essays; however, **project-based learning** initiatives, where students work on real-world projects as part of developing core content-area skills, may involve a **culminating assessment** task, such as writing and publishing a website or composing and sending a letter to a government official. Such tasks can be seen as **authentic assessment** activities because the written piece is not solely for the purpose of teacher assessment but also serves a real-life purpose.

Assessment of spelling proficiency may also take many forms, including the use of assessments like spelling tests to assess foundational knowledge or assessments in contexts, such as noting and providing feedback on students' spelling development within a written assignment on another topic.

Practice Question

12) A teacher wants to create an authentic assessment to evaluate students' skills with writing in coherent paragraphs. Which assignment would be BEST?
    A. directing students to give a presentation to the class on something they know how to do well
    B. asking students to analyze the way paragraphs are used in a newspaper article on a topic of their choice
    C. assigning students to write the draft of an email they will eventually send to someone
    D. having students use a graphic organizer to organize their thoughts into paragraphs before writing an essay about an assigned topic

Conventions of Language

Parts of Speech

Understanding the structure of language is an important part of effective oral and written communication. Students may not consistently use parts of speech correctly in their writing and speaking until well into their elementary years. Recall that within oral language development are phases in which children leave out needed articles, prepositions, and other linking words. Once speech becomes fully developed and students are generating their own sentences and paragraphs, basic rules of grammar can be introduced. Many structured language arts curriculum resources begin with a study of the eight parts of speech and their functions within a sentence; these are described below.

Nouns are words that indicate a person, place, thing, or idea. They may be common (*student, teacher, room, school*) or proper (*Blanca, Ms. Robinson, Idaho, Frederick Douglass Elementary School*). **Common nouns** are not capitalized, but **proper nouns** must be capitalized. Nouns may also be singular or plural, and students will need practice in forming the plural form of nouns by adding either *–s* or *–es*.

> **Check Your Understanding**
>
> What are the major phases of oral language development?

Pronouns are words that take the place of nouns. They may either serve as subjects (*I, you, he, she, it, we, they*) or as objects (*me, you, her, him, it, us, them*) and are known as **subject pronouns** or **object pronouns**, respectively. Pronouns should always have an **antecedent**, or noun to which they refer. Pronouns must agree in number, person, and gender with their antecedents. Pronoun errors are frequent in developmental writers, and ambiguous pronoun references, lack of pronoun-antecedent agreement, and incorrect use of subject and object pronouns are all common mistakes.

As discussed above, pronouns generally also indicate the perspective or person in which a piece is written. First-person writing generally uses pronouns such as *I, me, we,* and *our*, and second-person writing uses the pronoun *you*. Third-person texts use a variety of pronouns, such as *he, she, it,* and *them*. Shifts in pronoun person are common in student writing, and teachers need to provide help to students who unnecessarily change point of view in a writing assignment.

Verbs describe an action, state of being, or occurrence. They can be action verbs, which like their name implies, describe actions such as *walk, eat,* and *speak*, or linking verbs (*is, become, seem*), which describe states of being or link a subject to additional information. Some verbs may be action verbs or linking verbs depending upon their specific use. If verbs are merely linking a subject to further information, they are considered linking verbs, but if they are expressing an action, they are considered action verbs.

Examples:

This soup tastes bad.

In this sentence, the verb *tastes* links the subject *soup* to its predicate adjective *bad*, so *tastes* is being used as a linking verb.

I taste the soup.

In this sentence, *taste* is describing an action, so it is an action verb

Helping verbs always appear alongside another main verb and show the tense (*will* be, *had* eaten) or possibility (*may* be, *could* last, *might* enjoy) of another verb. Helping verbs are used to **conjugate**, or change, many verbs to different **tenses**. Unnecessary shifts in tense from present to past or future are prevalent in student writing, and English language learners and native speakers alike will need lots of practice with forming challenging tenses, such as the present and past perfect, and challenging irregular past tenses with verbs such as *to lie*.

Adjectives modify and describe nouns, and their use is essential to descriptive writing. Student errors with adjectives generally include using an incorrect comparative or superlative form ("He is tallest than me!") or confusing adjectives and adverbs ("She eats hungry/She eats hungrily.").

Adverbs modify adjectives, verbs, or other adverbs and frequently end in *–ly*. Student errors with adverbs are similar to those with adjectives and generally involve the incorrect use of comparatives and superlatives or the use of adjectives and adverbs interchangeably.

A **preposition** is a word that expresses a relationship between words, and it usually comes before a noun or pronoun. Prepositions help form links in speech and writing, and student errors most frequently involve their omission. Additionally, English language learners may find using prepositions challenging, particularly when they are part of colloquial expressions (e.g., driving me *up* the wall, a pig *in* a poke).

A **conjunction** joins words or sentence parts together. There are both coordinating conjunctions (*and, but, or, nor, for, yet, so*), which join two independent clauses to form compound sentences, and subordinate conjunctions (*e.g., before, while, because, as*), which join dependent clauses to independent clauses to form complex and compound-complex sentences.

Determiners are not parts of speech in themselves but have a similar function: explaining what a noun refers to. They may be adjectives that are used as articles, such as *a*, *an*, and *the*; possessive adjectives and pronouns (*my, his, ours, your*); demonstrative pronouns such as *this, that, these,* and *those*; or any other words that quantify, distribute, or show a difference (*a little, half, other, such, quite*).

Like prepositions, determiners are challenging for English language learners. In some languages, determiners are used in only some situations and not others, and some languages lack certain types of English determiners entirely. English language learners who struggle with determiners might benefit from being paired with a native speaker for peer review to help insert needed articles into a piece.

Additionally, variations exist across all parts of speech in different languages. American Sign Language, as just one example, does not use what we might think of as conjugated verbs to show tense; rather, a sign indicating now, next, before, and so on is inserted into the beginning of the sentence to show the intended meaning. It is important for teachers to understand that grammatical knowledge will be more challenging for some students, and they should strive to ensure the classroom is a place where all students are being supported in their learning.

Practice Questions

13) Which of the following is a preposition?
    A. our
    B. from
    C. has
    D. so

14) Which of the following skills do students need to master before they can determine whether an adjective or adverb is most appropriate to use in a sentence?
    A. understanding the difference between a noun and a verb
    B. understanding the difference between a noun and a pronoun
    C. understanding the function of prepositions
    D. being able to form compound sentences

Phrases and Clauses

A **phrase** is a group of words that communicates a partial idea and lacks either a subject or a predicate. Several phrases may be strung together, one after another, to add detail and interest to a sentence.

Example:

The animals crossed the large bridge to eat the fish on the wharf.

Phrases are categorized based on the main word in the phrase. A **prepositional phrase** begins with a preposition and ends with an object of the preposition; a **verb phrase** is composed of the main verb along with its helping verbs; and a **noun phrase** consists of a noun and its modifiers.

Examples:

prepositional phrase: The dog is hiding under the porch.

verb phrase: The chef would have created another soufflé, but the staff protested.

noun phrase: The big, red barn rests beside the vacant chicken house.

An **appositive phrase** is a particular type of noun phrase that renames the word or group of words that precedes it. Appositive phrases usually follow the noun they describe and are set apart by commas.

Example:

My dad, a clock maker, loved antiques.

Verbal phrases begin with a word that would normally act as a verb but is instead filling another role within the sentence. These phrases can act as nouns, adjectives, or adverbs.

Examples:

gerund phrase: Writing numerous Christmas cards occupies her aunt's time each year.

participial phrase: Enjoying the stars that filled the sky, Dave lingered outside for quite a while.

> **Helpful Hint**
>
> The word *gerund* has an *n* in it, a helpful reminder that the gerund acts as a noun. Therefore, the gerund phrase might act as the subject, the direct object, or the object of the preposition just as another noun would.

Infinitive phrase: <u>To visit Europe</u> had always been her dream.

Practice Question

15) Identify the underlined phrases in the following sentence:

<u>Wrapping packages for the soldiers,</u> the kind woman tightly rolled the tee-shirts <u>to see how much space</u>

remained <u>for the homemade cookies</u>.
- A. participial, infinitive, prepositional
- B. gerund, infinitive, prepositional
- C. gerund, prepositional, prepositional
- D. participial, prepositional, adverbial

Constructing Sentences

Good writers use a variety of sentence structures to convey their meaning. While young students will generally start with **simple sentences** consisting of a single, independent clause, older students should be encouraged to write more advanced sentences as appropriate. **Compound sentences** are made when two independent clauses are joined together using a comma and coordinating conjunction; a semicolon—either alone or with a transitional expression, such as *however* or *moreover*—or a colon. Generally, a semicolon alone is only used to join two closely related independent clauses ("My mother likes chocolate; she is a chocoholic."). A colon is generally only used to introduce a second independent clause which is an example or elaboration upon the first ("I have only one thing to say to you: I am very disappointed.").

Complex sentences are formed when a dependent clause is joined to an independent clause with a subordinating conjunction, relative pronoun, or other word. A **dependent clause** is so called because it cannot stand on its own as a sentence, unlike an **independent clause**. The dependent clause may be added anywhere: the beginning, the middle, or the end of the sentence.

Examples:

My mother, *who is a gardener*, likes to spend most of her time outdoors.

In this sentence, the dependent clause is "who is a gardener," beginning with the relative pronoun *who*.

Because she likes to spend most of her time outdoors, my mother is a gardener.

Here, the dependent clause is "[b]ecause she likes to spend most of her time outdoors," beginning with the subordinating conjunction *because*.

My mother is a gardener *as she likes to spend most of her time outdoors*.

In the sentence above, the dependent clause is "as she likes to spend most of her time outdoors," beginning with the subordinating conjunction *as*.

Compound-complex sentences are merely compound sentences with one or more dependent clauses ("My mother is a gardener, but she does not like to spend time outdoors because she has allergies.").

Sentence Structure	Independent Clauses	Dependent Clauses
Simple	1	0
Compound	2 +	0
Complex	1	1 +
Compound-complex	2 +	1 +

Practice Question

16) Which of the following is a compound sentence?
    A. Jeremy likes to fish by the ocean because he finds it peaceful and relaxing.
    B. I wish I could buy a new car, but I do not have enough money right now.
    C. Jenny is a writer, and she writes for thirty minutes every day because she has to keep motivated.
    D. While the train slowly chugged along the tracks, my little dog stared curiously out the window.

Punctuation

Many of the mechanical choices writers must make relate to **punctuation**. While creative writers have liberty to play with punctuation to achieve their desired ends, academic and technical writers must adhere to stricter conventions.

The **period** is the most common **terminal punctuation** mark, used to end declarative (statement) and imperative (command) sentences.

Examples:

Period

Sarah and I are attending a concert.

Meet me outside the concert hall one hour before the show.

Question Mark

The **question mark**, another common terminal punctuation mark, is used to end interrogative sentences (questions).

How many people are attending the concert?

While the difference between the period and the question mark is usually obvious, confusion sometimes occurs when questions are stated indirectly. In such cases, the period is usually preferable.

I wonder how many people are attending the concert.

Exclamation Point

Exclamation points end exclamatory sentences, in which the writer or speaker is exhibiting intense emotion or energy; thus, writers should carefully consider their use of exclamations. In fact, the exclamation point should be used reservedly or not at all in academic writing unless the exclamation point is within a quotation that a writer incorporates into the text. The emphatic usage of *what* or *how* without asking a question, however, demands the usage of the exclamation point.

> **Helpful Hint**
> The exclamation point has impact only in contrast to its frequency of usage. That is, if the exclamation point is used frequently, each exclamation will be less impactful. On the other hand, if the exclamation point is used sparingly, its use will draw the reader's attention and emphasize the information contained in the sentence.

What a great show that was!

Colon and Semicolon

The colon and the semicolon, though often confused, each have a unique set of rules surrounding their use. While both punctuation marks are used to join clauses, the construction of the clauses and the relationships between them vary.

The semicolon is used to show a general relationship between two independent clauses (IC; IC).

The disgruntled customer tapped angrily on the counter; she had to wait nearly ten minutes to speak to the manager.

When using the semicolon with a conjunctive adverb to join two independent clauses, the pattern is as follows: independent clause, semicolon, conjunctive adverb, comma, independent clause.

She may not have to take the course this <u>year; however,</u> she eventually will have to sign up for that specific course.

The colon, somewhat less limited than the semicolon in its usage, shows a relationship between two clauses and, moreover, to highlight the information contained in the second clause—usually a list, definition, or clarification. While the clause preceding the colon must be an independent clause, the clause that follows doesn't have to be.

Incorrect: *The buffet offers three choices that include: ham, turkey, or roast beef.*

Correct: *The buffet offers three choices: ham, turkey, or roast beef.*

Correct: *The buffet offers three choices that include the following: ham, turkey, or roast beef.*

A writer should also use the colon to separate a title from a subtitle (Title: Subtitle), to separate the hour and the minutes (9:30 a.m.), to follow certain parts of a letter or memo (To:, From:, Date:, RE:), and to follow a formal salutation (To whom it may concern:). Neither the semicolon nor the colon should be used to set off an introductory phrase from the rest of the sentence.

Incorrect: *After the trip to the raceway; we realized that we should have brought ear plugs.*

Incorrect: *After the trip to the raceway: we realized that we should have brought ear plugs.*

Correct: *After the trip to the raceway, we realized that we should have brought ear plugs.*

> **Helpful Hint**
>
> *Let's eat Grandma* OR *Let's eat, Grandma.* This humorous and well-known example demonstrates the importance of accurate comma usage.

Many people are taught that, when reading, a comma represents a pause for breath. While this trick may be useful as a way of helping young readers build fluency, it is not a helpful guide for comma usage when writing. Rather, proper comma usage is guided by a set of specific rules.

Important rules for comma usage, and examples of each, are summarized in the following list:

Examples:

1. Commas are used to separate two independent clauses along with a coordinating conjunction.

    George ordered the steak, but Bruce preferred the ham.

2. Commas are used to separate coordinate adjectives.

    The shiny, regal horse ran majestically through the wide, open field.

3. Commas are used to separate items in a series.

    The list of groceries included cream, coffee, donuts, and tea.

4. Commas are used to separate introductory words and phrases from the rest of the sentence.

    Slowly, Nathan became aware of his surroundings after the concussion.

    For example, we have thirty students who demand a change.

5. Commas are used to set off nonessential information and appositives.

    Estelle, our newly elected chairperson, will be in attendance.

6. Commas are used to set off introductory words from quoted words if the introductory words are not part of an independent clause.

    Elizabeth said sadly, "I want to go home right now for spring break."

7. Commas are used to set off the day and month of a date within a text.

    My birthday makes me feel quite old because I was born on February 16, 1958, in Minnesota.

8. Commas are used to set up numbers in a text of more than four digits.

    We expect 25,000 visitors to the new museum.

Quotation marks are used for many purposes, the most common of which are related to academic writing and citation. First, quotation marks enclose titles of short, or relatively short, literary works such as short stories, chapters, and poems. (The titles of longer works, like novels and anthologies, are italicized.) Additionally, quotation marks are used to enclose direct quotations within the text of a document where the quotation is integrated into the text. If a quotation is within another quotation, then the inner quotation uses single quotation marks.

Writers also use quotation marks to set off dialogue. Occasionally, quotation marks are used to enclose words used in special sense or for a non-literary purpose.

Example:

The shady dealings of his Ponzi scheme earned him his ironic name "Honest Abe."

When considering quotation marks versus italics in notating a title, the question of short versus long is a useful guide. A chapter title is written in quotation marks, while the book title itself is italicized. Short poetry titles are written in quotation marks; long epic poem titles are italicized. An article title is written in quotation marks, while the name of the newspaper is italicized.

Apostrophes, sometimes referred to as single quotation marks, have several different purposes:
- to show possession: *boy's watch, John and Mary's house*
- to replace missing letters, numerals, and signs: *do not = don't,* 1989 = '89
- to form plurals of letters, numerals, and signs—but only when adding the apostrophe would add clarity: *cross your t's and dot your i's*

Other marks of punctuation include the **en dash** (to indicate a range of dates, for example), the **em dash** (to indicate an abrupt break in a sentence and emphasize the words within the em dashes), the **parentheses** (to enclose insignificant information), the **brackets** (to enclose added words to a quotation and to add insignificant information within parentheses), the **slash** (to separate lines of poetry within a text or to indicate interchangeable terminology), and the **ellipses** (to indicate information removed from a quotation, to indicate a missing line of poetry, or to create a reflective pause).

Practice Question

17) Which punctuation mark should be added to the following sentence?

Freds brother wanted the following items for Christmas a red car a condo and a puppy.
- A. Fred's / Christmas; / car, /condo,
- B. Fred's / Christmas: / car, / condo,
- C. Fred's / Christmas: / car,
- D. Fred's / items' / Christmas: / car, / condo,

Literature and Informational Texts

Features of Different Text Genres

It is important that students of all ages be exposed to a wide variety of texts. **Informational texts**, or **nonfiction texts**, are texts about the world around us and generally do not use characters to convey information. Science and social studies texts fall into this category. These informational texts are often structured in such a way as to organize information in a format that is accessible and meaningful to students.

As part of an introduction to different types of texts, a teacher might ask elementary-aged students to analyze elements of their textbooks or workbooks. Do they have bold headings to help the reader understand when new ideas are being introduced? Do they have sidebars to give readers additional information alongside the main body of text?

In contrast, **literary texts**, or **fiction texts**, are usually stories made up by the author. While they may contain true elements or be based on actual events, they usually include plenty of elements designed to keep and capture the reader's interest. They generally have **characters**—which may be real or imagined—people, animals, or creatures, and a **plot**, or sequence of story events. The **setting** of fiction texts may be any time or place past, present, future, real, or imagined. While teachers may put a lot of focus on short stories that are highly accessible for young students, it is also important to expose children to other genres so that they can practice comprehending texts that are unfamiliar at first.

Fiction texts often employ special language to achieve desired effects. For example, **word choice** can have a significant impact on what the reader understands from the passage or the overall **tone**—the attitude the writer takes toward the subject of the work. Consider the following sentences and how word choice impacts meaning and tone:

- *She pulled the berry from the vine.*

versus

- *She yanked the berry from the vine.*

Similarly, **figurative language**, or groups of words not meant to be taken literally, are also often employed in works of fiction. Common types of figurative language include **similes**, or indirect comparisons between two unlike things often using the words *like* or *as*, and **metaphors**, or more direct comparisons between unlike things. **Hyperbole** is another type of figurative language, which employs exaggeration for emphasis. **Personification** involves ascribing human-like qualities to non-human entities.

Examples:

Simile: The woman's hair was like a spider web.

Metaphor: The woman's hair was a spider web.

Hyperbole: The woman's hair was so tangled that it contained every stick and bramble from the nearby wood.

Personification: The woman's hair plied and pirouetted in the wind.

Texts may also contain **analogies**, or comparisons to unlike things for the purpose of explanation. For example, a text may have the sentence, "You might not think a pet snake and a pet cat are similar, but snakes are like cats in their eating habits and desire to be left alone most of the time." Analogies are similar to similes; the primary difference is that analogies seek to explain while similes are often used to drive interest and description. Analogies are often employed in argumentative writing to make a point, as in the example above.

Allusions are another feature of some texts. Allusions are indirect references to something else. For example, a text may have the sentence, "The job of caring for her sister's pets was the cross she had to bear." The "cross" is an indirect reference to the Christian Bible. Many allusions are to religious or mythical texts; others are historical or to other popular literary texts.

In **drama**, most of the story is centered around dialogue between characters. They are usually separated into segments like chapters, known as **acts**, and smaller subsegments (generally with a consistent setting) known as **scenes**. Using drama in the classroom is a great way to get students interested in different types of texts. Teachers may consider setting up a simple **stage** in a kindergarten or elementary classroom as a natural outgrowth of a dramatic play center sometimes found in preschool classrooms. Acting out dramas not only helps students work on expressive reading (prosody), but it also reinforces social and emotional learning as students analyze the emotions and actions of characters.

While poetry may be associated with older children, even young students can appreciate and recognize **rhyme**. Poetry with rhyme can help reinforce phonological awareness and is a natural outgrowth of many young children's love of song. **Meter**—the rhythm, or beat, of the poem—can also be used to engage young students with different texts since a beat can be clapped to, stomped to, or even danced to! Many timeless books for children—such as *One Fish, Two Fish, Red Fish, Blue Fish* and *Each Peach Pear Plum*—have both rhyme and meter and give young children exposure to poetry. **Alliteration**, or the repetition of the same sound at the beginning of successive words, is also a feature of some poems. For example, a poem may contain a line such as "Nine new nurses needed nicer notebooks."

Recognizing genre is the ability to name the genre of a text (e.g., poetry, drama, picture book, graphic novel, folktale, myth, fairy tale, tall tale, historical fiction, science fiction) and the features of that genre. Readers who understand and recognize the characteristics of a variety of genres can gain additional insights into an author's purpose or message. For example, a reader is able to comprehend a text with a greater depth and breadth if she knows how the **rhyme scheme** (e.g., abab, aabb, aabba) and **meter** (i.e., basic rhythmic structure of the lines or verses in poetry) of a poem affect its tone or how **stage directions** develop the rising action in a play. Furthermore, skilled readers know how to speak about texts in different genres, such as **stanzas**, or groups of lines in poems that are similar to paragraphs in narrative texts.

> **Check Your Understanding**
>
> What is the difference between analogy, simile, and metaphor?

Children's literature is a genre in its own right. It tends to have characters who are children; if animals or mythical creatures are the characters, they tend to behave in the way a child would. The genre also tends to focus on characters who learn an important lesson, often one that is applicable to life as a whole. Other characteristics of children's literature include accessible vocabulary and situations or events that children can relate to and find appealing. Many children's books—even those for intermediate readers—often include vivid illustrations to help bring the plot to life.

Much of today's literature—both for young children and older children—is not entirely new but rather reconceptualizes or reinterprets timeless themes and traditions. For example, "coming of age" is an important milestone in many cultures throughout the world, celebrated and honored in myriad ways. Thus, it is a popular topic for many stories. Additionally, various cultural patterns, traditions, and symbols can be found in books and stories for children. Some, like the Cinderella legend, can be found in some form in literature from multiple places throughout the world.

Literature for children may also be based on mythologies from long ago, such as those from ancient Greece or Rome. These tales have often been reinterpreted in an accessible and contemporary format. Religious traditions from various cultures often underscore popular stories; as just one example, almost all cultures have some sort of origin or creation myth surrounding the natural world. Christian beliefs also influence some popular children's literature as do positive character traits that exist beyond any religious framework, such as treating others with kindness and respect.

Practice Question

18) Which sentence includes hyperbole?
   A. Harriet likes to go fishing on the weekends, though she has never caught anything.
   B. I generally enjoy reading a variety of literature types, but I like historical fiction the best.
   C. We need to determine the type of problem before we can think about solving it.
   D. You really must stop calling me five thousand times every day when I am at work.

Organizational Structures of Text

Authors organize information in such a way as to get their points across as clearly as possible. They tend to use a text structure that suits their purpose. This structure may be a **sequence** of events, such as a news story recounting the days leading up to an important event, or a thorough **description** of something, as in the opening pages of a novel, which might describe the main character in finite detail.

Many historical texts are written in a **cause-and-effect** pattern, where the cause is presented first, followed by a discussion of the result. A chapter in a social studies text about the Industrial Revolution, for example, may follow this pattern as the Industrial Revolution is cited as the cause for changes in working and living conditions in many cities.

Other works may be organized in a **problem-solution structure**. This might be taught through a collaborative activity where students identify a problem in the classroom, school, or community and then write a letter to a decision maker outlining both the nature of the issue and a possible solution.

Students could also be challenged to **compare and contrast**, or explain how two things from their everyday experiences are similar and different. Charts and other visual/graphic organizers can help students organize their thoughts. A teacher may ask students, for example, what the differences and similarities are between the first and second grades. This might even lead to a persuasive writing assignment about this topic.

While reading nonfiction texts is important, inciting a love of reading is often best accomplished through multiple exposures to high-interest fiction, both classic and contemporary. In order to facilitate deep comprehension of these narratives, teachers can help students understand key elements through a **plot diagram**. This type of graphic organizer helps students identify the **exposition**, or beginning, of the story, which sets up the reader for what is to come by describing the time, place, and main characters. The plot organizer will then help students move into the primary problem driving the story, or the **conflict**, and the **rising action**, or sequence of events leading to the eventual **climax**, or turning point, which is the apex of the diagram. The curve slopes sharply downward as the **falling action**, or results of the climax, unfolds. The diagram closes with the final **resolution**, or ending of the story. It is important to impart to students that the resolution might not always be happy, but all stories do have one.

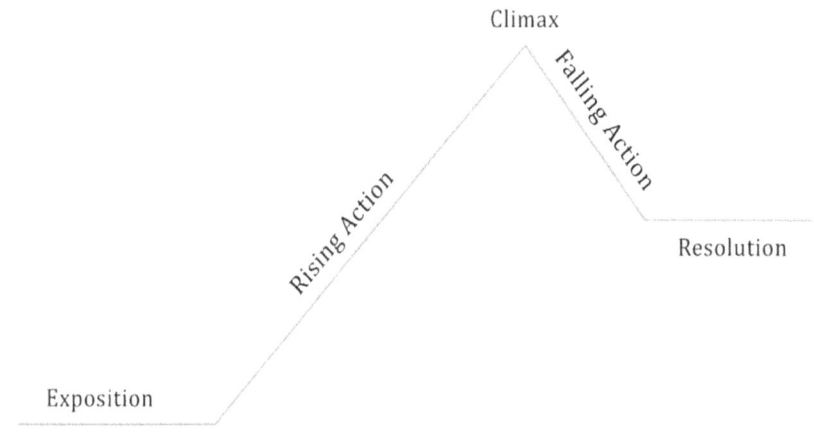

Figure 1.4. Plot Diagram

Introducing the plot diagram is easiest when students already have some background with a story. Teachers may draw on a popular children's movie or fairy tale to introduce these elements. If students are not struggling to comprehend a new text while being introduced to these elements, the understanding will likely come more quickly. Timeless stories with plots that students know by heart are ideal for an initial exploration of the plot diagram.

Practice Question

19) Ms. Jones wants to introduce her first-grade students to new types of text structures they have not seen before. Which activity would BEST meet her goal?
    A. asking students to go to the library and explain the different sections
    B. bringing in magazines, pamphlets, newspapers, and other items for students to explore
    C. having students compare and contrast two different storybook characters they have read about
    D. dividing students into groups and having them create a plot diagram about their favorite movie

Selecting Appropriate Texts

Most children's earliest experiences with reading are with **picture books**. Timeless titles such as *Have You Seen My Duckling?* and *Pancakes for Breakfast* can be appreciated by young children and their parents alike, and being read to from a young age is positively associated with future interest in reading. Picture books help young children engage in "pretend reading" by recounting a story from memory or using a picture book to "read" to a sibling or parent.

Did You Know?

Reading to children has a strong correlation to future achievement. According to the Program for International Student Assessment (PISA), results from fourteen countries indicate that students whose parents read books to them during the first year of school average fourteen points higher on a reading assessment taken at age fifteen.

It is important that educators avoid relegating picture books to the discard pile too early or chide children for their enjoyment of **graphic novels**. Graphics have a place in enhancing interest and the comprehension of texts and are prevalent in much of the written media that is consumed in daily life. In fact, **visual** literacy—the ability to comprehend visual texts—is an important predecessor to being able to comprehend more sophisticated written works.

Finding a balance between the complexity of a text and an individual student's current level of literacy development can be challenging. Many programs recognize this challenge and structure goal setting and student assessments in a growth-over-time approach. Regardless of the milestones laid out by a school or district, teachers should always aim for students to tackle ever more sophisticated texts as they develop the foundational skills they need to take on new challenges; however, this does not mean that students should be pushed beyond what they can decode. Giving students developmentally inappropriate texts may lead to a denigration of confidence and a lack of interest and enthusiasm for reading.

Many factors contribute to a text's complexity. Before determining appropriateness, texts should be evaluated qualitatively, quantitatively, and per their match to the reader. Quantitative measurements include anything for which a number can be calculated, such as **word frequency**, length of words and **sentence length**, average syllables per word, and so on. These quantitative calculations may result in a range or score being allotted to a text. The most popular of these is that calculated by MetaMetrics, a company that uses word frequency and sentence length in an equation that yields a score. MetaMetrics assigns scores to both readers and texts. Those assigned to readers typically come from standardized tests and measure a student's current level of reading ability; these are called reader measures.

MetaMetrics also assigns **Lexile ranges** to texts called Lexile test measures. While these ranges do not have a direct correlation to grade level in the strictest sense, charts can be used to glean the typical ranges for a given grade. The company purports that the best results come when the reader measure falls within a "sweet spot" range per the text measure.

More than likely, much of what students read (textbooks, passages in software programs, published children's literature) has already been assigned a Lexile text measure. Teachers can raise students' chances of enjoyment and comprehension of texts by ensuring that the Lexile text measure fits within the average range for the grade level and, more importantly, for the individual student's reader measure.

There are, of course, other metrics for measuring the readability of a text. Scales such as the Flesch-Kincaid Grade Level, the Gunning-Fog Index, and the ATOS and SMOG indexes may also provide text analytics. A specific program or school may also use other proprietary tools, such as Accelerated Reader Book Finder or Scholastic Book Levels.

Beyond the quantitative measures determined by Lexile and others are qualitative measures such as the layout of the text (illustrations, text size), the overall text **structure** (simple narrative chronology, more advanced argumentative essay), **sentence structure** (prevalence of simple or more complex sentences), **levels of meaning** (whether ideas are explicitly or implicitly communicated), and **knowledge demand** (the cultural knowledge or other ideas that the reader must already know). The overall language and **vocabulary** of the text also generally fall under qualitative measures, although some quantitative scales measure the frequency of vocabulary with which students of a particular age or grade are unlikely to be familiar.

No singular measure of any text is sufficient to determine appropriateness for all students. Consider, for example, that Lexile ranges do not take into account the prevalence of mature subject matter and that overall appropriateness must always be considered. Teachers should also always keep in mind the need to differentiate literacy instruction in the classroom.

Practice Question

20) A teacher wants to select a text for the class based on its qualitative measures. Which strategy should the teacher use?
   A. access the Lexile score and see if it falls within the suggested range for the grade level
   B. run the text through a program that provides a score such as ATOS or Flesch-Kincaid
   C. examine the text to determine the complexity of content-area vocabulary
   D. give an assessment to students to identify students' Lexile reading measure

Reading Literature and Informational Texts

Comprehension and Analysis of Literature

Expertise in language arts requires an ability to use key ideas and details from literary or informational texts to determine the moral, theme, or central idea; make inferences; and summarize information. Readers must also be able to analyze characters, setting, plot, and relationships among ideas, events, and concepts.

The **theme** of a literary text is the basic idea about society or the human condition that the author wants to convey. It weaves in and out of the text as the story, play, or poem unfolds. It expresses an underlying opinion related to the text's subject. On the other hand, the **moral** of a literary text is the lesson the author wants to teach the reader. It is more direct than a theme. The basic underlying idea of a text is referred to as the **central idea**. This is the major focus of the events described. Both literary and informational texts have a central idea, though typically informational texts do not have a theme.

Teachers help students to comprehend what is being read by teaching students a variety of comprehension strategies. One of these strategies is the ability to make **inferences**, or determine what an author is suggesting by using clues in text. It is the ability to understand what is not directly stated by an author.

Summarization is the distillation and condensation of a text into its main idea and key details. It is a short encapsulation of what the text is about to clarify; however, to properly summarize a literary text, it is important to **identify story elements**. More specifically, this means identifying the characters (e.g., main, minor, protagonist, antagonist, dynamic, static); setting (where the story takes place); and plot development (e.g., exposition, rising action, problem/climax, falling action, resolution) in a text.

Understanding the role of a character in a story via the character's actions, traits, relationship, and personality is **character analysis**. Analyzing how a character thinks and behaves allows a reader to understand his motivations and beliefs. Furthermore, **dialogue**, or the words spoken by the characters, is essential to understanding their motivations and beliefs. Incidents or events, such as a character refusing to do something or agreeing with another character, also reveal something about them.

An author uses a specific point of view to tell a story. When **identifying point of view**, readers use genre and pronoun clues to identify who is telling a story to best form accurate conclusions about the events of the story. Typically, authors use one of five points of view: first-person, second-person, third-person objective, third-person limited omniscient, and third-person omniscient.

In **first-person** point of view, one character tells the story from her direct experience using pronouns such as *I*, *my*, *mine*, and *we*. In **second-person** point of view, the perspective of the text is from an external "you," whether that be the reader or unknown other. In **third-person objective** point of view, a detached narrator relates the actions and dialogue of the story, but not the thoughts or feelings of any characters. In **third-person limited omniscient** point of view, a detached narrator tells the story from one character's point of view including that character's internal thoughts and feelings. In **third-person omniscient** point of view, a detached and all-knowing narrator tells the story from the point of view of all of the characters, including all of their thoughts and feelings. Any text told from a third-person point of view includes pronouns such as *he*, *she*, *it*, and *they*.

Authors also use certain techniques to drive reader interest. For example, an author may **foreshadow**, or hint at an event that will occur in the future to create interest and build suspense. Similarly, an author may use sarcasm or **irony**, each of which uses language that typically means the opposite in order to drive humor.

Practice Questions

21) Read the excerpt from *Treasure Island* by Robert Louis Stevenson.

I remember him as if it were yesterday, as he came plodding to the inn door, his sea-chest following behind him in a hand-barrow—a tall, strong, heavy, nut-brown man, his tarry pigtail falling over the shoulder of his soiled blue coat, his hands ragged and scarred, with black, broken nails, and the sabre cut across one cheek, a dirty, livid white.

This text is written from which point of view?
- A. second-person
- B. first-person
- C. third-person objective
- D. third-person omniscient

22) What is an inference based on?
- A. identifying the main idea of each paragraph of the text
- B. combining details in the text and the reader's knowledge
- C. understanding the author's purpose in writing the text
- D. recognizing the author's tone or attitude toward the subject

Comprehension and Analysis of Informational Text

Informational texts are distinct from literary texts in that they are nonfiction. Of course, this does not mean informational texts are always **expository** or limited to a presentation of facts and information. Some genres of informational texts, such as literary nonfiction, present real information in a story format.

Some informational texts also offer supplemental information outside of the main text. These **text features** include images like photographs, drawings, maps, charts, and graphs. They also include organizational features like chapter **headings**, titles, **sidebars** (boxes of explanatory or additional information set aside from the main text), and **hyperlinks** (highlighted sections or words in digital text that take a reader to another digital location or document for additional information). Readers should be able to **analyze text features** to better comprehend an author's message.

Finally, **analyzing text organization** is the ability to analyze the way in which a text is organized in order to better comprehend an author's purpose for writing. Different forms of textual organization facilitate an author's message. Some of the more common organizational structures are cause and effect, problem and solution, sequence of events (i.e., steps-in-a-process), compare and contrast, and description. Each **text structure** can be identified by the use of particular signal or transitional words (words that provide clues as to how the author has organized information) and features.

> **Helpful Hint**
>
> Students can be taught to skim an informational text before they begin by noting titles, bolded headings, and other text features. This prereading strategy can help students get a general idea of what they will learn and help them set a purpose for reading.

Like literary texts, informational texts have a central or main idea and can be summarized to build comprehension. Of particular importance in informational texts are content-specific words that students must understand to comprehend the article or passage. Students can be encouraged to use context clues, morphological clues, and other features sometimes present in informational texts, such as glossaries, footnotes, or definitions present in the running text.

One particular type of informational text is an argumentative text, or a text that presents and develops an argument on a topic. Argumentative texts typically introduce one or many **claims** or theses, which are key points made, and develop these claims with support. **Support** for claims may take the form of statistics or other facts, quotations, examples, or counter-examples. Quality argumentative texts may also introduce and refute a **counterclaim**, or the perspective opposite of what is being argued.

Students should practice analyzing argumentative texts to identify claims that are and are not supported with sufficient evidence.

Practice Question

23) What is one way students could determine the claim made in an argumentative text?
    A. by summarizing the passage beginning with "the passage is mostly about_____"
    B. by crossing out all irrelevant evidence
    C. by highlighting all sentences that mention the main topic
    D. by completing the sentence stem "the author believes that_____"

Writing

Writing Development

Like reading and spelling development, students typically develop writing skills in a somewhat linear process that corresponds with their overall cognitive and language development.

Table 1.7. Developmental Stages of Writing		
Stage	**Age**	**Students in this stage . . .**
Preconventional	3 – 5	<ul><li>are aware that print conveys meaning but rely on pictures to communicate visually,</li><li>can recognize shapes and letters on drawings, and</li><li>can describe the significance of the objects in the drawings.</li></ul>

Table 1.7. Developmental Stages of Writing

Stage	Age	Students in this stage . . .
Emerging	4 – 6	<ul><li>use pictures when drawing, but may also label objects;</li><li>can match some letters to sounds; and</li><li>copy print they see in their environment.</li></ul>
Developing	5 – 7	<ul><li>write sentences and no longer rely mainly on pictures,</li><li>attempt to use punctuation and capitalization, and</li><li>spell words based on sound.</li></ul>
Beginning	6 – 8	<ul><li>write several related sentences on a topic;</li><li>use word spacing, punctuation, and capitalization correctly; and</li><li>create writing that others can read.</li></ul>
Expanding	7 – 9	<ul><li>organize sentences logically and use more complex sentence structures,</li><li>spell high-frequency words correctly, and</li><li>respond to guidance and criticism from others.</li></ul>

Table 1.7. Developmental Stages of Writing

Stage	Age	Students in this stage . . .
Bridging	8 – 10	<ul><li>write about a particular topic with a clear beginning, middle, and end;</li><li>begin to use paragraphs; and</li><li>consult outside resources (e.g., dictionaries).</li></ul>
Fluent	9 – 11	<ul><li>write both fiction and nonfiction with guidance;</li><li>experiment with sentence length and complexity; and</li><li>edit for punctuation, spelling, and grammar.</li></ul>
Proficient	10 – 13	<ul><li>write well-developed fiction and nonfiction,</li><li>use transitional sentences and descriptive language, and</li><li>edit for organization and style.</li></ul>
Connecting	11 – 14	<ul><li>write in a number of different genres,</li><li>develop a personal voice when writing, and</li><li>use complex punctuation.</li></ul>
Independent	13 and older	<ul><li>explore topics in-depth in fiction and nonfiction,</li><li>incorporate literary devices in their writing, and</li><li>revise writing through multiple drafts.</li></ul>

In their overall plan for developing literacy in students, teachers should give students plenty of opportunities to practice writing alongside reading and analyzing texts. It is important to ensure conscious writing instruction and practice as research suggests that these are sometimes overlooked components of early-childhood literacy curriculum. Some studies even suggest that many prekindergarten and kindergarten students spend at least three minutes a day on writing practice. The overall process of learning to write involves three distinct components:

- conceptual knowledge (understanding the purpose of writing)
- procedural knowledge (understanding how to form letters and words)
- generative knowledge (using words to communicate a meaning)

> **Check Your Understanding**
>
> What are concepts of print? How can teachers encourage print awareness in their classrooms?

In helping young students develop conceptual knowledge of writing, teachers should focus on activities that show students the link between print and its intended purpose. Environmental print is a great resource for helping students develop this knowledge as teachers point out classroom signs and posters or those in the school building and on the playground. They can further build early conceptual knowledge by having students **draw** or **scribble** to communicate their own feelings and ideas.

Procedural knowledge involves the nuts and bolts of writing. Procedural knowledge-building activities are those that build awareness of

- basic letter formation,
- the knowledge that words are made up of letters,
- the knowledge that words have spaces between them, and
- the overall mechanics of writing.

Procedural knowledge and the alphabetic principle are entwined, and the letter sounds and names should be reinforced when consciously instructing correct letter formation.

Additionally, procedural knowledge of writing will coincide with the development of fine motor skills. Fine motor skills development in the classroom cannot be overemphasized, particularly in the preschool and kindergarten settings. As in any part of emergent literacy, teachers will have students with widely divergent levels of fine motor proficiency. It is essential that the classroom provides a variety of opportunities for students to build these skills through the use of manipulatives, such as alphabet boards and puzzles, and a variety of writing implements, such as crayons, markers, and pencils.

Practice Question

24) In which stage of writing development do students begin to write sentences?
    A. emerging
    B. developing
    C. beginning
    D. expanding

Types of Writing

There are four main writing **styles** that students often learn in elementary school. Each style is selected based on an author's **purpose** for writing—to explain, to entertain, to describe, or to persuade—and the needs of the **audience**, the people reading the material. Different audiences have different needs. For example, people reading a humor blog will most likely prefer an informal style, while the audience for a magazine article explaining environmental problems caused by deforestation will appreciate writing with a well-organized structure and paragraphs that expand on key issues. The four main styles of writing are as follows:

- **Expository Writing:** This style of writing is primarily used to explain an idea or concept, or to inform the reader about a topic. It is most often used in formal essays that include a main idea and supporting details based on fact.

- **Narrative Writing:** This style of writing is primarily used to tell a personal or fictional story that entertains the reader. The author includes descriptive details and figurative language in order to maintain the reader's attention with dynamic characters, interesting settings, and captivating plots. Poems that tell stories, or **narrative poems**, also use this writing style.
- **Descriptive Writing:** This style of writing emphasizes the production of imagery using words and figurative language that appeal to the reader's five senses. It is a writing style that produces vivid pictures in the reader's imagination and is often used to write poetry or detailed descriptions of experiences or events.
- **Persuasive Writing:** This style of writing is used to convince, or persuade, a reader to subscribe to the author's opinion or point of view. It follows a formal progression that aims to sway the reader into accepting the author's stance and often plays on the reader's emotions to achieve its goal. Persuasive writing is often used for **speeches** and **advertisements**. Persuasive writing is somewhat distinct from **argumentative writing** because persuasive writing has the purpose of encouraging the reader to take some action while argumentative writing merely presents the writer's view on a subject.

In addition, there is writing for school (i.e., **academic writing**), and **authentic writing** for a real-life purpose. Authentic writing activities may include writing for the purposes of communicating with others via letter or e-mail and writing related to obtaining a job or career, such as creating a resume, LinkedIn profile, or job application.

Practice Question

25) Which of the following can be classified as persuasive writing?
   A. an advertisement for a new product
   B. a research paper on the effects of climate on ecosystems
   C. a poem about the ocean on a foggy day
   D. an opinion piece describing the author's anger at high taxes

The Writing Process

Students should understand that writing is a process and that even professional writers go through several phases before their finished products are released. This **authoring cycle** generally includes several phases in which ideas are transformed into written form to effectively communicate meaning. Students first need to **brainstorm** ideas. This can take many forms, and teachers might have the entire class generate ideas for writing topics and record them on the board or screen as an initial step.

Students can then create their own webs or **outlines** to organize their ideas. This initial planning can help students organize their overall point and supporting details. These activities can be based on a book they have read, where they take a stance on the work (e.g., "I liked the book," "I did not like the book," "My favorite/least favorite part was...") and then list the reasons why or why not. Students might also write a simple expository piece in which they introduce an overall topic and then use supporting details to inform the reader. Brainstorming activities can also help students organize the events they wish to recount when writing narratives.

After the brainstorming is complete, students draft their piece and link their ideas together with an introductory statement, support, and concluding section or statement. With scaffolding, students must then go through a **revision** and **editing** process in which they strengthen their piece through the addition of more supporting details and connecting words (e.g., *because*, *also*, *then*) and proofread for capitalization, end marks, and spelling.

Teachers may aid students in the revision process by providing a simple checklist to help students ensure they have met certain criteria. One simple revision checklist is the **COPS** mnemonic. This stands for **c**apitalization, **o**rganization, **p**unctuation, and **s**pelling and is used with success in many early elementary classrooms. Teachers may also employ peer and/or teacher feedback as part of the overall revision process. Receiving feedback helps reinforce that the overarching purpose of writing is to communicate ideas, so the perceptions and suggestions of multiple readers must be taken into account when revising a piece.

Students should also **publish** their work after the final copy is created, particularly if the writing project is significant in scope. Having students read their work aloud is one simple and immediate way to publish a piece, as is posting it on a classroom or school bulletin board. Teachers may have students organize and bind their work into a simple book with string or brads or collect student work into a class-wide literary sampler.

If a teacher uses student portfolios in the classroom, he may have students prepare their pieces for inclusion into a digital or physical folder. This may involve transcribing the piece digitally, adding illustrations, or matting it on construction paper. Teachers should also emphasize to students that seminal to the idea of publishing is sharing the work with others. This is a great way to build a home–school connection while encouraging students to share their work with parents. Teachers should also show student work samples or portfolios at parent conferences to further build the connection between home and school.

> **Did You Know?**
>
> There are many intentionally fake sites on the internet designed to help students practice determining whether online information is legitimate. One example is found at https://zapatopi.net/treeoctopus, where students can learn about the Pacific Northwest Tree Octopus.

Practice Question

26) Which option is NOT a way to publish student writing?
   A. hosting a poetry night where students read their work aloud
   B. submitting a student-authored essay to a writing contest
   C. asking students to type their piece on the computer
   D. having students trade a bound book they have created with a friend to read and enjoy

Research

Research Basics

As students grow as writers, they begin to learn how to cite sources to support their ideas in research papers. The research paper is an expository essay that contains references to outside materials that legitimize claims made in the essay. Students learn to **paraphrase** supporting information, or briefly restate it in their own words, in order to avoid **plagiarism**, which is the intentional copying and credit-taking of another person's work. They also learn to include **citations** that name original sources of new information and are taught how to differentiate between primary sources, secondary sources, reliable sources, and unreliable sources.

Primary sources are original materials representative of an event, experience, place, or time period. They are direct or firsthand accounts in the form of text, image, record, sound, or item. **Secondary sources** inform about events, experiences, places, or time periods, but the information is provided by someone who was not directly involved and who used primary sources to discuss the material.

Reliable sources are trustworthy materials that come from experts in the field of study. These sources have **credibility** because they include extensive bibliographies listing the sources used to support the information provided. Some examples of reliable sources are published books, articles in credible magazines, and research studies provided by educational institutions. **Unreliable sources** are untrustworthy materials from a person or institution that does not have the educational background, expertise, or evidence of legitimate sources to support a claim. Some examples of unreliable sources are self-published materials, studies done to sell products, and opinion pieces.

Practice Question

27) Which of the following is considered a reliable source for research about California?
   A. a personal blog about living in California
   B. a research paper published by the State of California
   C. an advertisement for California real estate
   D. a letter to the editor about California roadways

The Research Process

Research and library skills are an important part of developing overall student literacy. Generally, there are seven steps in the research process:

1. **Identifying and focusing on the topic:** This might be as simple as having students pick a topic they want to learn more about or develop a research question they wish to answer—before searching online.

2. **Finding background information and conducting a preliminary search:** This involves getting a general overview of a topic and possible subtopics. During this stage, students may Google a topic or read the *Wikipedia* page devoted to a particular topic.

3. **Locating materials:** This could involve work at the library and online. Teachers should encourage students to explore a wide variety of possible resources, such as books, articles, and web pages devoted to a topic.

4. **Evaluating sources:** Students need to determine if certain sources are useful and accessible to them. For example, a library database may generate results for articles in publications to which the library does not have a subscription. Some resources may be inaccessible to students as they may be overly technical or written for an older audience. Students should also make sure they have credible sources written by experts. This stage in the research process might be a good time to introduce the different types of information available on the internet and the qualities that help increase reliability (e.g., listed author, .edu or .org domain, publication date).

5. **Note-taking:** Note-taking may involve using formal note cards or simply jotting down main ideas.

6. **Writing:** This includes organizing all the notes into sentences and paragraphs. Students need to be cognizant of the overall organization of their work as they introduce a focused topic,

provide support, and write a conclusion. Depending on the age group with which teachers work, they may have students make a poster or use another outlet instead of a formal paper to present their research.

7. **Citing sources:** This may include in-text **citations** and preparing a bibliography. To simplify these elements for young students, teachers might use a simpler works cited/bibliography page where students simply list titles of books and authors. Students in the upper elementary grades may work to develop more sophisticated bibliographies in MLA style, as it is generally regarded as the simplest citation style and the one to which students are first introduced.

Practice Question

28) A teacher has just provided students a general overview of a research project due at the end of the semester. Which of the following is MOST appropriate as a first task?
    A. selecting a topic
    B. developing an outline
    C. choosing reliable primary and secondary resources
    D. formulating appropriate research questions on a topic

Presenting Research

The use of varied media often makes a message clearer and more engaging. Many national and state standards require students to work on media projects such as presentations, videos, posters, charts, graphs, and audio recordings. Often, these types of projects promote curricular integration as students use media skills to analyze and present information across content areas.

Teachers should help students learn to create high-quality and engaging multimedia projects to present their research findings. Effective presentations should

- contain an appropriate balance of media elements;
- use sound, images, and video aligned with the overall message of the presentation;
- offer opportunities for audience participation, if possible; and
- be aligned with the project's purpose and audience.

Students should strive to use media in their work for a specific purpose—often to elaborate on a point or help the audience visualize something. The use of media elements as "decoration" or "fluff" is generally not a best practice. Students should therefore be taught to recognize and evaluate effective presentations, both those they make themselves and those made by others. Rubrics customized for specific types of media can be very helpful for both teacher and student evaluation of media.

With the increased use of media comes more responsibility. Students should use appropriate online etiquette and must learn to navigate fair-use issues in the digital space.

Students creating and posting media must follow basic **netiquette** protocols, meaning they should use a communication style appropriate to the online environment. Most schools and districts have netiquette policies, which might include the following:

- keeping the people behind digital communications in mind at all times;
- remembering that nothing posted online is private or temporary;
- using an appropriate tone for the audience;
- maintaining the privacy and confidentiality of others; and
- avoiding the use of all caps, emojis, or slang.

When creating media, students must also learn how to correctly use and cite media sources. **Copyright** is the legal ownership of a work of art. Copyrighted works can only be reproduced or repurposed under specific conditions.

Fair use refers to the legal use of **copyrighted** work without the permissions of the rights-holder in certain circumstances. Fair use doctrine follows four main guidelines:

> **Helpful Hint**
>
> Types of art that CAN be copyrighted include written works, painting, photographs, musical compositions, movies, and sound recordings. Things that CANNOT be copyrighted include recipes/formulas, ideas, slogans, and common knowledge.

1. Purpose and character of use: Education and nonprofit use of copyrighted works is usually permitted. Works that are transformative—meaning they add something substantially new—are also usually able to use copyrighted materials.

2. Nature of the work: Personal, creative works of art are less likely to be considered for fair use.

3. Amount and substantiality of the work: Using small portions of copyrighted works is often permitted.

4. Effect of the use on the market for copyrighted material: Reproduction of copyrighted materials that substantially affects the ability of the original creators to market their products is not allowed.

Classroom use of copyrighted content often falls under fair use guidelines because it is for educational purposes; however, the principles of fair use must still be considered. For example, it may be appropriate for students to use properly cited images in a slide presentation given to the class. It would not, however, be appropriate for students to use those copyrighted images on their personal websites without the copyright-holder's permission. In these cases, the material has two different purposes: one is a limited educational setting; the other is the broad online dissemination of someone else's work.

Of course, not all media is copyrighted. Work that is in the **public domain** is free for use because its copyright has expired, was forfeited, or never existed. Students can be directed to sites that offer photos and images in the public domain.

Additionally, some work falls under a **Creative Commons** license. Creative Commons (CC) is a nonprofit that helps content creators designate how their work may be used. All CC content must be attributed to its creator. Further, there are multiple types of CC licenses that dictate how the work may be used. Some require that the content only be used for noncommercial purposes or that it only be reused if the new work will also fall under a Creative Commons license.

Students and teachers should also be aware of liability before using images or videos featuring other students. Schools and districts will typically have a media release policy and associated forms that parents must sign. Without such documentation, photos and videos of students should not be posted on any online platforms, including class websites or social media pages.

Practice Question

29) A teacher assigns an activity wherein student groups create a website highlighting the life and work of a well-known author of the past. What should the teacher advise students before they begin?
   A. They can use any type of media on the site because it is for educational purposes and thus falls under fair use.
   B. They should avoid the use of any images on their website because of the risk of copyright infringement.
   C. They should seek out image sources that are in the public domain or that have certain types of CC licenses.
   D. They can use most types of media on the site but should provide links to the original sources for proper citation.

Non-Written Communication

Analyzing Media

Media literacy is the ability to find and effectively analyze media content. All types of media—from magazines to movies to podcasts—can be analyzed in much the same way as traditional texts. Students should learn to assess both the content and context of the media they consume. Import aspects of media analysis include

- the message or main idea of the content,
- the intent or purpose of the people who produce the content,
- the effect the media has on the audience, and
- the techniques used to produce this effect.

Teachers often begin the process of analyzing media by explaining to students that no media is completely neutral—every piece has a **message**. Students should be able to identify the key information communicated in a piece of media and understand how it builds the message.

To place media's message in the proper context, students must look for the **intent** of its producers—who made this piece of media and why? Every piece of media has a purpose. Like informational texts, media can inform, persuade, or entertain.

To identify the purpose of a piece of media, students should first identify the person or organization behind it. Knowing this information allows students to assess the producer's **bias** so they can evaluate the strength of the content. Asking the following types of questions can help students determine bias:

- Is the producer a person or company with a vested interest in the subject matter?
- Are the producers experts in their fields, or do they have any professional qualifications?
- Is the producer a magazine or news organization with a known political bias?
- How are the producers funded and how might this affect their biases?

> **Helpful Hint**
>
> As part of a media literacy program, students should learn how advertising drives content in digital media. Often, the intent of producers is simply to attract viewers and raise ad revenue.

Once the creator is identified, the intent of the media can be analyzed. For example, if a notable scientific study is being covered in media, the intent of the media creator will determine how that study is presented:

- The university that did the study may promote it with an upbeat article on its website.
- A news site may drive traffic to its site by focusing on sensationalized aspects of the study.
- A company may use the study to advertise their own products.
- Social media accounts may use the study to promote a specific political agenda.

Media can have many different **effects** on the consumer and can affect an individual's knowledge, attitudes, beliefs, and behaviors. These effects might change the way an individual thinks or behaves or reinforce existing beliefs and behaviors.

> **Helpful Hint**
>
> **Propaganda** is communication designed to influence public opinion, often through partial truths—or even total falsehoods. Students should learn to identify propaganda and become familiar with the various logical fallacies it often uses.

To help students develop skills in evaluating various types of media, they should be exposed to multiple sources of information and learn how to compare and contrast them. For example, an informational article or podcast could be compared to a documentary film on the same topic. Similarly, advertisements across various platforms like radio, print, and film—both past and present—could be compared to identify techniques used and how those impact the viewer, reader, or listener.

Along with comparing media representations of various topics, students should be taught to confirm facts from a variety of sources and spot examples of media messages that contain lies or claims that cannot be verified through other sources. Again, the availability of technology can be a help. For example, in the past, the public often had to rely on word of mouth to confirm the claims of advertisers about a product or service; now, online reviews can reveal much and help consumers make informed purchases.

Practice Question

30) A teacher wants to design an activity to help students confirm the accuracy of information in an online video about a historical topic. Which activity is MOST appropriate?
   A. having students compare the information in the video to multiple photographs covering the same topic
   B. assigning students the task of creating their own videos on the same topic
   C. encouraging students to use the information in the video to create a multimedia presentation on the same topic
   D. asking students to compare the information in the video with that found in multiple print sources

Speaking and Listening

Some students may be introverted and others more extroverted; however, all children need help to develop basic skills in speaking and listening to enable them to become effective communicators. There will be times when students must employ **passive listening**, where they listen to a speaker or presentation without conversing. These occasions might be at school assemblies, when watching a movie, or when listening to a storyteller. Passive listening, so long as it is done intently, is not necessarily bad; it just implies a lack of two-way communication. In fact, some occasions, such as being a respectful audience member, will require students to employ passive listening skills.

Active listening, on the other hand, should be employed whenever there is two-way communication. Active listening is used in many positive behavioral support programs, so if a school or program employs one of these, active listening may become a skill about which teachers are daily reminding students. The goal of active listening is to ensure that the listener has correctly understood the speaker. This is often extended to include an understanding of and empathy with this speaker. Generally, active listening involves making appropriate **eye contact** with the speaker, waiting for the speaker to finish, and then responding in a way that shows understanding.

Not only should teachers be active listeners to ensure they understand what students are thinking and feeling, but they should also encourage students to employ these techniques whenever they are listening to directions or holding conversations. Active listening can also help students avoid conflict with each other as they refrain from interrupting and practice valuing the thoughts and opinions of others.

Part of listening and responding may involve different **types of questioning** as listeners check for understanding. Speakers generally employ either open-ended questions ("What does your house look like?"), which require a significant response, or closed-ended questions ("Do you like fried chicken?"), which generally require only a simple one-word answer. Speakers may even ask rhetorical questions, which do not require a response but are designed to make the listener think.

Language arts teachers should design curriculum to develop students' speaking skills in conjunction with reading and writing skills. Specific strategies are used to develop proficiency in the areas of active listening, oral presentation, and the use of **multimedia** (combined mediums of expression) to support speech. Across the duration of an oral presentation assignment, teachers should cover the following:

- **Delivery:** posture, intonation, volume, eye contact, articulation (clarity of speech) and expression
- **Organization:** a logical presentation structure with
    - a brief, attention-grabbing hook that captures the audience's interest (e.g., an amusing thought, an interesting prop, an intriguing fact, or a thought-provoking statement);
    - an introduction that states the topic and gives a brief overview of what will be covered;
    - a body of evidence and/or details that correlate to and support the topic; and
    - a conclusion that summarizes the presentation's main points.
- **Claims and Evidence:** accuracy of content, strength of argument, use of source material, correlation between main idea and supporting details, logical progression of ideas, facts, and reasoned judgments
- **Audience Awareness:** preparedness, appropriateness, and ability to hold audience attention

- **Visuals and/or Audio:** supporting materials that reinforce content (e.g., props, posters, digital media, photographs, music)

Students are provided with opportunities to strengthen listening skills during classmates' oral presentations. They are tasked with providing **constructive feedback**—positively worded suggestions—derived from previously agreed-upon criteria.

> **Think About It**
>
> How would you design an oral presentation research project for first-grade students?

Practice Question

31) Which of the following is an active listening strategy that can be taught to kindergarten students?
    A. emphasizing proper articulation
    B. maintaining eye contact
    C. using open-ended questioning
    D. practicing oral presentations

Answer Key

1) B: All languages are learned by human babies at roughly the same time.

2) B: The prefix *mono–* means "one," and the root word *graph* means "written," so a monograph is a written document about one subject.

3) A: The prefix *poly–* means "many," and the suffix *–glot* means "in a language or tongue." Therefore, the sentence is explaining that the sister speaks many languages.

4) D: In the holophrastic stage, children use one word to denote a broader desire or meaning. This is the stage after babbling.

5) D: Marlin's interest in conversation and his ability to self-correct indicate that he is moving towards advanced fluency and has reached the intermediate stage.

6) C: The strategy of phoneme segmentation requires students to separate the phonemes in a word.

7) C: Experts concur that by the end of third grade, students should make the shift from the transitional stage to the intermediate stage of literacy development.

8) D: Having students act out a play from a script would give them practice reading expressively.

9) A: The word *skim* may suggest that a text was not read thoroughly and only glanced over for surface meaning.

10) A: The pattern is *g* (consonant) *a* (vowel) *p* (consonant).

11) B: When students say the onset and rime together, they are blending both phonemes together.

12) C: Assigning students to write the draft of an email they will eventually send to someone is an assignment that is authentic because students will actually send the email to someone, so the assessment has a real-world application. It also allows the teacher to assess the students' use of paragraphs.

13) B: The word *from* is a preposition.

14) A: Because adjectives modify nouns and adverbs modify verbs, adjectives, or other adverbs, this is a foundational understanding that must precede a discussion of when using an adjective or adverb is most appropriate. The other options are not relevant to adjective versus adverb use.

15) A: The underlined phrases are participial, infinitive, and prepositional, respectively.

16) B: In this sentence option, two independent clauses are joined with a comma and the coordinating conjunction *but*.

17) B: To be possessive, *Freds* requires an apostrophe before the *s* (*Fred's*). *Christmas* needs a colon to indicate the upcoming list (*Christmas:*), and *car and condo* should be followed by commas since they are items in a series (*car, condo*).

18) D: The phrase "five thousand times a day" is an exaggeration, or hyperbole.

19) B: Bringing in magazines, pamphlets, newspapers, and other items for students to explore allows for hands-on learning and will help Ms. Jones explain how these different texts are structured for their intended purposes.

20) C: The complexity of content-area vocabulary is a qualitative feature of the text; the others are all quantitative measures.

21) B: The first-person point of view is written directly from the perspective of one character.

22) B: In order to read between the lines, readers must use their own knowledge as well as draw on the information provided.

23) D: The claim is the author's opinion or take on the topic, so this strategy would be most effective.

24) B: In the developing stage of writing, between the ages of 5 and 7, students begin to write in sentences.

25) A: Persuasive writing is aimed at getting the reader to take action, such as buying a product.

26) C: Asking students to type their piece on the computer does not necessarily share the piece with others; it merely formats it in a different way.

27) B: A published study by a government institution is a reliable research source.

28) A: The first step in any research project is to select a topic of interest. Once general information on a topic is understood, a relevant question can be formulated.

29) C: In order to prevent students from infringing on copyrighted information, the teacher should advise students that they must seek out image sources that are considered public domain or those which have certain types of Creative Commons (CC) licenses.

30) D: Students should confirm facts in popular media by using multiple sources to ensure the accuracy of the information and note inconsistencies.

31) B: Maintaining eye contact is a core part of active listening and can help kindergarten students focus on a speaker. The other activities listed are not a part of active listening.

2. History and Social Science

World History

Ancient (Classical) Civilizations

Classical civilizations have had a lasting influence on human history. Ancient civilizations in the Fertile Crescent (including ancient Egypt), Greece and Rome, Africa, India, and China have had a tremendous impact on the world.

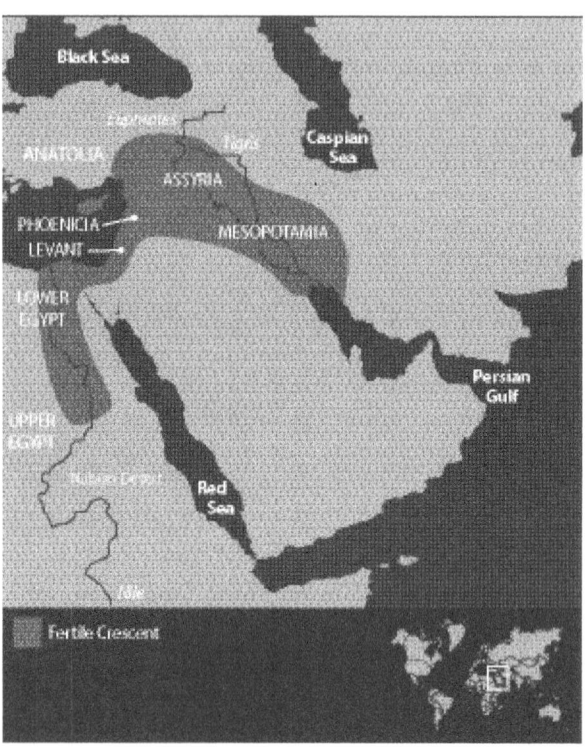

Figure 2.1. The Fertile Crescent

> **Did You Know?**
>
> Hammurabi's Code contained 282 rules, including those that defined standards for commercial interactions.

Around 2500 BCE (or possibly earlier) the **Sumerians** emerged in the Near East (eventually expanding into parts of Mesopotamia). The Sumerians developed irrigation and advanced agriculture as well as **cuneiform**, the earliest known example of writing to use characters to form words. Sumer featured city-states, the potter's wheel, early astronomy and mathematics, early education, literary and artistic developments, and religious thought. Cuneiform also allowed advanced governance and administration. Later, **Assyria** and **Babylonia** developed as important empires in the region. The Assyrians had based much of their culture on Sumer, contributing unique sculpture and jewelry, establishing military dominance, and playing an important role in regional trade. Babylonia also inherited elements of Sumerian civilization and developed them further. In the eighteenth century BCE, King Hammurabi in Babylonia had developed courts and an early codified rule of law—**the Code of Hammurabi**—which meted out justice on an equal basis: "an eye for an eye, a tooth for a tooth."

Egypt

Meanwhile, development had been under way in the **Nile Valley** in ancient **Egypt**. The fertile land on the banks of the Nile River allowed the early Egyptians to develop settled communities thanks to agriculture and irrigation. Known for their pyramids, art, use of papyrus as paper, and pictorial writing (**hieroglyphs**), the ancient Egyptians emerged as early as 5000 BCE and were united under one monarch, or **pharaoh**.

Figure 2.2. Hieroglyphs

Around 2500 BCE, Egypt's civilizational institutions, administrative structure, written language, art, and architecture were becoming well developed. In addition, the religious framework of ancient Egypt had become established, with a complex mythology of various gods. The ancient Egyptians also developed astronomy and the twenty-four-hour system of measuring time. It was during this period that the famous **pyramids** were erected at Giza; these structures were actually burial tombs for pharaohs. Major pharaohs included Hatshepsut, Thutmose III, Akhenaten, and Ramesses II.

Egyptian architecture also influenced many civilizations in the Western world. The use of columns in Pharaoh Hatshepsut's temple in Luxor is an example. It influenced Greek architectural design, which was copied by the Romans and many civilizations since.

The Hebrews

In the land of Canaan (present day Palestine), another important civilization, the **Hebrews**, emerged. Though the early source of information on this civilization is largely the Pentateuch, or the first five books of the Christian bible, scholars date this civilization to sometime close to 1900 BCE. Its founder, or patriarch, was a man named Abraham who is said to have made a covenant with a god named Yahweh, beginning the religious history of the Hebrew people.

The Hebrew people were largely nomadic in their earliest civilization and often shared their goods and wealth in common. The Hebrew people organized into clans or tribes (the twelve tribes of Israel per the religious texts). They did eventually appoint a series of kings, including the famed Kings David and Solomon, who founded a capital in Jerusalem and a temple that was the center of religious life. The Hebrew kingdom was relatively wealthy due to its location along major trade routes, but resentment against Solomon's taxation grew. After the death of Solomon, the kingdom split into two, with ten of the twelve clans or tribes splitting from the rest. The new partitioned kingdoms were the kingdom of Israel in the north and the kingdom of Judah in the south.

While the Hebrews are not most remembered for their art or technological developments as some earlier civilizations, their monotheistic religion (believing in and worshipping only one god) would impact many other civilizations. It also stands as the first time in documented human history that monotheism was widely practiced by any civilization.

Africa

Elsewhere in Africa, the **Kush**, the oldest known civilization in the sub-Saharan region, flourished from roughly 2500 – 1500 BCE. This period, sometimes called the first Kingdom of Kush, saw rise of the capital settlement of **Kerma**, located in the Upper Nubian region. Kush flourished when Egypt was weakest, and historians often note the period of declining Egyptian control of the region when the Kush conquered and ruled Egypt (roughly 750 – 350 CE) as the Second Kingdom of Kush.

The Kush kingdom was heavily influenced by its northern Egyptian neighbors, who were important trade partners. The Egyptians also influenced the culture of the Sudanese Kush, though Kushites had their own language and gods, even though they also worshipped Egyptian gods and at one time used Egyptian hieroglyphics to record their language before developing their own script. The Kush were known for their wealth from ivory, gold, and incense, which were traded with their northern neighbors and others.

India

Though less is known about the ancient Indian civilization called the **Indus Valley** civilization, it is believed to have existed from roughly 2500 – 1700 BCE. As compared with the Egyptian and Mesopotamian civilizations, the Indus civilization spanned a much larger territory, encompassing the major cities of Harappa and Mohenjo-daro and at least 100 other smaller settlements. The Indu people practiced agriculture, making use of irrigation from the Indus River. While confirming evidence from this civilization is scant, many believe that the civilization had a centralized political system and standard singular language. The Indus Valley civilization produced great amounts of art, including terra-cotta figurines, which may have represented their pantheon.

China

In **China**, the Shang Dynasty, the first known dynasty, emerged around the second millennium BCE and developed the earliest known Chinese writing, which helped unite Chinese-speaking people throughout the region. Like other early civilizations, the Shang Dynasty featured the use of bronze technology, horses, wheeled technology, walled cities, and other advances. Later, under the Zhou dynasty, China developed the concept of the **Mandate of Heaven**, in which the emperor had a divine mandate to rule, based on an understanding that land was divinely inherited. **Confucius** lived toward the end of this dynasty (c. 551 – 479 BCE). His teachings would be the basis for Confucianism, the foundational Chinese philosophy emphasizing harmony and respect for hierarchy.

The Qin dynasty (221 – 206 BCE) was characterized by a centralized administration, expanded infrastructure, standardization in weights and measures, writing, currency, and strict imperial control. The administrative bureaucracy was established by the first emperor, **Qin Shihuangdi**, and it was the foundation of Chinese administration until the twentieth century. In addition, the emperor constructed the **Great Wall of China**; his tomb is guarded by the famous **terracotta figurines**.

Figure 2.3. Great Wall of China

Greece

Ancient Greece was composed of small **city-states** like **Athens**, the first known **democracy**, and the military state **Sparta**. Around 460 BCE, Athens became a revolutionary democracy controlled by the poor and working classes. In fact, the term *democracy* comes from the Greek word *demokratia*—"people power." It was participatory rather than representative; officials were chosen by groups rather than elected. Athenian ideals have influenced politics and governance throughout history.

Athens was the strongest of the many small political bodies (in fact, the word *political* comes from the Greek word *polis* meaning "city-state" or "community"), and much of Greece became unified under Athens following the Peloponnesian war between Athens and Sparta. It was during this period, the **Golden Age** of Greek civilization, that much of the Hellenic art, architecture, and philosophy known today emerged, including the **Parthenon** and other masterpieces of ancient Greek sculpture and architecture.

Socrates began teaching philosophy, influencing later philosophers like **Plato** and **Aristotle**, establishing the basis for modern Western philosophical and political thought. Mathematical advances included the Pythagorean Theorem, Euclidean geometry, and the calculation of the circumference of Earth. Playwrights like **Sophocles** and **Euripides** emerged; their work later influenced Western literature. The Greeks practiced the Olympic Games to honor their gods, a diverse panoply of deities with a detailed mythology.

The Greeks established numerous colonies across the Black Sea, southern Italy, Sicily, and the eastern Mediterranean, spreading Greek culture throughout the Mediterranean world; it was eventually conquered by the rising Mediterranean power, Rome.

Rome

Originally a kingdom, Rome became a republic in 509 BCE; as such, Romans elected lawmakers (senators) to the **Senate**. The Romans developed highly advanced infrastructure, including aqueducts and roads, some still in use today. Economically powerful, Rome began conquering areas around the Mediterranean, including Greece, with its increasingly powerful military and began expanding westward to North Africa. With conquest of territory and expansion of trade came increased slavery, and working-class Romans were displaced; at the same time, the wealthy ruling class became more powerful and corrupt.

The people, or *Populare*, wanted a more democratic republic. As the Senate weakened due to its own corruption, **Julius Caesar**, a popular military leader widely supported by the *Populare*, emerged. Forcing the corrupt Senate to give him control, Caesar began to transition Rome from a republic to what would become an empire. Caesar was assassinated in 44 BCE; however, in that short time he had been able to consolidate and centralize imperial control. His nephew Octavian eventually gained control of Rome in 27 BCE, taking the name **Augustus Caesar** and becoming the first Roman emperor.

Figure 2.4. Pax Romana

At this time, Rome reached the height of its power, and the Mediterranean region enjoyed a period of stability known as the ***Pax Romana***. Rome controlled the entire Mediterranean region, Europe, and much of the Middle East and North Africa. Latin literature flourished, as did art, architecture, philosophy, mathematics, science, and international trade throughout Rome and beyond into Asia and Africa.

> **Check Your Understanding**
>
> What were similarities among ancient civilizations that allowed societies to grow and flourish?

A series of Barbarian invasions led to an empire already in decline splitting into an East and West in 395 CE. After the western empire was pillaged by Visigoths in 410, the fall of Rome was in full force with the date of its end cited as 476 CE by many scholars. The eastern empire, or Byzantium, would continue for many years to come.

Why the great empire of Rome fell remains of interest to historians. Though it remains too challenging to point to a single factor for the great end of Rome, several problems plagued the civilization near its end. Christianity began to spread, which created some disunity and weakened certain Roman traditions rooted in the ancient Roman pantheon. Economic problems, caused by over-expansion, mismanagement, and over-reliance on enslaved labor, also contributed to the decline. Raids by Barbarian tribes could not be defended by the weakened Roman legions or the series of incompetent and weakened leaders. Taken together, these many realities contributed to the fall of the great empire.

Practice Questions

1) According to Confucianism, an ideal society
    A. is based on respect for authority and wisdom, making harmonious interaction a priority.
    B. allows respectful debate and discussion to encourage learning and the development of wisdom.
    C. encompasses a diverse group of people, to gather wisdom from different cultures.
    D. values hierarchy and enforces a caste system.

2) During the Pax Romana, the Mediterranean region was all of the following EXCEPT
    A. experiencing a period of relative stability under Roman rule.
    B. a center of commercial activity.
    C. ruled by Augustus Caesar.
    D. under the control of a powerful Senate.

Medieval and Early Modern Times

The Eastern Roman Empire later became the Byzantine Empire, a strong civilization and a place of learning based in Constantinople, a strategically located commercial center connecting Asian trade routes with Europe. The Western Roman Empire eventually collapsed: the Christian church remained important politically and culturally, but different rulers took power throughout Europe.

> **Check Your Understanding**
>
> What were some of the factors that contributed to the collapse of Rome?

In Europe, the early **Middle Ages** (or Dark Ages) from the fall of Rome to about the tenth century was a chaotic, unstable, and unsafe time. What protection and stability existed were represented and maintained by the Catholic Church and the feudal system.

Society and economics were characterized by decentralized, local governance, or **feudalism**, a hierarchy where land and protection were offered in exchange for loyalty. In exchange for protection, **vassals** would pledge fealty, or pay homage to **lords**, landowners who would reward their vassals' loyalty with land, or **fiefs**. Economic and social organization consisted of manors, self-sustaining areas possessed by lords but worked by peasants. The peasants were **serfs**, not slaves but not entirely free. Tied to the land, they worked for the lord in exchange for protection; however they were not obligated to fight. Usually they were also granted some land for their own use. While not true slaves, their lives were effectively controlled by the lord.

Warriors who fought for lords, called **knights**, were rewarded with land and could become minor lords in their own right. Lords themselves could be vassals of other lords; that hierarchy extended upward to kings or the Catholic Church. The Catholic Church itself was a major landowner and political power. In a Europe not yet dominated by sovereign states, the **pope** was not only a religious leader, but also a political one.

There were, however, limits on sovereign power. In 1215, long before the revolution, English barons forced King John to sign the **Magna Carta**, which protected their property and rights from the king and was the basis for today's parliamentary system in that country. The Magna Carta also established what was known as the **rule of law**, which established equality before the law of all citizens, including the monarch.

Small kingdoms and alliances extended throughout Europe, and stable trade was difficult to maintain. The Celts controlled Britain and Ireland until the invasion of the Saxons; around 600 CE, the Saxons conquered Britain while the Celts were pushed to Ireland, Scotland, and Brittany in northwest France. While the Church was gaining power, it was insecure in Italy as the Germanic tribes vied for control in Germany and France. Monasteries in Ireland and England retained and protected classical learning in the wake of the fall of Rome and insecurity in Italy. The Germanic tribes themselves were threatened by Asian invaders like the Huns, increasing instability in central and eastern parts of Europe, where Slavs also fought for supremacy north of Byzantium.

One exception to the chaos was the Scandinavian **Viking** civilization. From the end of the eighth century until around 1100, the Vikings expanded their influence from Scandinavia, ranging from the Baltic Sea to the East to the North Sea through the North Atlantic, thanks to their extraordinary seafaring skills and technology. The Vikings traded with the Byzantine Empire and European powers. They traveled to and sometimes raided parts of Britain, Ireland, France, and Russia.

Meanwhile, by the eighth century the North African **Moors**, part of the expanding Islamic civilization, had entered Iberia and were a threat to Christian Europe. **Charles Martel**, leader of the Franks in what is today France, defeated the Moors at the **Battle of Tours (or Poitiers)** in 732 CE, effectively stopping any further Islamic incursion into Europe from the south. After Martel's death, **Charlemagne**, the son of a court official, eventually took over the kingdom.

Charlemagne was able to maintain Frankish unity and extend his rule into Central Europe, even defending the Papal States in central Italy. In what is considered the reemergence of centralized power in Europe, parts of Western and Central Europe were organized under Charlemagne, who was crowned emperor of the Roman Empire by the pope in 800 CE. While in retrospect this seems long after the end of Rome, at the time many Europeans still perceived themselves as somehow still part of a Roman Empire.

It was also under Charlemagne that the feudal system became truly organized, bringing more stability to Western Europe. In 962 CE, the **Holy Roman Empire** was formed in Central Europe, a confederation of small states which remained an important European power until its dissolution in 1806.

In 1066, **William the Conqueror** left Normandy in northwest France. The Normans established organization in England, including a more consolidated economy and kingdom supported by feudalism. They also consolidated Christianity as the local religion. English possessions included parts of France; however, conflict between Britain and France would continue for several centuries, while rulers in Scandinavia and Northwest Europe consolidated power.

Practice Question

3) In feudal Europe, serfs were
   A. enslaved by the lords and knights.
   B. bonded to the land but under the protection of the lords.
   C. forced to fight for the lords.
   D. able to purchase their freedom from the knights in exchange for support with fighting.

Conflict and Cultural Exchange

Meanwhile, Arab-Islamic empires characterized by brisk commerce, advancements in technology and learning, and urban development arose in the Middle East.

In Arabia itself, the Prophet **Muhammad** was born in Mecca around 570; he began receiving messages from God (Allah), preaching them around 613 as the last affirmations of the monotheistic religions and writing them as the **Qur'an**, the Islamic holy book. Driven from **Mecca** to Medina in 622, Muhammad and his followers were able to recapture the city and other major Arabian towns by the time of his death, establishing Islam and Arab rule in the region.

After Muhammad's death in 632 CE, his followers went on to conquer land beyond Arabia north into the weakening Byzantine Empire. The Arab-Islamic empires, or caliphates, were first based in Damascus. The first caliphate, the Umayyad, was overthrown by the Arab-Muslim Abbasid family, which established a new capital in Baghdad.

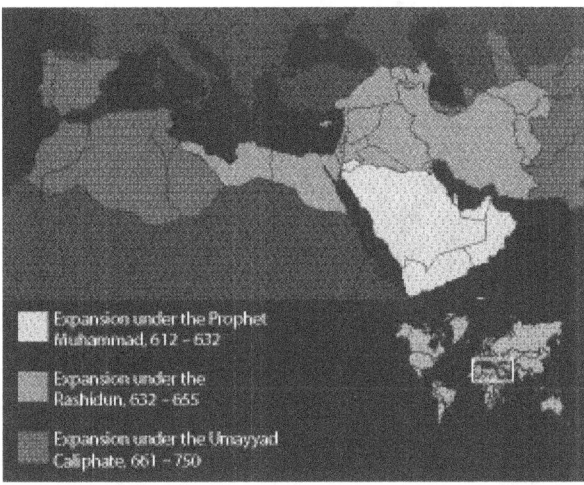

Figure 2.5. Islamic Expansion

Building on the Umayyad Caliphate, Abbasid administration was highly organized, allowing efficient taxation. The administration and stability provided by the caliphates fostered an Arabic literary culture. Stability permitted open trade routes, economic development, and cultural interaction throughout Asia, the Middle East, North Africa, and parts of Europe, while other parts of Europe remained relatively unstable following the collapse of Rome.

Thanks to the universality of the Arabic language, scientific and medical texts from varying civilizations—Greek, Persian, Indian—could be translated into Arabic and shared throughout the Islamic world. Arab thinkers studied Greek and Persian astronomy and engaged in further research. Arabs studied mathematics from around the world and developed algebra, enabling engineering, technological, and architectural achievements. Finally, Islamic art is well known for its geometric designs.

Around this time, China experienced tremendous development and economic growth. Characterized by increasing urbanization, Song Dynasty China featured complex administrative rule, including the difficult competitive written examinations required to obtain prestigious bureaucratic positions in government. China engaged not only in overland trade along the Silk Road, exporting silk, tea, ceramics, jade, and other goods, but also sea trade with Korea, Japan, Southeast Asia, India, Arabia, and even East Africa.

International commerce was vigorous along the **Silk Road**, trading routes which stretched from the Arab-controlled Eastern Mediterranean to Song Dynasty China. The Silk Road reflected the transnational nature of Central Asia: the nomadic culture of Central Asia lent itself to trade among the major civilizations of China, Persia, the Near East, and Europe. Buddhism and Islam spread into China.

Chinese, Islamic, and European art, pottery, and goods were interchanged—essentially, early globalization. The Islamic tradition of the **hajj**, or the pilgrimage to Mecca, also spurred cultural interaction. Islam had spread from Spain throughout North Africa, the Sahel, the Middle East, Persia, Central Asia, India, and China; peoples from all of these regions traveled and met in Arabia as part of their religious pilgrimage.

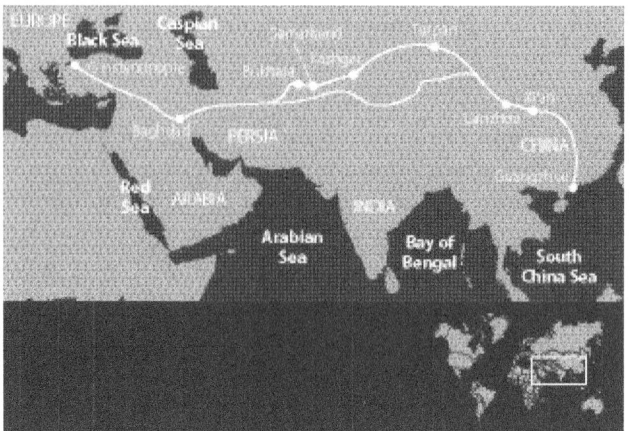

Figure 2.6. Silk Road

Islam also spread along trans-Saharan trade routes into West Africa and the Sahel. Brisk trade between the gold-subrich **Kingdom of Ghana** and Muslim traders based in Morocco brought Islam to the region around the eleventh century. The Islamic **Mali Empire** (1235 – 1500), based farther south in Timbuktu, eventually extended beyond the original Ghanaian boundaries all the way to the West African coast and controlled the valuable gold and salt trades. At the empire's peak, the ruler **Mansa Musa** made a pilgrimage to Mecca in 1324; however, by 1500, the **Songhai Empire** had overcome Mali and eventually dominated the Niger River area.

Check Your Understanding

How did the Silk Road and Islam both contribute to global cultural exchange?

Loss of Byzantine territory to the Islamic empires meant loss of Christian lands in the Levant—including Jerusalem and Bethlehem—to Muslims. In 1095 CE, the Byzantine Emperor asked the pope for help to defend Jerusalem and protect Christians. With a history of Muslim incursions into Spain and France, anti-Muslim sentiment was strong in Europe and Christians there were easily inspired to fight them in the Levant, or **Holy Land**. The Pope offered lords and knights the chance to keep lands and bounty they won from conquered Muslims (and Jews) in this **Crusade**. He also offered Crusaders **indulgences**—forgiveness for sins committed in war and guarantees they would enter heaven.

Despite conflict in Europe, Christians found they had more in common with each other than with Muslims, and were able to unite to follow the Pope's call to arms to fight in the Middle East. The decline of the Abbasids had left the Levant vulnerable, and Christian Crusaders were able to establish settlements and small kingdoms in Syria and on the Eastern Mediterranean coast, conquering major cities and capturing Jerusalem by 1099 in the **First Crusade**.

The Crusades continued over several centuries. While they never resulted in permanent European control over the Holy Land, they did open up trade routes between Europe and the Middle East, stretching all the way along the Silk Road to China. This increasing interdependence helped lead to the European Renaissance.

Ongoing interactions between Europeans and Muslims exposed Europeans to improved education and goods and, thanks to international trade, Europeans could now afford these. However, the **Bubonic (Black) Plague** also spread to Europe as a result of global exchange, killing off a third of its population from 1347 – 1351. The plague had a worldwide impact as empires fell in its wake.

> **Did You Know?**
>
> During the Hundred Years' War, **Joan of Arc** led the French in the 1429 Battle of Orléans, reinvigorating French resistance to English incursions.

Back in Europe, conflict reached its height throughout the thirteenth and fourteenth centuries known as the **Hundred Years' War** (1337 – 1453). France was in political chaos during the mid-fourteenth century, decentralized and at times without a king, suffering the effects of the Black Plague, and periodically under English rule. While conflict would continue, England lost its last territory in France, Bordeaux, in 1453.

In Al-Andalus (Spain), despite some coexistence between Christians and Muslims under Muslim rule, raids and conflict were ongoing during the lengthy period of the **Reconquista**, which did not end until 1492 when Christian powers took Grenada. From the zenith of Muslim rule, Christian raids continued. The marriage of Ferdinand of Castilla and Isabella of Aragon in 1479 connected those two kingdoms, and the monarchs were able to complete the Reconquista by taking Grenada and uniting Spain.

Practice Questions

4) While the Crusades enriched Europe in many ways, what did they NOT do?
   A. bring new knowledge to the West
   B. result in lasting land gains
   C. provide religious indulgences for crusaders
   D. offer the opportunity to gain personal wealth

5) The Kingdom of Mali developed due to its
   A. control of the trans-Saharan trade routes.
   B. ability to repel Islamic influences from the north.
   C. control over gold and salt resources.
   D. control of the trans-Saharan slave trade.

Empires in Transition

The collapse of the Abbasid Caliphate in the thirteenth century led to instability and decentralization of power in Mesopotamia, Persia, and Central Asia; smaller sultanates (territories ruled by sultans, regional leaders) emerged, and production and economic development declined. China closed its borders and trade on the Silk Road declined.

Despite the lack of political cohesion, Islam remained a unifying force throughout the region, and political instability and decentralization paradoxically allowed local culture to develop, particularly Persian art and literature.

The Mongols

The **Mongol Empire** was based in Central Asia. Led by **Genghis Khan**, the Mongols expanded throughout Asia thanks to their abilities in horsemanship and archery. Despite the rich history of transnational activity across Asia, the continent was vulnerable. Central Asia lacked one dominant culture or imperial power; Southwest Asia was fragmented following the decline of the Abbasids. These weaknesses allowed the Mongols to take over most of Eurasia.

In China, the Mongols destroyed local infrastructure, including the foundation of Chinese society and administration—the civil service examinations (which were eventually reestablished). However, the Mongol **Yuan Dynasty** maintained most of the administrative policy of the preceding Song Dynasty. The Yuan did, however, upend Chinese social hierarchy, placing Mongols at the top followed by non-ethnic Han Chinese and then Han Chinese. Yet attempts at imperial expansion, threats from the Buboninc Plague, financial problems, and flooding, led to the decline of the Yuan Dynasty and the rise of the ethnic Chinese **Ming Dynasty** in 1368.

> **Did You Know?**
>
> Genghis Khan wasn't Genghis Khan's first name. He was originally named Temujin, which means "blacksmith." He got the name Genghis Khan in 1206 after becoming the "universal ruler" of the Mongols, which is how most historians translate the

The Ming reasserted Chinese control and continued traditional methods of administration; the construction of the **Forbidden City**, the home of the emperor in Beijing, helped consolidate imperial rule. The Ming also recharged international trade; demand for ceramics in particular, in addition to silk and tea, was high abroad, and contact with seafaring traders like the Portuguese and Dutch in the sixteenth century was strong. China itself explored the oceans.

Russia

Mongol decline was not only isolated to China; in Russia, **Ivan the Great** brought Moscow from Mongol to Slavic Russian control, achieving Moscow's independence in 1480 and consolidating a Russia that was the foundation for an empire and a sovereign nation that sought diplomatic status with Europe. A century later, the first tsar, **Ivan the Terrible**, expanded Russian territory farther into Europe. Ivan reformed government, the military, and strengthened Russian Orthodox Christianity; however, his despotic reputation gave him his name.

India

In India, the **Mughal Empire** developed from the small kingdoms that made up the Subcontinent. The Mughals would rule India from the sixteenth century until the eighteenth century and nominally control parts of the country until British takeover in the nineteenth century.

Despite the instability inland, Indian Ocean trade routes had continued to function since at least the seventh century. The ocean acted as a unifying force throughout the region, and the monsoon winds permitted Arab, Persian, Indian, and Chinese merchants to travel to East Africa in search of slaves and goods, such as ivory and gold.

The Slave Trade

Despite the achievements of the Islamic empires, China, and the Central Asian and Indian empires that would emerge from the Mongols, the **East African slave trade** remained vigorous until the nineteenth century. Arabs, Asians, and other Africans kidnapped African people and sent them to lives of slavery throughout the Arab world and South Asia. Later, Europeans would take part in the trade, forcing

Africans into slavery in colonies throughout South and Southeast Asia, and on plantations in Indian Ocean islands such as Madagascar.

2.8. Indian Ocean Slave Trade

The major East African port was Zanzibar, from which slaves, gold, coconut oil, ivory, and other African exports made their way to Asia and the Middle East. However, enslaved persons from Sub-Saharan Africa were also forced north overland to markets in Cairo, where they were sold and dispersed throughout the Arab-Islamic, Fatimid, and Ottoman empires.

The Ottoman Empire

Further north, the Ottoman Turks represented a threat to Central Europe. Controlling most of Anatolia from the late thirteenth century, the Ottomans spread west into the Balkans. In 1453 they captured Istanbul, from which the **Ottoman Empire** would come to rule much of the Mediterranean world.

Under the leadership of **Mehmed the Conqueror** in the fifteenth century and his successors, the Ottomans would conquer Pannonia (Hungary), North Africa, the Caucasus, the Levant and Mesopotamian regions, western Arabia, and Egypt. Under **Suleiman the Magnificent** (1520 – 1566), the **Ottoman Empire** consolidated control over the Balkans, the Middle East, and North Africa and would hold that land until the nineteenth century.

The capture of Istanbul (Constantinople) had represented the true end of the Byzantine Empire. The remaining Christian Byzantines, mainly isolated to coastal Anatolia, Constantinople, and parts of Greece, fled to Italy, bringing Greek, Middle Eastern, and Asian learning with them and enriching the emerging European Renaissance.

Japan

Medieval **Japan** (roughly 1185 – 1603 CE), like the other empires described, experienced many changes in this period. A new samurai warrior class that served **shogun** military rulers emerged, which largely replaced the power of emperors and aristocrats. This social structure was similar to that of Europe, and shogun-owned lands were provided to warriors in return for military service in a feudalist system. Agriculture and trade flourished during this period, which saw the improvement and modification of many tools and techniques including the use of fertilizers, more efficient tools, and new crop strains.

The religion of medieval Japan was primarily **Buddhism**, a belief system without a god or deity that is centered around an understanding that ending suffering in life comes with an end to craving worldly attachments. **Shinto** was often practiced alongside Buddhism and may be considered as more of a worldview than a religious devotion. Shinto emphasizes respect of family and the good of the group over the good of the individual.

The Americas

The **Maya**, who preceded the Aztecs in Mesoamerica, had dominated the Yucatan peninsula around 300 CE. They developed a complex spiritual belief system accompanied by relief art, a detailed calendar, a written language, and pyramidal temples that still stand today. In addition, they studied astronomy and mathematics. Maya political administration was organized under monarchial city-states from around 300 until around 900, when the civilization began to decline.

As smaller Mesoamerican civilizations had weakened and collapsed, the **Aztecs** had come to dominate Mexico and much of Mesoamerica. Their military power and militaristic culture allowed the Aztecs to dominate the region and regional trade. The main city of the Aztec empire, **Tenochtitlan**, was founded in 1325 and, at its height, was a major world city home to several million people.

Meanwhile in the Andean highlands, the **Incas** had emerged. Based in **Cuzco**, the Incas had consolidated their power and strengthened in the area, likely due to a surplus of their staple crop maize from their highly-effective terrace irrigation system, around 1300. Inca engineers built the citadel of **Machu Picchu** and imperial infrastructure, including roads throughout the Andes. In order to subdue local peoples, they moved conquered groups elsewhere in the empire and repopulated conquered areas with Incas.

Practice Questions

6) How did Russia build its empire?
    A. by strengthening its navy to colonize overseas
    B. by expanding overland, moving eastward into Asia and Siberia and westward into Europe
    C. by remaining isolated, avoiding expansion and focusing on industrialization instead
    D. by converting Asian peoples from Islam to Russian Orthodox Christianity

7) Which of the following was a result of the rise of the Ottoman Turks?
    A. Christian Byzantines left Constantinople for Western Europe, bringing classical learning with them.
    B. The Ottomans were able to conquer large areas, establishing a vast Islamic empire.
    C. The Ottomans represented an Islamic threat to European Christendom.
    D. all of the above

The European Renaissance

The **Renaissance**, or *rebirth,* included the revival of ancient Greek and Roman learning, art, and architecture in Europe. However, the roots of the Renaissance stretched further back to earlier interactions between Christendom, the Islamic World, and even China, during the Crusades and through Silk Road trade. Not only did the Renaissance inspire new learning and prosperity in Europe, enabling exploration, colonization, profit, and later imperialism, but it also led to scientific and religious questioning and rebellion against the Catholic Church and, later, monarchical governments.

Reinvigoration of classical knowledge was triggered in part by Byzantine refugees from the Ottoman conquest of Constantinople, including scholars who brought Greek and Roman texts to Italy and Western Europe. The fall of Constantinople precipitated the development of **humanism** in Europe, a mode of thought emphasizing human nature, creativity, and an overarching concept of truth.

Art, considered not just a form of expression but also a science in itself, flourished in fifteenth-century Italy, particularly in **Florence**. Major figures who explored anatomy in sculpture, design and perspective, and innovation in architecture included Leonardo da Vinci, Botticelli, and Michelangelo. In addition to his artistic achievements, Leonardo is particularly known for his scientific pursuits.

Meanwhile, scholars like Galileo, Isaac Newton, and Copernicus made discoveries in what became known as the **Scientific Revolution**, rooted in the scientific knowledge of the Islamic empires, which had been imported through economic and social contact initiated centuries prior in the Crusades. Scientific study and discovery threatened the power of the Church, whose theological teachings were often at odds with scientific findings and logical reasoning.

> **Check Your Understanding**
>
> The Scientific Revolution changed European thinking. What was the impact of using reason and scientific methodology rather than religion to understand the world?

Also in the mid-fifteenth century, in Northern Europe, Johann Gutenberg invented the **printing press**. With the advent of printing, texts could be more widely and rapidly distributed, and people had more access to information beyond what their leaders told them. Combined with humanism and increased emphasis on secular thought, the power of the church and of monarchs who ruled by divine right was under threat. Here lay the roots of the **Enlightenment**, the basis for reinvigorated European culture and political thought that would drive its development for the next several centuries—and inspire revolution.

Transnational cultural exchange had also resulted in the transmission of technology to Europe. During the sixteenth century, European seafaring knowledge, navigation, and technology benefitted from Islamic and Asian expertise; European explorers and traders could now venture beyond the Mediterranean. Trade was no longer dependent on the Silk Road. Europeans eventually arrived in the Western Hemisphere, heretofore unknown to the peoples of Eurasia and Africa.

Practice Question

8) Major influences on the European Renaissance included
    A. cultural discoveries in North America.
    B. African music and culture.
    C. the ideas of the Greek Orthodox Church.
    D. scientific knowledge from the Islamic empires.

Colonization of the Western Hemisphere

Interest in exploration grew in Europe during the Renaissance period. Technological advancements made complex navigation and long-term sea voyages possible, and economic growth resulting from international trade drove interest in market expansion. Global interdependence got a big push from Spain when King Ferdinand and Queen Isabella agreed to sponsor **Christopher Columbus's** exploratory voyage in 1492 to find a sea route to Asia in order to speed up commercial trade there. Instead, he stumbled upon the Western Hemisphere, which was unknown to Europeans, Asians, and Africans to this point.

Columbus landed in the Caribbean; he and later explorers would claim the Caribbean islands and eventually Central and South America for Spain and Portugal. However, those areas were already populated by the major American civilizations.

In Mexico, the ruler **Montezuma II** led the Aztecs during their first encounter with Spain; explorer **Hernan Cortés** met with him in Tenochtitlan after invading other areas of Mexico in 1519. Spain was especially interested in subduing the Aztec religion, which included ceremonies with human blood and human sacrifice, and in controlling Mexican and Mesoamerican gold. Cortés arrested Montezuma; Spain then began the process of colonizing Mexico and Central America, and the Aztec Empire collapsed.

In South America, as in Mexico and Central America, the Spanish were interested in economic exploitation and spreading Christianity, accessing the continent in the early sixteenth century. In 1533, the Spanish conquistador **Francisco Pizzaro** defeated the Inca king **Atahualpa** and installed a puppet ruler, marking the decline of the Inca Empire. While the empire remained nominally intact for several years, the Spanish installed Christianity and took control of the region.

Spain took over the silver- and gold-rich Mesoamerican and Andean territories, as well as the Caribbean islands, where sugar became an important cash crop. Thus developed **mercantilism**, whereby the colonizing or *mother country* took raw materials from the territories they controlled for the colonizers' own benefit. Governments amassed wealth through protectionism and increasing exports at the expense of other rising colonial powers. This eventually involved developing goods and then selling them back to those colonized lands at an inflated price. The *encomienda* system granted European landowners the "right" to hold lands in the Americas and demand labor and tribute from the local inhabitants. Spreading Christianity was another important reason for European expansion. Local civilizations and resources were exploited and destroyed.

> **Check Your Understanding**
>
> What was destructive about the *encomienda* system?

The **Columbian Exchange** enabled mercantilism to flourish. Conflict and illness brought by the Europeans—especially smallpox—decimated the Native Americans, and the Europeans were left without labor to mine the silver and gold or to work the land. African slavery was their solution.

Slavery was an ancient institution in many societies around the world; however, with the Columbian Exchange, slavery came to be practiced on a mass scale the likes of which the world had never seen. Throughout Africa and especially on the West African coast, Europeans traded for slaves with some African kingdoms and also raided the land, kidnapping people. European slavers took captured Africans in horrific conditions to the Americas; those who survived were enslaved and forced to work in mining or agriculture for the benefit of expanding European imperial powers.

The Columbian Exchange described the **triangular trade** across the Atlantic: European slavers kidnapped African people and took them to the Americas, sold them at auction, and exchanged them for sugar and raw materials; these materials were traded in Europe for consumer goods, which were then exchanged in Africa for slaves (and also sold in the colonies), and so on.

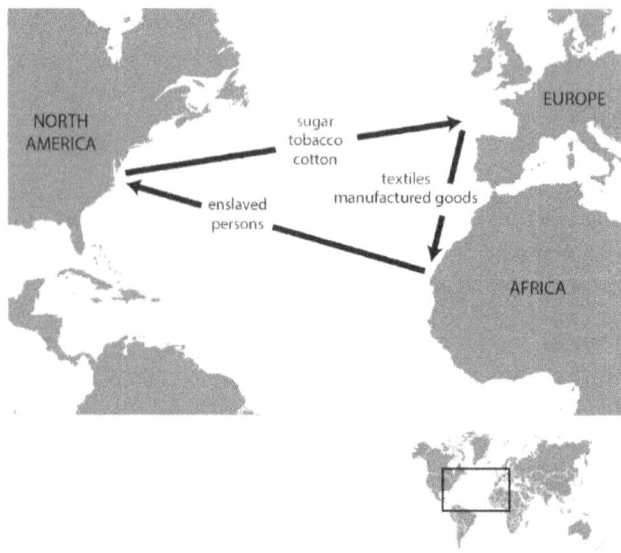

Figure 2.7. Triangular Trade

Throughout this period, Africans resisted on ships and later, in the Americas: **Maroon communities** of escaped slaves formed throughout the Western Hemisphere. The **Underground Railroad** in the nineteenth-century United States helped enslaved persons escape the South, and **Toussaint L'Ouverture** led a successful slave rebellion in Haiti, winning independence from the French for that country in 1791.

However, the slave trade continued for centuries. The colonies and independent countries of the Western Hemisphere continued to practice slavery until the nineteenth century; oppressive legal and social restrictions based on race continue to affect the descendants of slaves to this day throughout the hemisphere. The slave trade also had consequences in the sub-Saharan African communities from which people were captured and forcibly relocated. Because slave traders offered incentives for human chattel, warlords looking for economic gain emerged and perpetuated violence and chaos. Further, because the humans most desired as enslaved laborers were young, healthy men and women of reproductive age, those left in some African societies were largely elderly or infirm. This reality had drastic demographic and labor consequences, leading to economic development struggles in some communities.

> **Check Your Understanding**
>
> Explain the Columbian Exchange.

During the eighteenth century, Spain and Portugal were preeminent powers in global trade thanks to colonization and **imperialism**, the possession and exploitation of land overseas. Later, Great Britain became an important presence in North America and on the seas; it would later dominate the oceans and amass colonies worldwide throughout the nineteenth century. Likewise, France gained territory in North America and in the West Indies; despite losses to Britain in the eighteenth century, that country would also expand its own global empire in the nineteenth century.

Practice Questions

9) Slaves were originally brought to the Americas as part of the triangular trade in order to do all of the following EXCEPT
    A. work on cotton plantations.
    B. work on sugar plantations.
    C. work in colonists' homes.
    D. work in textile factories.

10) In South America, how was the Inca Empire able to consolidate its power?
    A. The Inca used advanced military technology to conquer neighboring peoples.
    B. The Inca converted people to their own religion, gaining followers and loyal subjects.
    C. The Inca used their mastery of high-altitude transportation to expand their empire.
    D. The Inca grew their empire by bringing in migrants from other parts of South America.

Reformation and New Europe

While Spain and Portugal consolidated their hold over territories in the Americas, conflict ensued in Europe. With the cultural changes of the Renaissance, the power of the Catholic Church was threatened; new scientific discoveries and secular Renaissance thought were at odds with many teachings of the church. The Catholic monk **Martin Luther** wrote a letter of protest to the pope in 1517 known as the **Ninety-Five Theses**, outlining ways he believed the church should reform; his ideas gained support, especially among rulers who wanted more power from the church. Triggering the **Reformation**, or movement for reform of the church, Luther's ideas led to offshoots of new versions of Christianity in Western Europe, separate from the Orthodox churches in Russia and Greece.

The English **King Henry VIII** developed the Protestant **Church of England**, further consolidating his own power, famously allowing divorce, and marrying several times himself. His reign initiated a chain of events leading to the consolidation of Protestantism in England and eventually civil war and the empowerment of Parliament.

Conflict between Protestants and Catholics was fierce on the Continent as well. The **Thirty Years' War** (1618 – 1648) began in Central Europe between Protestant nobles in the Holy Roman Empire who disagreed with the Catholic Holy Roman Emperor, Ferdinand II. Ferdinand was a leader of the 1619 **Counter-Reformation**, attempts at reinforcing Catholic dominance throughout Europe during and after the Reformation in the wake of the Renaissance and related social change. Ferdinand was also closely allied with the Catholic **Habsburg Dynasty**, which ruled Austria and Spain.

At the same time, despite France's status as a Catholic country, it came into conflict with its Habsburg-ruled neighbors, Spain and Austria. As part of the Counter-Reformation, Spain had defeated Protestant powers in Central Europe in 1634, dominating the region. Thus, the Habsburgs controlled territory surrounding France, representing a military threat. As a result, despite their religious commonalities, France declared war on Spain in 1635 and shortly after on the Habsburg-supported Holy Roman Empire. This political tactic represented a break from the prioritization of religious alliances and a movement toward emphasis on state sovereignty.

The tangled alliances among European powers resulted in war between not only France and Spain, but also Sweden and Austria, with the small states of the weakening Holy Roman Empire caught in the middle. The war had been centered on alliances and concerns about the nature of Christianity within different European countries. However, upon signing the 1648 **Treaty of Westphalia**, the European powers agreed to recognize state sovereignty and practice noninterference in each other's matters—at the expense of family and religious allegiances. The year 1648 marked a transition into modern international relations when politics and religion would no longer be inexorably intertwined.

The end of the Thirty Years' War represented the end of domination of the Catholic Church over Europe and the concept of religious regional dominance, rather than ethnic state divisions. Over the next several centuries, the church—and religious empires like the Ottomans—would eventually lose control over ethnic groups and their lands, later giving way to smaller nation-states.

As state sovereignty became entrenched in European notions of politics, so too did conflict among states. Conflict over control of the Habsburg territories led to the **Seven Years' War** in 1756. In Europe, this war further cemented concepts of state sovereignty and delineated rivalries between European powers engaged in colonial adventure and overseas imperialism—especially Britain and France. It would kick-start British dominance in Asia and also lead to Britain's loss of its North American colonies.

European concepts of social and political organization became constructed around national sovereignty and nation-states. European economies had become dependent upon colonies and were starting to industrialize, enriching Europe at the expense of its imperial possessions in the Americas, in Africa, and increasingly in Asia.

Industrialization and political organization allowed improved militaries, which put Asian governments at a disadvantage. The major Asian powers—Mughal India, China, the Ottoman Empire, and Persia—would eventually succumb to European influence or come under direct European control.

Practice Questions

11) The power of the Catholic Church was diminished during the Reformation due to which of the following?
   A. its unwillingness to protect the Indigenous peoples of the Americas
   B. the discoveries of the Scientific Revolution
   C. the growth of Islam in Western Europe
   D. its failure to capture the Holy Land during the Crusades

12) Which of the following BEST describes the motivation for the reformer Martin Luther?
   A. He originally sought to develop a new form of Christianity separate from the Catholic Church.
   B. He tried to reform the Catholic Church because he was unhappy with its teachings and its corruption.
   C. He was influenced by European political leaders, who used him to limit the power of the Church.
   D. He tried to topple the Catholic Church, believing it to have become too corrupt.

The Age of Revolutions

Monarchies in Europe had been weakened by the conflicts between Catholicism and Protestant faiths; despite European presence and increasing power overseas, as well as its dominance in the Americas, instability on the Continent and in the British Isles made the old order vulnerable. Enlightenment ideals like democracy and republicanism, coupled with political instability, would trigger revolution against **absolute monarchy**. Revolutionary actors drew on the philosophies of enlightenment thinkers like John Locke, Jean-Jacques Rousseau, and Montesquieu, whose beliefs—republicanism, the social contract, the separation of powers, and the rights of man—would drive the Age of Revolutions.

In 1642, the **English Civil War** broke out between the Royalists, who supported the monarchy, and the Parliamentarians, who wanted a republic. Eventually, the Royalists succumbed to the Parliamentarians. The **1689 English Bill of Rights** established constitutional monarchy in the spirit of the Magna Carta.

The American Revolution, heavily influenced by **Locke**, broke out a century later. (See the section below on US history for details.)

The French Revolution was the precursor to the end of the feudal order in most of Europe. **King Louis XIV**, the *Sun King* (1643 – 1715), had consolidated the monarchy in France, taking true political and military power from the nobility. Meanwhile, French Enlightenment thinkers like **Rousseau**, **Montesquieu**, and **Voltaire** criticized absolute monarchy and the repression of freedom of speech and thought; in 1789, the French Revolution broke out.

The power of the Catholic Church had weakened and the Scientific Revolution and the Enlightenment had fostered social and intellectual change. Colonialism and mercantilism were fueling the growth of an early middle class: people who were not traditionally nobility or landowners under the feudal system were becoming wealthier and more powerful thanks to early capitalism. This class, the **bourgeoisie**, chafed under the rule of the nobility, which had generally inherited land and wealth (while the bourgeoisie earned their wealth in business).

> **Did You Know?**
>
> Louis XIV built the palace of Versailles to centralize the monarchy and to contain and monitor the nobility.

2. History and Social Science

In France, the problem was most acute as France had the largest population in Europe at the time. At the same time, France had one of the most centralized monarchies in Europe and entrenched nobilities. With a growing bourgeoisie and peasant class paying increasingly higher taxes to the nobility, resentment was brewing.

The French government was struggling financially and proposed taxing the nobility. In 1787, an unwilling council of nobles instead called for the **Estates-General** to be convened. This weak, representative assembly reflected French society: the clergy, the nobility, and the **Third Estate**—the middle class and the poor peasants, or *commoners*. The burden of taxation traditionally fell on the Third Estate. In fact, peasants had to **tithe**, paying ten percent of their earnings to the nobles.

The Third Estate eventually declared itself the National Constituent Assembly. At the same time, panic over dwindling food supplies and suspicion over a conspiracy against the Third Estate triggered the **Great Fear** among the peasants in July 1789. Suspicion turned to action when the king sent troops to Paris, and on July 16 the people stormed the **Bastille** prison in an event still celebrated in France and symbolic of the overthrow of tyranny. The peasantry then revolted in the countryside; consequently the National Constituent Assembly officially abolished the feudal system and tithing. Furthermore, the Assembly issued the **Declaration of the Rights of Man and of the Citizen**, the precursor to the French constitution assuring liberty and equality in the model of Enlightenment thought.

Another idea—that of a **representative democracy**—also began to permeate certain French circles in the 1790s. Though this idea was not new (as evidenced by ancient Rome), it was somewhat novel at the time. This idea of a government not led by one powerful monarch but rather by elected representatives of the people was not limited to France. James Madison was writing about the same idea in his *Federalist Papers*, which predate the French Revolution.

> **Helpful Hint**
>
> An important tenet of the revolutionary ethos in France was the concept of self-determination, or the right of a people to rule themselves, which threatened other rulers who feared revolution in their own countries.

Nevertheless, the French Revolution inspired revolutionary movements throughout Europe and beyond; indeed, the revolutionary principle of self-determination drove revolutionary France to support its ideals abroad. The country declared war on Austria in 1792, but following severe defeats the people became suspicious of the unpopular queen **Marie Antoinette**. The people imprisoned the royal family, and the republic was established later that year. The monarchy was abolished.

Fearful of counterrevolutionaries in France and instability abroad, the republican government created the Committee for Public Safety in 1793 and the Reign of Terror began. Thousands of people were executed by **guillotine**, including the king and Marie Antoinette.

In 1804, **Napoleon Bonaparte** emerged as emperor of France and proceeded to conquer much of Europe throughout the **Napoleonic Wars**, changing the face of Europe. French occupation of Spain weakened that country enough that revolutionary movements in its colonies strengthened; eventually Latin American colonies, inspired by the Enlightenment and revolution in Europe, won their freedom. **Simón Bolivar** led or influenced independence movements in Venezuela, Colombia (including what is today Panama), Ecuador, Peru, and Bolivia in the early part of the nineteenth century.

Napoleon's movement eastward also triggered the collapse of the Holy Roman Empire; however, the powerful state of Prussia emerged in its wake, and a strong sense of militarism and Germanic nationalism took root in the face of opposition to seemingly unstoppable France.

Nationalism is a sentiment of loyalty to one's own cultural or ethnic group above others. This was a new concept in a Europe that had previously been dominated by religious affiliation (Catholic and Protestant) and empires, where a ruler may have been from a different linguistic or cultural group (e.g., the Habsburgs had ruled both in Central Europe and Spain; the Austro-Hungarian Empire controlled parts of the Balkans where neither German nor Hungarian was spoken).

Nationalism triggered a sense of local identity; people did not identify with a power based in a faraway capital. Likewise, nationalism could be a unifying factor; numerous smaller German-speaking states in Central Europe connected with Prussia, empowering that country. A **nation-state** is a sovereign territory ruled by an ethnic majority, in contrast to previous models of imperial rule in which one ethic group governed many others. Under the concept of a nation-state, individuals with shared experience (including ethnicity, language, religion, and cultural practices) should be unified under one government.

Helpful Hint
Prussia had a particular rivalry with France, having lost several key territories during the Napoleonic Wars. In 1870, the militarily powerful kingdom went to war against France in the **Franco-Prussian War**, during which Prussia took control of Alsace-Lorraine, mineral rich and later essential for industrial development.

Prussia had come to dominate the German-speaking states that once comprised the Holy Roman Empire. Prussia, a distinct kingdom within the Holy Roman Empire since the thirteenth century, had become a powerful Central European state by the eighteenth century. It had become main rival of Austria for influence in the Germanic lands of Central Europe. By the nineteenth century and due in part to emphasis on military prowess, Prussia became an important military power and a key ally in the efforts against Napoleon.

Napoleon was finally defeated in Russia in 1812 and was forced by the European powers to abdicate in 1813. He escaped from prison on the Mediterranean island of Elba and raised an army again.

Practice Question

13) Simon Bolivar is remembered for his role in which of the following?
    A. the spread of nationalism throughout Europe
    B. the French Revolution
    C. the Latin American Independence movement
    D. the Spanish Civil War

Industrial Revolution

Meanwhile, raw goods from the Americas fueled European economic growth and development, leading to the **Industrial Revolution** in the nineteenth century. This economic revolution began with textile production in Britain, fueled by cotton from its overseas territories in North America, and later India and Egypt. The first factories were in Manchester, where **urbanization** began as poor people from rural areas flocked to cities in search of higher paying unskilled jobs in factories.

Early industrial technology sped up the harvesting and transport of crops and their conversion to textiles. This accelerated manufacturing was based on **capitalism**, the *laissez-faire* (or free market) theory developed by **Adam Smith**, who believed that an *invisible hand* should guide the marketplace—that government should stay out of the economy, as the market would eventually automatically correct for inequalities, price problems, and any other problematic issues.

Technology exponentially increased the amount of cotton that workers could process into yarn and thread. The **steam engine** efficiently powered mills and ironworks; factories no longer had to be built near running water to access power. Advances in iron technology allowed for stronger machinery and would later support the **Second Industrial Revolution** in the late nineteenth and early twentieth centuries; this revolution was based on heavy industry, railroads, and weapons.

To access the raw materials needed to produce manufactured goods, Britain and other industrializing countries in Western Europe needed resources, which drove imperialism. Cotton was harvested in India and Egypt for textile mills; minerals were mined in South Africa and the Congo to power metallurgy.

Furthermore, as industrialization and urbanization led to the development of early middle classes in Europe and North America, imports of luxury goods like tea, spices, silk, precious metals, and other items from Asia increased to meet consumer demand. Colonial powers also gained by selling manufactured goods back to the colonies from which they had harvested raw materials in the first place, for considerable profit.

Largely unbridled capitalism had led to the conditions of the early Industrial Revolution; workers suffered from abusive treatment, overly long hours, low wages or none at all, and unsafe conditions, including pollution. The German philosophers **Karl Marx** and **Friedrich Engels**, horrified by conditions suffered by industrial workers, developed **socialism**, the philosophy that workers, or the proletariat, should own the means of production and reap the profits, rather than the bourgeoisie, who had no interest in the rights of the workers at the expense of profit and who did not experience the same conditions.

Marx argued for the abolition of the class system, wages, and private property. He argued instead for collective ownership of both the means of production and products, with equal distribution of income to satisfy the needs of all. Later, Marx and Engels wrote the *Communist Manifesto*, a pamphlet laying out their ideas and calling for revolution. It inspired the formation of socialist groups worldwide.

> **Check Your Understanding**
>
> How are communism and socialism similar and different?

A different version of socialism would later help Russia become a major world power. The Russian intellectuals **Vladimir Lenin** and **Leon Trotsky** would take the theories of Marx and Engels further, developing **Marxism-Leninism**. They embraced socialist ideals and believed in revolution; however, they felt that **communism** could not be maintained under a democratic governing structure. Lenin supported dictatorship, more precisely the *dictatorship of the proletariat*, paving the way for the political and economic organization of the Soviet Union.

Practice Question

14) According to Adam Smith, in a free market
   A. the government does not interfere with the economy.
   B. workers own the means of production.
   C. wages and private property have been abolished.
   D. a dictatorship is necessary to maintain a strong economy.

United States History

Native Americans

Prior to European colonization, diverse Native American societies controlled North America; they would later come into economic and diplomatic contact—and military conflict—with European colonizers and United States forces and settlers.

Major civilizations that would play an important and ongoing role in North American history included the **Iroquois** in the Northeast, known for longhouses and farming in the Three Sisters tradition; they consisted of a confederation of six tribes. The **Algonquin** were another important northeastern civilization; rivals of the Iroquois, the Algonquin were important in the fur trade. Algonquin languages were spoken throughout the Great Lakes region.

Farther west, the **Shawnee** were an Algonquin-speaking people based in the Ohio Valley; however their presence extended as far south and east as the present-day Carolinas and Georgia. While socially organized under a matrilineal system, the Shawnee had male kings and only men could inherit property. Also matrilineal and Algonquin-speaking, the **Lenape** were considered by the Shawnee to be their "grandfathers" and thus accorded respect. Another Algonquin-speaking tribe, the **Kickapoo** were originally from the Great Lakes region and moved west. The Algonquin-speaking **Miami** moved from Wisconsin to the Ohio Valley region, forming settled societies and farming maize. They too took part in the fur trade as it developed during European colonial times. These tribes later formed the Northwest Confederacy to fight US westward expansion.

In the South, major tribes included the **Creek**, **Chickasaw**, and **Choctaw**, the descendants of the **Mississippi Mound Builders** or Mississippian cultures, and societies which built mounds from around 2,100 to 1,800 years ago as burial tombs or the bases for temples. Sharing similar languages, all the tribes would later participate in an alliance—the Muscogee Confederacy—to engage the United States. The Chickasaw and Choctaw were matrilineal; the former also engaged in Three Sisters agriculture like the Iroquois.

Figure 2.8. Mississippi Mounds

Another major southern tribe, the **Cherokee** spoke (and speak) a language of the Iroquoian family. It is thought that they migrated south to their homeland in present-day Georgia sometime long before European contact, where they remained until they were forcibly removed in 1832. Organized into seven clans, the Cherokee were also hunters and farmers like other tribes in the region and would later come into contact—and conflict—with European colonizers and the United States of America.

The nomadic tribes of the Great Plains, like the **Sioux**, **Cheyanne**, **Apache**, **Comanche**, and **Arapaho** lived farther west. These tribes depended on the **buffalo** for food and materials to create clothing, tools, and domestic items; therefore they followed the herds. While widely known for their equestrian skill, horses were introduced by Europeans and so Native American tribes living on the Great Plains did not access them until after European contact. Horseback riding facilitated the hunt; previously, hunters surrounded buffalo or frightened them off of cliffs.

In the Southwest, the **Navajo** controlled territory in present-day Arizona, New Mexico, and Utah. As pastoralists, they had a less hierarchical structure than other Native American societies. The Navajo were descendants of the **Ancestral Pueblo** or **Anasazi** (pictured on the following page), who practiced Three Sisters agriculture and stone construction, building cliff dwellings.

Figure 2.9. Ancestral Pueblo Cliff Palace at Mesa Verde

In the Pacific Northwest, Native American peoples depended on fishing and used canoes. Totem poles depicted histories. The **Coast Salish**, whose language was widely spoken throughout the region, dominated the Puget Sound and Olympic Peninsula area. Farther south, the **Chinook** controlled the coast at the Columbia River.

Practice Question

15) Which of the following did NOT contribute to the destruction of Native American populations in North America?
    A. the colonists overuse of natural resources such as bison and timber
    B. the transfer of smallpox from Europeans to Native Americans
    C. violent conflict over land and resources between Europeans and Native Americans
    D. geographical displacement by colonists

Early Colonization

When European settlers came to North America in the 1600s, they found an already populated continent. An estimated 60,000 Native Americans lived in the area that would become the first New England colonies. Early relationships between Native peoples and European colonists, however, were not always centered around conflict. For example, the famous Plymouth Colony, established in 1620, shared a meal with members of the Wampanoag tribe in what would become known as the first Thanksgiving.

Reciprocal relationships were often established in these early years of European encroachment. Colonists needed trading partners to lay the infrastructure of their settlements, and Native Americans sought potential military alliances.

However, conflict-free relationships did not last. European-brought microbes, such as measles and smallpox, began to ravage Native communities. Tensions over the religious zeal of many colonists and the Native American way of life along with ongoing encroachment on the land of Native peoples led to what is sometimes referred to as **The First Indian War**. The conflict lasted over a year (1675 – 1676) and led to large loss of life on both sides: Plymouth Colony in Massachusetts and the Native American alliance that included the Wampanoag, Mohegans, and Mohawk.

Though a treaty ended the war, the relationship between early European colonists and Native Americans remained a complicated one, with vacillations between conflict and cooperation. In some ways, the colonists had a military advantage during military conflicts, having both firearms and a single, shared language allowing for easier alliance-making. However, as time went on and trade continued, Native American groups adopted modern weaponry and formed powerful alliances of their own.

The impacts of early colonization on Native Americans varied by location. Communities in New England had to face land seizure or "purchase" as well as more direct contact via war, trade, and nearby settlements. However, even Native peoples living in areas somewhat removed from early settlement were impacted by the diffusion of goods, ideas, and disease.

Practice Question

16) Which statement BEST describes the relationship between Native Americans and early European colonists?
    A. near constant warfare
    B. near constant peace
    C. vacillation between conflict and cooperation
    D. vacillation between armed and diplomatic conflict

Development of Slavery

The first enslaved Africans were brought to Jamestown, Virginia as early as 1619. This system coexisted for some years alongside the **indentured servitude** of White colonists, or the practice of being bound to an individual for a set period of time to pay off a debt, such as the cost of transport to the colonies.

The slave trade offered a way for colonists to exploit the potential for agricultural bounty in the rich soil of the southern colonies. Laws permitting African slavery were enacted throughout the colonies throughout the 1660s. **Tobacco**, which was grown in Virginia and Maryland, and **rice**, grown in the Carolinas, required a large labor force and exacerbated the expansion of the "cruel institution."

> **Did You Know?**
>
> Most indentured servants had a term of 4 – 6 years; however, indentured servants who were convicted of crimes often served at least seven years.

Enslaved people living in the colonies were treated as chattel and subject to multiple restrictions governing almost every aspect of their lives. Though some colonial governments began to outlaw the African slave trade in the early eighteenth century, the sale of enslaved persons already in the colonies only increased. This led to the breakup of families and other atrocities perpetrated against enslaved persons.

The experience of slavery varied by location to some degree. Often southern colonies contained large plantations with large numbers of enslaved people who tended the fields and the household. In northern colonies, households had fewer numbers of enslaved persons, some of whom were skilled trade and craftspeople.

Enslaved people resisted in myriad ways, including active means such as running away, rebelling, or staging armed uprisings as well as passive means, such as stealing from the estate, feigning illness, or even forming relationships with slave owners to encourage better treatment. Similarly, enslaved people kept their African traditions alive in different ways through community activities like song and dance and the retention of African religious customs. Others converted (either voluntarily or by force) to Christianity but kept their religious beliefs alive by **religious syncretism**, or the blending of different religious beliefs or practices together.

Practice Question

17) What was a central difference between slavery in the northern versus the southern colonies?
    A. Enslaved people lived in smaller groups in the North.
    B. Enslaved people lived in better conditions in the North.
    C. Enslaved people tended cash crops in the North.
    D. Enslaved people had more freedoms in the North.

The War for Independence

European powers had begun colonizing North America in the sixteenth century to access fur and agricultural resources; by the eighteenth century, Britain controlled most of the east coast of the continent, including the Thirteen Colonies, which became the original United States. France and Britain battled for control of northeastern North America, and following the **French and Indian War**, Great Britain consolidated its control over much of the continent.

Despite British victory in the French and Indian War, it had gone greatly into debt. Furthermore, there were concerns that the colonies required a stronger military presence following Native American attacks and uprisings like **Pontiac's Rebellion** in 1763. Consequently, **King George III** signed the

Proclamation of 1763, an agreement not to settle land west of the Appalachians, in an effort to make peace; however much settlement continued in practice.

King George III enforced heavy taxes and restrictive acts in the colonies to generate income for the Crown and eventually to punish disobedience. England expanded the **Molasses Act** of 1733, passing the **Sugar Act** in 1764 to raise revenue by taxing sugar and molasses, which were widely consumed in the colonies. In 1765, Britain enforced the **Quartering Act**, forcing colonists to provide shelter to British troops stationed in the region.

The 1765 **Stamp Act**, the first direct tax on the colonists, triggered more tensions. Any document required a costly stamp, with the revenue reverting to the British government. Colonists felt the tax violated their rights, given that they did not have direct representation in British Parliament. As a result, they began boycotting British goods and engaging in violent protest. **Samuel Adams** led the **Sons and Daughters of Liberty** in violent acts against tax collectors and stirred up rebellion with his **Committees of Correspondence**, which distributed anti-British propaganda.

Protests against the Quartering Act in Boston led to the **Boston Massacre** in 1770, when British troops fired on a crowd of protestors. By 1773, in a climate of continued unrest driven by the Committees of Correspondence, colonists protested the latest taxes on tea levied by the **Tea Act** in the famous **Boston Tea Party** by dressing as Native Americans and tossing tea off a ship in Boston Harbor. In response, the government passed the **Intolerable Acts**, closing Boston Harbor and bringing Massachusetts back under direct royal control.

In response to the Intolerable Acts, colonial leaders met in Philadelphia at the **First Continental Congress** in 1774 and presented colonial concerns to the king, who ignored them. However, violent conflict began in 1775 at **Lexington and Concord**, when American militiamen (**minutemen**) gathered to resist British efforts to seize weapons and arrest rebels in Concord. On June 17, 1775, the Americans fought the British at the **Battle of Bunker Hill**; despite American losses, the number of casualties the rebels inflicted caused the king to declare that the colonies were in rebellion. Troops were deployed to the colonies; the Siege of Boston began.

In May 1775, the **Second Continental Congress** met at Philadelphia to debate the way forward. Debate among leaders like Benjamin Franklin, John Adams, Thomas Jefferson, and James Madison centered on the wisdom of continued efforts at compromise, negotiations, and declaring independence. Again, the king ignored them. By the summer of 1776, the Continental Congress agreed on the need to break from Britain; on July 4, 1776, it declared the independence of the United States of America and issued the **Declaration of Independence**.

Preamble to the Declaration of Independence:

When in the Course of human events, it becomes necessary for one people to dissolve the political bands which have connected them with another, and to assume among the powers of the earth, the separate and equal station to which the Laws of Nature and of Nature's God entitle them, a decent respect to the opinions of mankind requires that they should declare the causes which impel them to the separation.

We hold these truths to be self-evident, that all men are created equal, that they are endowed by their Creator with certain unalienable Rights, that among these are Life, Liberty and the pursuit of Happiness. That to secure these rights, Governments are instituted among Men, deriving their just powers from the consent of the governed, that whenever any Form of Government becomes destructive of these ends, it is the Right of the People to alter or to abolish it, and to institute new

Government, laying its foundation on such principles and organizing its powers in such form, as to them shall seem most likely to effect their Safety and Happiness. Prudence, indeed, will dictate that Governments long established should not be changed for light and transient causes; and accordingly all experience hath shewn, that mankind are more disposed to suffer, while evils are sufferable, than to right themselves by abolishing the forms to which they are accustomed. But when a long train of abuses and usurpations, pursuing invariably the same Object evinces a design to reduce them under absolute Despotism, it is their right, it is their duty, to throw off such Government, and to provide new Guards for their future security.--Such has been the patient sufferance of these Colonies; and such is now the necessity which constrains them to alter their former Systems of Government. The history of the present King of Great Britain is a history of repeated injuries and usurpations, all having in direct object the establishment of an absolute Tyranny over these States. To prove this, let Facts be submitted to a candid world.

> **Check Your Understanding**
>
> Which instructional strategies could be used to help students analyze the preamble to *The Declaration of Independence*?

Americans were still divided over independence: **Patriots** favored independence while those still loyal to Britain were known as **Tories**. **George Washington** had been appointed head of the Continental Army and led a largely unpaid and unprofessional army; despite early losses, Washington gained ground due to strong leadership, superior knowledge of the land, and support from France.

Initially, the British seemed to have many advantages in the war, including more resources and troops. Britain won the **Battle of Brooklyn** (Battle of Long Island) in August 1776 and captured New York City. The tide turned in 1777 at **Valley Forge**, when Washington and his army survived the bitterly cold winter and managed to overcome British military forces.

A victory at **Saratoga** led the French to help the rebels in 1778. France was an important player in the Revolutionary War, sending supplies and troops to aid the Continental Army from 1778 – 1782. Its assistance is viewed by some scholars as crucial to the ultimate success of Patriot forces.

After Saratoga, fighting shifted south. Britain captured Georgia and Charleston, South Carolina; however, British forces could not adequately control the country as they proceeded to Yorktown, Virginia in 1781. At the **Battle of Yorktown**, British forces were defeated by the Continental Army with support from France and were forced to surrender.

Meanwhile, the British people did not favor the war and voted the Tories out of Parliament; the incoming Whig party sought to end the war. After troops fought for two more years, the **Treaty of Paris** ended the revolution in September 1783. In 1787, the first draft of the Constitution was written, and George Washington became the first president of the United States two years later. The American Revolution would go on to inspire revolutions around the world.

The Revolutionary War also had impacts on the new nation. In the spirit of freedom and liberty sparked by popular rhetoric, movements for abolition of slavery began to grow. Other groups began to argue for expanded rights for women. The Anglican Church, or the Church of England in the colonies, largely ceased to exist as its head was the British monarch. Other traditions of the mother country, such as laws dictating land inheritance, were abolished. New markets beyond England were also opened for the goods of American farmers and merchants. Additionally, new land in the western territories became "open" for conquest and settlement by Americans.

Practice Questions

18) The Intolerable Acts included all of the following EXCEPT
    A. the Boston Port Act.
    B. the Quartering Act.
    C. the Alien and Sedition Acts.
    D. the Massachusetts Government Act.

19) What advantage did the colonists have over the British in the American Revolution?
    A. vast financial wealth
    B. superior weaponry
    C. strong leadership and knowledge of the terrain
    D. a professional military and access to mercenaries

The Government of the Early Republic

Dominating American political thought since the American Revolution, **republicanism** stresses liberties and rights as central values, opposes corruption, rejects inherited political power, and encourages citizens to be civic-minded and independent. It is based on **popular sovereignty**, that is, the concept that the people are the source of political power. These ideas helped to form not only the Declaration of Independence but also the Constitution.

The colonies had broken away from Britain because of what they viewed as an oppressive, overbearing central government. As a result, the first government they created, whose framework was called the **Articles of Confederation**, was an intentionally weak, democratic government. Called a "firm league of friendship," it was designed to create a loose confederation between the colonies (now states) while allowing them to retain much of their individual sovereignty.

As a result, the Articles established a weak government with extremely limited authority: it did not have the power to levy taxes or raise an army. The legislature was intentionally and clearly subordinate to the states. Representatives were selected and paid by state legislatures.

It quickly became clear that this government was too weak to be effective, and by 1787, the new government of the United States was already in crisis. Without the power to levy taxes, the federal government had no way to alleviate its debt burden from the war. In addition, without an organizing authority, states began issuing their own currencies and crafting their own, competing trade agreements with foreign nations, halting trade and sending inflation through the roof. Without a national judicial system, there was no mechanism to solve the inevitable economic disputes. Furthermore, there were uprisings in the country.

A convention of the states was called to address problems in the young United States. At the **Constitutional Convention** in 1787, a decision was made to completely throw out the old Articles and write a new governing document from scratch.

The states did not want a central government that was so strong that it would oppress the states or the people, so they decided to prevent the concentration of power by dividing it. **Separation of powers** limited the powers within the federal government, dividing power among three branches: the executive, the legislative, and the judicial. In addition, each branch was given powers that would limit the power of the other branches in a system called **checks and balances**.

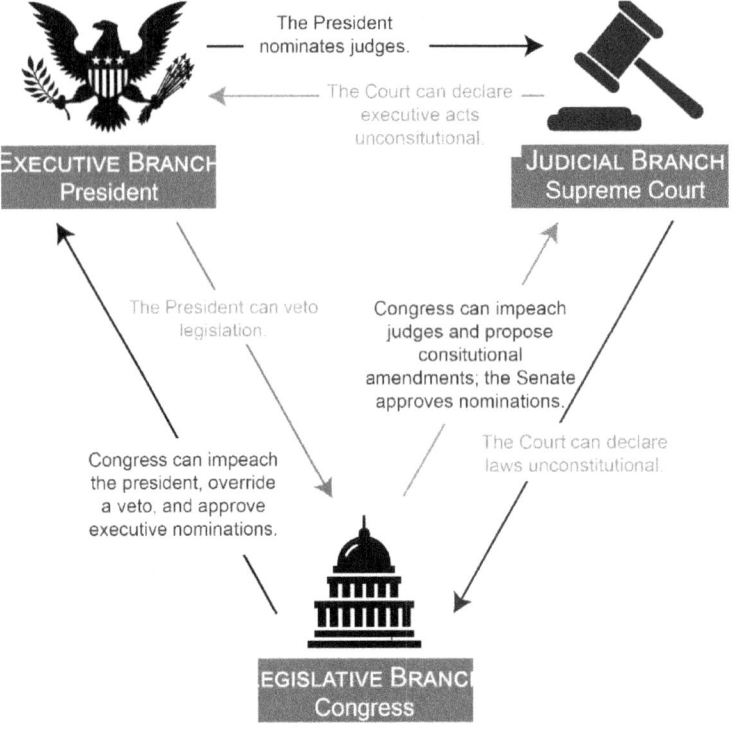

Figure 2.10. Checks and Balances

The executive branch—via the role of president—has the power to veto (reject) laws passed by the legislature. The legislative branch, consisting of Congress, can override the president's veto (with a two-thirds vote) and pass the law anyway. Finally, the judicial branch, consisting of the Supreme Court and other courts, can determine the constitutionality of laws (**judicial review**).

At the writing of the Constitution, the branch of the federal government endowed with the most power was the legislative branch, which makes laws. Simply called **Congress**, this branch is composed of a bicameral legislature (two houses). While this structure was not originally adopted under the Articles of Confederation, the framers chose it when reorganizing the government, mainly due to a dispute at the convention over the structure of the legislative body—specifically the voting power of each state.

Small states advocated equal representation, with each state having the same number of representatives, each with one vote; however, the more populous states argued for a plan based on **proportional representation**. Each state would be assigned a number of representatives based on its population (enslaved people deprived of their rights would even be counted among the population, benefiting those states with large slave populations). In the end, the **Great Compromise** was reached. There would be two houses: the **House of Representatives** (the lower house) would have proportional representation, and the **Senate** (the upper house) would have equal representation.

This system had two other advantages: the House of Representatives would also be directly elected by the people, and the Senate by the state legislatures. This supported the federal structure of the government: one house would serve the needs of the people directly, and the other would serve the needs of the states.

> **Check Your Understanding**
>
> How many representatives does California have in the US Congress?

Also, it curbed federal power by fragmenting it and slowing down the legislative process. Today, senators are also directly elected by the people.

Under the Constitution, the federal government is charged with matters that concern the population at large, such as managing federal lands, coining money, and maintaining an army and navy. It also handles conflicts between the states via the federal judiciary and by regulating interstate trade. Matters of regional or local concern are handled by state or local governments. This relationship is best codified in the Tenth Amendment, which states that any powers not explicitly given to the federal government are reserved for the states. The written Constitution can only be amended by a super majority.

State governments are generally modeled after these three branches, with the executive branch headed by the governor, the legislative branch headed by elected representatives, and the judicial branch headed by the state supreme court. **Local governments** have elected officials and generally follow charters that state constitutions have adopted. As they do with the federal government, the people vote for their state and local government representatives.

It took three years for all states to ratify the Constitution, with Rhode Island being the last to ratify on May 29, 1790. Much of the debate was over the lack of guarantees of basic civil rights in the Constitution. As a solution, James Madison introduced twelve amendments to the Constitution in 1789. Ten of these twelve are known as the Bill of Rights:

- **The First Amendment** protects **freedom of speech**. Congress may not pass laws that prohibit people from exercising freedom of religion, the press, assembly, or the right to petition against the government.

- **The Second Amendment** allows citizens to bear arms.

- **The Third Amendment** stops the government from quartering troops in private homes.

- **The Fourth Amendment** protects citizens from searches and seizures without a warrant.

- **The Fifth Amendment** ensures that citizens cannot be punished or subject to criminal prosecution without due process. Citizens also have the power of eminent domain, which means that private property cannot be seized for public use without proper compensation.

- **The Sixth Amendment** gives citizens a right to a fair and fast trial by jury, the right to know the crimes for which they are charged, and the right to confront witnesses. Citizens also have the right to legal representation and to gather testimonies from witnesses.

- **The Seventh Amendment** allows civil cases to be tried by jury (in the Articles of Confederation, only criminal trials could be tried by jury).

- **The Eighth Amendment** disallows excessive bail or fines; it also prohibits cruel and unusual punishment.

- **The Ninth Amendment** gives all rights not specifically enumerated in the Constitution to the people; it provides that the list of rights is not exhaustive.

- **The Tenth Amendment** provides that all other powers not provided to the federal government in the Constitution belong to the states.

Though the Constitution sought to create a healthy balance of power between state and federal government, the **nullification crisis** of 1832 – 33 revealed that states were not always happy with federal authority. After the passage of a tariff that was unfavorable to the southern states, South Carolina Senator Robert Hayne argued that states had a right to nullify or make void federal rulings that overstepped state's rights. He also maintained that states had the right to **secede** or leave the United States if their rights were not protected.

South Carolina adopted an ordinance to nullify the federal tariff and declared any force by the federal government would lead to its secession. President Andrew Jackson, who hoped to avoid Civil War, responded by lowering the tariff. South Carolina rescinded the ordinance of nullification; however, this crisis remains a pivotal event that illustrates the shaky balance between state's rights and the power of the federal government. It would also be a prelude of things to come.

Practice Question

20) Which of the following is NOT one of the amendments in the Bill of Rights?
    A. Citizens have the right to bear arms.
    B. The Senate must have equal representation.
    C. Citizens have the power of eminent domain.
    D. The government cannot quarter troops in private homes.

Expansion

In the nineteenth century, the idea of **Manifest Destiny**, or the sense that it was the fate of the United States to expand westward and settle the continent, pervaded. In 1803 President Thomas Jefferson oversaw the **Louisiana Purchase**, which nearly doubled the size of the United States. **Meriwether Lewis** and **William Clark** were dispatched to explore the western frontier of the territory—Jefferson hoped to find an all-water route to the Pacific Ocean (via the Missouri River). While this route did not exist, Lewis and Clark returned with a deeper knowledge of the territory the US had come to control.

> **Helpful Hint**
>
> Teaching about **Sacagawea**, the Lemhi Shoshone woman who joined the Lewis and Clark expedition, is one way to bring diverse historical actors into classroom instruction.

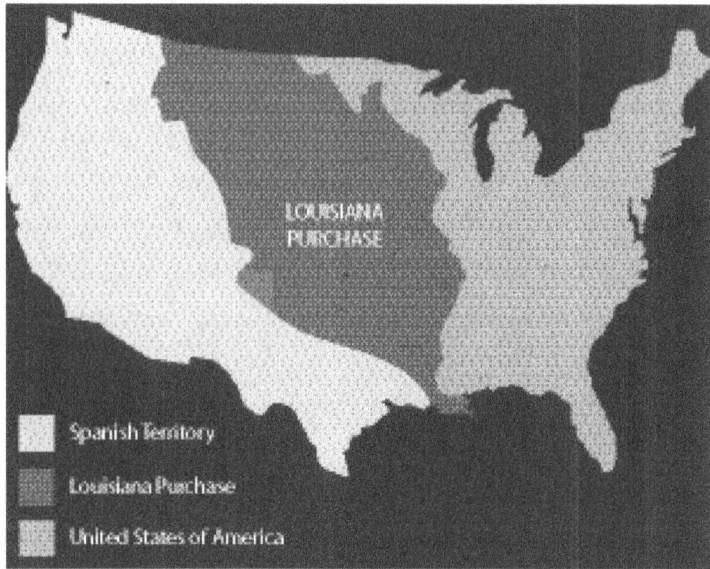

Figure 2.11. Louisiana Purchase

Later, British provocation at sea and in the northwest led to the **War of 1812** between the United States and Britain, which was allied with the Shawnee-led Northwest Confederacy. Growing nationalism in the

United States pressured Madison into pushing for war; Congress declared war under President Madison with the intent to defend the United States, end unfair trade practices and poor treatment of Americans on the high seas, and penetrate British Canada. Despite the Confederacy's alliance with Britain, the United States prevailed.

The war resulted in no real gains or losses for either the Americans or the British, yet at the war's end, the United States had successfully defended itself as a country and reaffirmed its independence. Patriotism ran high, strengthening the idea of Manifest Destiny. In 1819, following the Seminole War, the United States purchased Florida from Spain in the **Adams-Onis Treaty** (conflict with the Seminole would continue). The **Monroe Doctrine**, President James Monroe's policy that the Western Hemisphere was "closed" to any further European colonization or exploration, asserted US power in the region.

With westward expansion came questions over the expansion of slavery. In 1820, the **Missouri Compromise** allowed Missouri to join the union as a slave state but provided that any other states north of the thirty-sixth parallel 36°30' would be free. However, more tension and compromises over the nature of slavery in the West were to come.

With continental expansion came more conflict with Native Americans. Despite legal resistance by the Cherokee, President Andrew Jackson enforced the 1830 **Indian Removal Act**, forcing Cherokee, Creek, Chickasaw, Choctaw, and others from their lands in the Southeast. Thousands of people were forced to travel to Indian Territory (today, Oklahoma) on the infamous **Trail of Tears** to make way for White settlers.

The United States continued to grow throughout the nineteenth century. In 1845, the United States annexed Texas, which contributed to the outbreak of the Mexican-American War the next year. As a result, it gained California and the Utah and New Mexico territories in the 1848 Treaty of Guadalupe Hidalgo. In 1846, the United States and Britain agreed on the Oregon Treaty, which established a border at the forty-ninth parallel.

Practice Question

21) What did the Missouri Compromise accomplish?
    A. It admitted Missouri as a free state.
    B. It admitted California as a free state.
    C. It allowed slavery in New Mexico and Utah to be decided by popular sovereignty.
    D. It banned slavery north of the thirty-sixth parallel.

Life in the Early Republic

The country was increasingly divided over slavery; **sectionalism** grew, strengthening disunity between the North and the South. Reform movements continued to include **abolitionism**, the ending of slavery. The former slave **Frederick Douglass** advocated for abolition. An activist leader and writer, Douglass publicized the movement along with the American Anti-Slavery Society and publications like Harriet Beecher Stowe's *Uncle Tom's Cabin*. He and other activists, like **Harriet Tubman**, helped free slaves using the **Underground Railroad**. An estimated 100,000 slaves escaped the South between 1810 and 1850 through a system of safe houses, even though these actions violated state laws. The radical abolitionist **John Brown** led violent protests against slavery. Abolitionism became a key social and political issue in the mid-nineteenth century; slavery was the main cause of the **Civil War**.

Distinct regional identities were not only centered around beliefs about slavery. Complex historical, economic, and geographic factors all contributed to the sectional divide. Because the land in the southern states was rich and the climate hospitable to certain cash crops, these states focused on agriculture and, according to some scholars, developed a culture centered around a rigid view of morality and social conservatism.

In the northern states where the climate was less hospitable to mass agriculture, industry and manufacturing were prioritized. The need for a labor force led to the growth of cities and more **immigration**, particularly from European nations like Ireland and Germany. In the two decades prior to the Civil War, an estimated 4.5 million Europeans immigrated to the United States, many settling in the northern states or the Midwest. Immigration and urbanization impacted the culture of the northern states, which some say began to embrace more progressive causes, such abolition and the improvement of educational and political institutions.

Upheaval in Europe and limited opportunity, as well as the promise of land or high-paying industrial jobs, drew these immigrants to the United States, as did the democratic ideals upon which the United States was founded. These immigrants faced challenges, such as learning a new language and discrimination fueled by fears of "foreignness" and economic competition.

Free African Americans also faced discrimination via the laws and actions of White Americans; however, the lives of free African Americans varied considerably based on location. In the South, discrimination often prevented their participation in many facets of society. While discrimination against free men and women also existed in the North, the region offered more opportunities for African Americans to own land and businesses, serve in the military, and participate in the social life of the nation.

The antebellum period also began the era of Native "Americanization and assimilation." The United States government made agreements with many religious and reform groups to establish missions and schools on or near reservations. These efforts are today criticized for their attempted decimation of Native American culture and often abhorrent treatment of children. Native Americans who chose to live among Whites were not recognized as citizens with equal protections under the law and were often treated with hostility and suspicion.

White **women** in the pre-Civil War era experienced continuity and change. On the one hand, they had few rights even over their own property and children, and they could not make wills or sign contracts. On the other hand, the abolition movement involved many women who began to take on advocacy roles outside of their homes and families. Education reforms of the era, led by **Horace Mann**, sought to increase access to education for women. Meanwhile, social change in the Northeast and growing Midwest continued. As the market economy and early industry developed, so did an early **middle class**. Women asserted their rights: activists like **Susan B. Anthony** and **Elizabeth Cady Stanton** worked for women's suffrage, culminating in the 1848 **Seneca Falls Convention**.

Children also benefitted from educational reform as part of the common school movement. This movement, led by Mann, sought to develop public schools for all citizens—except African Americans and Irish Catholics. Nevertheless, many children worked in factories or on farms and had little labor protections.

However, as the nineteenth century marched on, slavery became the central issue in American society. Antislavery factions in Congress had attempted to halt the extension of slavery to the new territories obtained from Mexico, but they were unsuccessful. In the Compromise of 1850, Congress decided that the voters in some new territories

> **Check Your Understanding**
>
> What types of primary sources might help students understand what life was like for women and children in Antebellum America?

would be allowed to decide whether slavery should be legal or determined by popular sovereignty. In 1854, Congress passed the **Kansas-Nebraska Act**, effectively repealing the Missouri Compromise of 1820 by allowing these states to now decide slavery by popular sovereignty as well. In response, the new **Republican Party** emerged. One of its members, **Abraham Lincoln**, was elected president in 1860 on an antislavery platform.

Practice Question

22) Which of the following effectively repealed the Missouri Compromise?
    A. the Dred Scott decision
    B. the Compromise of 1850
    C. the Kansas-Nebraska Act
    D. the Fugitive Slave Act

Civil War

Following Lincoln's election, South Carolina immediately seceded, followed by Mississippi, Alabama, Florida, Louisiana, Georgia, and Texas. They formed the Confederate States of America, or the **Confederacy**, on February 1, 1861, under the leadership of **Jefferson Davis**, a senator from Mississippi.

Figure 2.19. The Civil War

Shortly after the South's secession, Confederate forces attacked Union troops in Sumter, South Carolina; the **Battle of Fort Sumter** sparked the Civil War. As a result, Virginia, Tennessee, North Carolina, and Arkansas seceded and joined the Confederacy. West Virginia was formed when the western part of Virginia refused to join the Confederacy.

The reasons for the Civil War were both complex and simple. On the one hand, slavery was the central issue; however, slavery was a part of deeper divisions related to notions of states' rights (see previous information about the nullification crisis). Though states' rights are seemingly a political issue, they reflect the different economic interests of northern and southern states. Slavery was central to the cash-crop economy of the South but much less central to the more industrialized North that relied on non-forced labor. At the outset of the conflict, each side had distinct advantages and disadvantages:

- The North had a larger population of 21 million versus the South's 9 million.
- The North had almost ten times as many manufacturing plants as the South.
- The North had 70 percent of all rail lines.
- The South had a "home field" advantage.
- The South had a long coastline that made blockades a challenge.
- Some historians also believe the southern states had better military leadership.

Both sides believed the conflict would be short-lived; however, after the **First Battle of Bull Run**, when the Union failed to route the Confederacy, it became clear that the war would not end quickly. Realizing how difficult it would be to defeat the Confederacy, the Union developed the **Anaconda Plan**, a plan to "squeeze" the Confederacy, which included building a naval blockade and taking control of the Mississippi River. Since the South depended on international trade in cotton for much of its income, a naval blockade would have serious economic ramifications for the Confederacy.

The Second Battle of Bull Run was a tactical Confederate victory led by General Robert E. Lee and Stonewall Jackson. The Union army remained intact, but the loss was a heavy blow to morale. The Battle of Antietam was the first battle to be fought on Union soil. Union General George B. McClellan halted General Lee's invasion of Maryland but failed to defeat Confederate forces. Undaunted, on January 1, 1863, President Lincoln decreed the end of slavery in the rebel states with the **Emancipation Proclamation**. The **Battle of Gettysburg** was a major Union victory. It was the bloodiest battle in American history up to this point, and the Confederate army would not recover.

Meanwhile, following the **Siege of Vicksburg**, Mississippi, Union forces led by General Ulysses S. Grant gained control over the Mississippi River, completing the Anaconda Plan. The Battle of Atlanta was the final major battle of the Civil War; victorious, the Union proceeded into the South, and the Confederacy fell. In April 1865, General Lee surrendered to General Grant at Appomattox, Virginia, and the war ended.

Practice Questions

23) What assets did the Confederacy have during the Civil War?
    A. The Confederacy had superior weaponry and production resources.
    B. The Confederacy maintained brisk trade with Europe, enabling it to fund the war.
    C. The Confederacy benefitted from strong military leadership and high morale among the population.
    D. The Confederacy's strong infrastructure allowed it to transport supplies and people efficiently throughout the South.

24) In the Emancipation Proclamation, President Lincoln declared an end to slavery
    A. in Kentucky and Missouri.
    B. in the Union only.
    C. in slave states that had not seceded from the Union.
    D. in the rebel states.

Reconstruction

Reconstruction after the war would bring huge changes in the South and redefine how African Americans fit into American society. The South was in economic ruins; many Southerners, especially newly freed slaves and other African Americans, sought better economic opportunities by moving to the North. Congress passed the Civil Rights Act in 1866, recognizing the rights of former slaves as US citizens; it also passed the Reconstruction Acts the next year, enforcing military occupation of the South. These acts laid out the process for readmission to the Union. Among other requirements, states had to ratify the Thirteenth, Fourteenth, and Fifteenth Amendments. These made slavery illegal, recognized equal rights, and permitted African American males to vote, respectively.

Still, agriculture and infrastructure were ruined, and many were bitter over Northern occupation and involvement. Even though the South was forced to accept the end of slavery, Southern states created "Black codes" which restricted the rights of Black Americans. African Americans faced ongoing discrimination and violence in the South, including segregation and threats from hate groups like the Ku Klux Klan. Thus, while African Americans could vote by law, most could not in practice as they faced threat of violence or death.

Violence toward African Americans and Reconstruction reforms led by **Radical Republicans** from the North proved almost insurmountable. Tired of war, the troops sent to assist in the effort were inadequate in number, mismanaged, and often instructed to refrain from engagement. The goal of Reconstruction was largely to rebuild the Union, not necessarily to protect or enfranchise free African American men and women in the South. Thus, conciliation was prioritized and the aims of "Radical Reconstruction" were unrealized.

Instead, the southern states institutionalized racism and segregation via law. **Black Codes** were the first laws passed in 1865 to limit the movements, work, and earnings of Black southerners. Such laws expanded in the aftermath of Reconstruction, and new **Jim Crow Laws** legalized and laid out the practices of racial segregation. These laws made segregation the way of the South until the civil rights movement of the 1960s.

Practice Question

25) Which of the following was NOT a result of Reconstruction?
   A. Southern states made new laws.
   B. American troops came to the South.
   C. African American Southerners began voting in large numbers.
   D. Segregation became the norm in public places in the South.

Industrialization and Nativism

The end of the Civil War also brought on an increase in **industrialization**. A British phenomenon, industrialization made its way to the United States. Machines replaced hand labor as the main way of manufacturing, exponentially increasing production capacities. Later in the nineteenth century, the US began developing heavy industry.

The **assembly line** developed by Henry Ford enabled **mass production**. Factors that contributed to this boom included the invention of new products (e.g., the automobile, the telephone, and the electric light); the improvement of production methods; an abundance of natural resources and infrastructure (railways opened the West further and connected factories and markets to raw materials); and banking (more people wanted to invest in booming businesses, and banks were financing them).

Did You Know?

Toilets for waste disposal may date back to the Indus Valley civilization, but they only became popular in the mid-nineteenth century after outbreaks of cholera and typhoid began to ravage England.

Several inventions changed life in America in the Industrial Age. Railroads, which were a key factor in the Union victory, allowed people and goods to travel farther and more easily than ever before. The typewriter, invented in 1867, changed administrative and office work, as did the cash register and adding machine, invented in the subsequent decades, that changed the world of retail. Innovations like the "water closet" improved health and decreased reliance on unsanitary methods of waste disposal, such as outhouses.

In industry, the **Bessemer Process** allowed American industrialists to make steel more efficiently and cheaply. Such innovation allowed for the construction of more rail lines and bigger and longer-lasting buildings. Other inventions, such as home electricity, began to impact life as the technology began to make its way into homes. Quality of life improved for many Americans in the Industrial Age, but it is important to mention that such improvements impacted wealthy urbanites more than rural Americans, Native Americans, African Americans, and poor Americans.

New cities and towns became larger as people started to live and work in urban areas, attracted by employment opportunities. Unfortunately, lack of planning for this phenomenon—**urbanization**—led to inadequate sanitation (which contributed to cholera and typhoid epidemics), pollution, and crime. However, overall, the economy of the US was growing, the middle class was becoming larger, and industry and technology were developing.

Immigration also continued in the decades following the Civil War. Around 5.2 million immigrants arrived in the United States in the 1880s alone. These "new immigrants" were different from those of the past. From southern and eastern Europe and places like Italy, Poland, and Russia, these people were often Catholic or Jewish and faced discrimination from some Protestant Americans.

As a downturn in the American economy during the 1870s led to fears that these immigrants were taking jobs from "native" Americans, a **nativist** movement began to take hold. Nativists supported restrictions on immigration and an extended waiting period prior to naturalization. In the mid-1850s, a nativist political party, originally known as the **Know-Nothing Party** and later rebranded the Native American and American Party, formed. This party believed, among other xenophobic conspiracies, that there was a Catholic conspiracy to undermine freedom of religion in the United States.

Practice Question

26) The Bessemer Process is related to which of the following?
    A. steel manufacturing
    B. administrative processes
    C. retail management
    D. human hygiene

Early California History

Pre-Columbian Peoples

The earliest people of California were the descendants of those humans who first crossed the Bering Strait from Asia into North America. Due to the particular geography of the state, the Native Peoples of California had a different existence than did many other Native Peoples of North America, such as those who lived in the Great Plains region of what is now the United States. Because of the myriad landforms in the state, including deserts and mountain ranges that prevented easy travel, the Native Peoples of present-day California often settled in smaller, isolated units.

Unlike the history of the Native Peoples of the Great Plains, large confederacies and alliances are largely absent from the story of California before European colonization. The state's abundant resources often prevented conflict over real or perceived scarcity, so Indigenous groups of California, who lived apart from one another in regions with distinct geographical barriers, had little incentive to engage in warfare.

Several distinct cultural groups inhabited the land that would become California. Most groups lacked a central political structure and instead were organized into smaller tribal groups (sometimes referred to as **tribelets**). Depending on the size of these groups, which could range from the hundreds to the thousands, people lived in a single village or a group of villages organized around one central or capital village. The types of structures and daily lives of these groups varied based on the region and its natural resources. Where trees were plentiful, such as in the north, homes were built of wood; where trees were scarce, homes were built of mud, brush, or palm—some were even built underground. Similarly, the climate and ecology of the region dictated daily life:

- Tribes in the Northwest constructed canoes out of the redwoods to fish for salmon.

- Centrally located tribes in the rich valley engaged in agriculture and hunting.
- Tribes that lived along the coast fished and traded with other tribes.

Some tribes had advanced techniques of food preservation, including leaching and hermetic sealing, which allowed for food to be stored for longer periods. Families traded food and other goods within the tribelet, but many communities also had a group of merchant traders who bought and sold goods from other regions.

Most tribelets had a chief who managed domestic affairs. Shamans, who organized religious rituals, were also important members of many communities. Religious beliefs varied among tribelets, but scholars note that some religious traditions were more common than others. The **Kuksu** faith, which dominated in the northern region, and the **Toloache** faith, more common in the southern part of what would become California, were two such belief systems.

The Kuksu and Toloache were religious traditions that spanned tribal affiliation and involved a formal initiation of devotees through ritual. In the Northwest, many tribes also practiced a similar religion dominated by myths and renewal rituals.

Many tribelets had highly developed cultural systems. Members composed and performed oral prose and poetry and created visual arts of many sorts. Rock paintings, pottery, and elaborate costumes, often used in religious rituals and ceremonies, were common in many tribelets in the region.

Basket weaving is the art that the Indigenous Peoples of California are perhaps best known for. These baskets are remarkable for their watertightness, strength, and durability. The Central Valley region inhabitants are believed to have made the most elaborate and varied baskets. This long tradition of artistry and skill has survived to this day, and fine baskets made by expert Native American craftspeople are displayed in museums and highly coveted among collectors.

Table 2.1. Major Tribes of California
Northeast
- Modoc
- Atsugewi
- Achomawi
Northwest
- Wiyot
- Chilula
- Chimariko
- Karuk
- Shasta
- Tolowa
- Yurok Hupa Whilkut
South
- Kitanemuk
- Serrano
- Gabrielino Luiseno Cahuilla
- Kumeyaay
- Chumash
- Alliklik

2. History and Social Science

Table 2.1. Major Tribes of California
- Mojave
Central
- Pomo
- Miwok
- Wappo
- Yuki
- Kato
- Maidu
- Yahi
- Yokut
- Yana
- many others

Though many Native groups of California were destroyed in the process of conquest and colonization (and the diseases brought to the Americas via these processes), the state today has more Native Americans than any other, which includes some 360,000 people with over one hundred tribal affiliations. Some of California's Native Peoples currently live on small reservations or trust allotments throughout the state; these areas make up less than 1 percent of the state's total land area. The Native Peoples of California have contributed much to the state's culture and fabric.

Did You Know?

The Yurok tribe, with five thousand members, is believed to be the largest of California's Indigenous communities.

Practice Question

27) Which statement BEST describes the distribution of California's Native American population before European arrival?
  A. densest in the Great Valley, where Native Peoples lived in large villages
  B. spread all over the state, where Native Peoples lived in small tribelets
  C. spread all over the state, where Native Peoples lived in large villages
  D. densest in the coastal regions, where Native Peoples lived in small tribelets

Spanish Colonization and Mexican California

The Spanish arrived in Baja, California, in the 1530s and made their way to Alta California in the 1540s. Early conquistadors claimed the land for the Spanish Crown and brought diseases that quickly spread and ravaged Indigenous populations. Still, there were few attempts to colonize this remote part of the new empire. The wealth of Mexico and Peru occupied Spaniards eager to exploit the gold and silver found there, and California was far removed from the center of the Spanish colonial empire. Thus, most Native Californians had few, if any, direct interactions with Europeans during the early colonial period.

Things began to change, however, after the **Seven Years' War**, or the **French and Indian War** (1754 – 1763), as it was called in North America. The war pitted French and British colonies against their Indigenous allies, which resulted in a British victory. The end of the war and the resulting Treaty of Paris of 1763 made Great Britain the dominant concern in North America, which tipped the uneasy balance of European power and incited the Spanish to action.

The fear of British expansion meant that Spain had to secure the land it had already claimed, including more remote areas like California. In 1769, the first permanent Spanish settlement, a **presidio**, or military fort, accompanied by a church formed by **Father Junípero Serra**, was established in San Diego. More presidios were established in Monterey (1770), San Francisco (1776), and Santa Barbara (1782).

Presidios offered some military protection and thus attracted Spanish settlers in communities known as **pueblos**. Pueblos not directly tied to presidios were established in the late eighteenth and early nineteenth centuries at San José, Los Angeles, Branciforte, and Sonoma.

Presidios and pueblos were important for bringing in settlers, but the center of Spanish interaction with the Native Peoples of California was the **mission**. By 1823, there were twenty-one of these religious settlements.

Franciscan priests operated Spanish missions to bring Native Peoples into the fold of Catholicism and convert them to a European way of life. In theory, the missions were to be temporary establishments, and Native Peoples who lived in missions were to become sufficiently Europeanized so they could then establish their own communities and live as the White settlers did. In reality, few Native Peoples were converted to the European way of life to the degree the Spanish missionaries would have liked. Thus, missions often became more permanent living and working arrangements.

Conditions in missions were often very poor, and missionaries were known to use force to achieve conversion and extract labor from their flock. Disease flourished in crowded missions, and Indigenous Peoples with no immunity to European pathogens became ill at alarming rates. In response to these conditions, Native Peoples tried different ways to resist forced assimilation, including continuing to worship their deities, escaping, and even directly rebelling against missionaries and other colonial authorities. Nevertheless, the labor of Native Peoples was central to the economy of Spanish California. Missions often produced the agricultural products that supplied the neighboring presidios and pueblos and formed the bedrock of the colonial economy.

Did You Know?

Scholars now believe that the knowledge of California's Native Peoples and their ability to live off the rich resources of the land influenced the success of Spanish colonialism in California.

Spanish California also included nonmilitary and nonreligious settlements in the form of ranchos. **Ranchos** were large tracts of land given to Spanish Californians, often in exchange for prior military service. These ranchos were not outright land grants during the Spanish period but rather the extension of grazing rights in a large area. Under the Spanish rancho system, the land would return to the Crown after the grantee's death. After Mexican independence from Spain in 1821, the rancho system was changed, and the rancheros—those living and working at ranchos—received legal titles to the land. After Mexico won independence from Spain, California came under a new political authority:

- The Franciscan mission system was quickly dismantled.
- Land grants increased, and the rancho system expanded.
- Cattle ranching became a central economic activity.

Rancheros traded beef and hides with American merchants via the Pacific Coast for the manufactured goods they needed. These wealthy, landed elite stood atop the social hierarchy and came to be known as **Californios**.

The economy of California was no longer self-sufficient as it had been during the Spanish colonial period. There was a tremendous reliance on trade to obtain certain goods; however, consistency in the labor force endured. Native Californians often worked on the ranchos as agricultural laborers or by raising and tending cattle.

Settlement of California was opened to foreigners during the Mexican national period, and Europeans and Americans began to arrive throughout the 1830s and 1840s to avail themselves of the land's richness.

The first American in California was believed to be adventurer **Jedediah Smith**, who led a group of trappers on an expedition in 1826. He was soon followed by other American settlers. By 1846, California was likely home to fourteen thousand non-Native Peoples, two thousand of whom were Americans.

However, California was not only the frontier of New Spain; it was also the frontier of Mexico. Far-removed from the seat of government, Mexico struggled to rule California effectively, and by the mid-1840s, California had established a degree of political independence.

Practice Question

28) Why did Spain begin to take more of an interest in the settlement of California in the eighteenth century?
   A. a desire to exploit the natural resources of the region
   B. a fear that it was losing political control over the Native Peoples
   C. a need to solidify colonial possessions after the British victory in the French and Indian War
   D. a desire to better ally itself with the French following the outbreak of the French and Indian War

The Mexican–American War and Statehood

Prelude to War

Americans moved not only to California in the nineteenth century but also to remote Mexican territories. One of these was Texas. The Mexican government initially welcomed Americans to Texas; few Mexicans had an interest in settling there because the Comanche and Apache peoples who inhabited the land were seen as a threat.

To encourage settlement in light of this perceived barrier, the Mexican government passed the **Imperial Colonization Law** in 1823, which permitted slavery in Texas and provided exemptions for settlers on various tariffs and taxes.

The relationship between settlers and the Mexican government quickly soured, however. As settlers poured in, the Mexican government feared a loss of control and passed new laws to curb settlement and reimpose taxes. A new dictator-like figure, **Antonio López de Santa Anna**, became the Mexican president in 1833 and quickly repealed the existing constitution. This prompted further concerns in Texas, where many American settlers who valued democratic ideals saw Santa Anna as a threat to their rights and freedoms.

In 1836, Texas declared independence from Mexico. After seven months of fighting, the Texans declared victory and became an independent republic. Though many, including Texas president Sam Houston, supported joining the United States, the existence of slavery in Texas posed a problem for the US government. Debates over the expansion of slavery into new territories were central to the political landscape of the time. In 1845, Texas joined the Union as a slave state.

President James K. Polk also looked to California, at this time still part of Mexico, as another possible way to expand the United States. In 1845, he sent **John Charles Frémont** and a group of army engineers to survey the Sierra Nevada.

For reasons debated, and perhaps at the direct instruction of Polk, Frémont and his men entered California in 1846 and told settlers there that he would support their rebellion against Mexico. On June 10, Frémont's men and a group of settlers attacked a lieutenant in the Mexican army. The Mexicans quickly surrendered, and the California Republic, or the **Bear Flag Republic**, as it was known because of its flag depicting a bear, existed for twenty-five days.

Figure 2.12. California Republic Flag

The **Mexican-American War**, or Mexican War (1846 – 1848), broke out largely over the annexation of Texas and disputed Texas-Mexico borders.

While US general **Zachary Taylor** focused on the border region, Colonel **Stephen Kearny** and his troops moved into California and New Mexico. In July of 1846, American marines arrived in California and claimed the land for the United States. Frémont and his troops joined American forces in their fight against Mexico, and the Bear Flag Republic ended.

The Mexican governor of California, Don Pío de Jesús Pico, known as **Pío Pico**, fled the state in August of 1846 after Americans took control of Los Angeles; however, Mexican Californio troops eventually regained the city, only to have it retaken in January of 1847. The surrender of the remaining Californio troops quickly followed, and the **Treaty of Cahuenga** was signed on January 13, 1847, ending Mexican Californio and American fighting in California. In September of 1847, Mexico City was captured by American troops under General Winfield Scott, and the war was largely won by the United States.

In 1848, the United States and Mexico negotiated the **Treaty of Guadalupe Hidalgo**. As a result, the United States gained territory—New Mexico, Arizona, Colorado, Utah, Nevada, and California—in exchange for fifteen million dollars. Mexico abandoned any claims to Texas.

> **Did You Know?**
>
> Mexico ceded 55 percent of its territory in the Treaty of Guadalupe Hidalgo.

Mexican citizens living in the ceded territories had the choice of moving back to Mexico, staying in their homes and becoming American citizens, or staying in their homes and retaining their Mexican citizenship. They had one year to make the choice. The majority, likely some one hundred thousand or more, chose to stay and accept American citizenship, though it is estimated that around three thousand people did return to land that was still part of Mexico.

Zachary Taylor, who had gained fame as a war hero, became the US president in 1848. The issue of California's formal entry into the Union was of particular importance to his government because gold had been discovered in the territory that same year.

The newly acquired territory, however, brought further debates over the expansion of slavery into new American territories. The proposed **Wilmot Proviso** would prohibit slavery in any of the areas acquired by the Treaty of Guadalupe Hidalgo. Though it was never enacted, it was vigorously debated by both abolitionists and proponents of slavery.

The American government was fiercely divided over whether to permit slavery in the enormous new territory obtained following the Mexican-American War; however, the desire to exploit the resources of these lands and open them to settlement drove leaders to compromise.

In the **Compromise of 1850**, Congress strengthened the **Fugitive Slave Act**, which provided for the return to bondage of enslaved persons found in free states; however, it also abolished the slave trade in Washington, DC. This compromise established the borders of Texas as they stand today.

Most important for California, the Compromise of 1850 admitted California as a free state, with slavery to be decided by popular sovereignty, or the will of the people in the state, in the Utah and New Mexico Territories.

Practice Question

29) Why did the American government want to quickly decide the issue of California becoming a state?
   A. Gold was discovered in California.
   B. The Mexican War began.
   C. A future California revolt was feared.
   D. The border with Mexico was disputed.

From the Gold Rush to the Present

The Discovery of Gold

On January 24, 1848, **James Marshall**, who was contracted to build a sawmill along the American River in California Territory, saw a glint of something in the stream. News of his discovery quickly spread, and a rush to the state began. California's population grew rapidly with the **Gold Rush** as people from all over the world descended on the region in search of riches.

Nearly one hundred thousand people moved to California in 1849. Known as "**forty-niners**," these people came from the United States, Europe, China, Australia, and beyond. Those who came from the United States had two choices: a long sea route or an even longer overland route. Immigrants with families often chose the overland path, bringing entire households with them. Many Americans also came to California to sell goods and services to these gold seekers.

With little guidance from the US government, the people of California drafted and approved their own state constitution in 1849, even before official statehood. However, finding gold—not establishing governmental bureaucracy—was the most pressing matter, and it largely fell to small mining camps to govern themselves. They did so fairly effectively, though vigilante justice was not unheard of.

After California became a state in 1850, it elected **Peter Hardeman Burnett** as its governor. His first order of business was eliminating the Native Californians he saw as standing in the way of the state's settlement and prosperity. He spread anti–Native American rhetoric and collected a cache of weapons, which he subsequently distributed to local militias to wage war on Native Peoples.

Local militias then began a process of extermination. The US Army and even civilian settlers joined in this mass slaughter of Native Peoples. Some White people formed official paramilitary groups, whose sole purpose was to find and kill Native Peoples.

As a result, the largely peaceful Native population of California was diminished by two-thirds in the first two years of the Gold Rush, a loss of some one hundred thousand men, women, and children. This period of violence and slaughter is now called the **California genocide**. Fortune was the ultimate goal of many who participated in the California genocide. They saw Native Peoples as "uncivilized" and standing in their way of mining for gold.

Despite the miners' goal of riches, California gold mining began very primitively. The earliest techniques often centered around a simple gravity method known as **panning**, whereby heavier gold could be separated from lighter water and silt. A system of panning multiple buckets at once with a device known as a **rocker box**, by which a screen identified gold in alluvial or water deposits, followed simple panning as a newer technique.

Once surface-level gold was exhausted, miners used picks and shovels to look for gold under the earth's surface. As mining became more complicated and less gold was available, miners banded together in large and small companies for greater chances of success.

The Gold Rush brought fortune to the lucky few, but it also had broader impacts on California and the United States. Transportation and communication grew to meet the needs of prospectors. New roads, bridges, ferries, and ships were constructed to transport people and goods. The **Pony Express** was founded during this period to deliver packages and correspondence from California to the Midwest. Retail and wholesale businesses of many sorts, from lumber to textiles, also sprang up.

Though gold brought people to California, the rich land and favorable climate are what led many to stay, and several of California's vineyards and farms emerged during this era. Additionally, the Gold Rush led to an international economic boom of sorts. Nations far and wide began to trade more with both Californians and other Americans. New banks and financial service industries sprang up to take advantage of this boom.

> **Did You Know?**
> The Gold Rush netted an estimated $216 million.

However, not every result of the Gold Rush and its aftermath was positive, as the genocide of Native Peoples clearly shows. Additionally, the Gold Rush also created environmental concerns because the landscape was ravaged to extract gold as quickly as possible with no consideration for long-term impacts. In many places, there were also rampant labor shortages since many Americans left their farms and workplaces to flock to California.

And, of course, one of the impacts of the Gold Rush was more gold in circulation, which led to inflation in the gold-backed currency system and thus higher prices for many consumer goods.

Practice Question

30) Which of the following was NOT a result of the California Gold Rush?
    A. new transportation networks
    B. labor shortages in other parts of the country
    C. environmental degradation
    D. lower prices for consumer goods

Nineteenth-Century Migration

Though people immigrating to California from Europe or Asia had no choice but to use sea travel, many Americans came overland. The **California Trail** system, spanning some 5,665 miles and ten states, was the most-used route. The remnants of this trail system can still be seen in many places.

Families using the trail from its beginnings in Missouri had a roughly 2,400-mile journey to California that could take up to six months. Along the way, they had to navigate deserts and mountains. Few towns existed along the route, forcing these settlers to depend on their resourcefulness to meet basic needs. An estimated two hundred thousand people traveled this route in the 1840s and 1850s. Some of them made it to their destination, but others perished from disease, starvation, or accidents along the way.

Americans were not the only people to feel the lure of the Gold Rush or other broader opportunities in the American West. Immigrants from Chile and Mexico in search of gold and a better life also came to California, where they joined Spanish-speaking Californios already living there.

During this era, Californios who had lived in the region under Mexico lost their land and were denied many of the rights that White people enjoyed—even though they had been promised US citizenship and equal rights under the Treaty of Guadalupe Hidalgo. They also suffered from racial and ethnic discrimination and were often wrongly portrayed as foreigners, though they were not immigrants.

Europeans also came to California, fleeing the wave of anti-monarchy revolutions of 1848 in Europe that left some nations in chaos. These immigrant groups, though often non-English-speaking, were generally accepted by White American Californians to a greater degree than were immigrants from Asia and Latin America. They were also more widely accepted than Californios. There was an irony to this: unlike the Californios who were in fact American citizens, these people were true American immigrants.

Tens of thousands of **Chinese migrants** came to California hoping to secure a future for their families as well; these migrants also became the target of xenophobia. White Americans in California feared and sometimes even outright despised these immigrants, whom they saw as having less right to the spoils of the American West than they did. As a result, a law passed in 1850 required non-Americans to hold a foreign mining license, which cost $20 per month, a hefty sum for the time. White Europeans—even immigrants like those fleeing the revolutions of 1848—could be exempted from the tax by becoming American citizens. This same option was not extended to Chinese Californians.

Unable to pay this tax, many Chinese migrants gave up mining and became businesspeople, establishing a thriving business sector in San Francisco dubbed "**Chinatown**." Eventually, the tax was lowered significantly, but anti-Chinese sentiment continued in California.

California was the land of opportunity because of its gold and other plentiful resources, but it remained largely removed from the rest of the United States throughout its earliest years of statehood. The California Trail provided a way to reach the American West, but it was far less efficient and more treacherous than rail travel. Things changed in 1863 with the construction of a transcontinental railroad. The Central Pacific Railroad would build 690 miles of track from Sacramento to connect at Promontory Summit, Utah, with the 1,085 miles being constructed by the Union Pacific from Omaha/Council Bluffs, Iowa. The Union Pacific employed a labor force that included Irish immigrants and Civil War veterans, but the Central Pacific relied largely on the labor of Chinese immigrants.

These Chinese American rail workers, who eventually made up 90 percent of the workforce laying the line, had a challenging job: they had to lay track through the Sierra Nevada mountains, which required the use of explosives. Historians estimate that at least one thousand employees died doing this dangerous work. Chinese rail workers were also paid less than half of what White workers made.

These conditions led to the largest organized labor movement of its time when a group of Chinese rail workers went on strike in June 1867, demanding safer and better working conditions and pay equal to that of White workers. The strike lasted eight days but was eventually squashed when the Central Pacific Railroad director diverted supplies like food to the demonstrating workers.

Despite these labor conditions, tens of thousands of Chinese workers helped complete the transcontinental railroad on May 10, 1869. The newly "connected" California continued to grow and change. With a transportation network by which to ship their produce and new and improved methods by which to irrigate land, large farms began to dot the state. Chinese laborers were now drawn to these large commercial farms, and many shifted from rail work to agricultural work.

However, an economic downturn and drought hit California in the 1870s. As unemployment swept the state, White Californians viewed Chinese Californians as competition for scarce jobs and began to stage numerous anti-Chinese campaigns. Mounting pressure from these groups led to the **Chinese Exclusion Act** of 1882, which prohibited emigration from China for ten years and dictated that Chinese-Americans, largely concentrated in California, could not become naturalized American citizens. This was quickly followed by the **Geary Act** of 1892, which prohibited Chinese immigration for another ten years and required Chinese Americans to obtain and carry documents known as "certificates of residence" at all times or face imprisonment or deportation. As a result, Chinese immigration to California declined sharply.

Practice Question

31) Which development led to the growth of large farms in California?
    A. European immigration
    B. the transcontinental railroad
    C. the Geary Act
    D. the growth of "Chinatown"

Constitutional and Political Development

Californians wrote their first state constitution in 1849 at the **Constitutional Convention of Monterey**. It was the basis for the subsequent constitution, drafted at the **Sacramento Convention** of 1878 – 1879. The resulting state constitution, adopted in 1879 and revised many times since, has become well known for two reasons: its extreme length and its specific provisions for individual rights that many interpret as going even beyond the Bill of Rights.

> **Did You Know?**
>
> The first state constitution was written in both English and Spanish.

The constitution was the result of many forces, most notably a desire for progressive reform. The California state legislature was dominated by the private interests of railroad and industry barons in the 1870s. The "everyday working people" of California resented this. In fact, many of the delegates at the Sacramento Convention were members of the **Workingmen's Party of California**, founded by **Denis Kearney**, a labor organizer. Though Kearney and his supporters often used a virulent anti-Chinese rhetoric, they were initially also concerned with the rights of labor and the need to hold politicians accountable for their actions.

The resulting document was criticized. Some felt the constitution was too detailed and issues would have been better sorted out through subsequent legislation. Others protested its blatant disregard of the Fourteenth Amendment; the document stripped Chinese Californians of the basic rights guaranteed to all Americans, a notable result of Kearney's influence.

Further changes were made to the constitution in 1911. Unlike the US Constitution, California's Constitution, after these amendments, empowers voters with initiative, referendum, and recall:

- **Initiative** refers to the voters' rights to begin legislative action by petition. If the petition has a certain number of signatures, the proposed law can be brought before voters, and, if passed, it can become law. This process completely bypasses the legislature.

- **Referendum** is similar to initiative in that the public votes on a law either before it has been enacted (legislative referendum) or after it has been enacted and has been challenged (popular referendum).

- **Recall** is a process by which the public can, by petition, call for an election to remove a public official.

These provisions in the California Constitution were a direct attempt to limit the power of state government and were part of broader American **Progressive Era** reforms aimed at promoting growth and prosperity while keeping corruption and private interests in check.

> **Did You Know?**
>
> One of the most famous California recalls was the 2003 recall of Governor Gray Davis, which resulted in Arnold Schwarzenegger being elected governor of California.

The Progressive movement in California was largely led by Governor **Hiram Johnson**, who served from 1911 to 1917. Under his government, California passed the **Workman's Compensation, Insurance, and Safety Act** in 1913, which solidified the role of state government in protecting workers. He also created a state kindergarten program and teacher pension fund.

Despite progressive reform, Chinese Californians, Black Californians, and Native and Hispanic Californians still experienced marginalization and discrimination; however, women of California had some rights beyond other American women. The 1849 constitution had established the rights of women to control property. In 1911, California women earned the right to vote.

Practice Question

32) Which statement BEST describes the recall provision in the constitution of California?
    A. Citizens can begin legislative action by petition.
    B. Citizens can vote on a law after it has been enacted.
    C. Citizens can force the removal of an elected official.
    D. Citizens can enact a new law by popular vote.

Twentieth Century

As California moved into the twentieth century, much had been accomplished, but more work remained. The state was no longer the frontier—by 1900, California was one of many growing western states. San Francisco was a particularly thriving city, but that peace and prosperity abruptly ended on April 18, 1906, with one of the most significant earthquakes in American history:

- The **San Francisco earthquake** formed a rupture of 296 miles along the Pacific coast and had a magnitude of 7.9 on the Richter scale.

- The quake was quickly followed by a four-day fire that consumed an estimated twenty-eight thousand buildings, or five hundred blocks of the city.

- The earthquake killed an estimated three thousand people and left another quarter of a million people without homes.

- Though destruction was severe and widespread, the city was rebuilt quickly, largely with earthquake-resistant construction methods.

Despite the threat of earthquakes, California continued to be a land of opportunity for many. Since California was a large state, land was cheaper there than elsewhere. Though larger agricultural operations were the norm, people also immigrated to the state to start small farms.

Large farms often relied on migrant workers. In California, many of these laborers came from the Philippines during the early twentieth century. The Filipino workers would work for less than White workers, which made them an attractive workforce to many landowners. This also made them a threat to White farm laborers who feared lowered wages. Tensions came to a head periodically: during the **Salinas Lettuce strike of 1934,** violence broke out between Filipino and White workers.

Mexican migrants fleeing the **Mexican Revolution** (1910 – 1920) also came to California in the early twentieth century, drawn by the prospect of work in the agricultural sector. Though the **Immigration Act** of 1924 sought to limit immigration, agricultural magnates in California and other states had a strong lobby and were able to ensure that Mexican migrants were exempted from these restrictions.

Many of these migrants settled in California permanently; others returned to Mexico throughout the early decades of the twentieth century, having earned what they had hoped to or responding to changing economic conditions.

Oil was discovered in California in the nineteenth century, and production increased rapidly as new pockets were found throughout the 1920s. By 1923, this oil boom made California America's leading oil producer and brought more migrants to the state. Many settled in Los Angeles, which grew and expanded with roads, highways, and suburban communities. This growth was due in large part to the new, lower cost of automobiles resulting from Henry Ford's assembly line manufacturing process. The state highways were built largely via bond issues throughout the early twentieth century.

> **Helpful Hint**
>
> State highways and the national highway system brought tourists to California. Known for its beautiful weather and picturesque beaches, the state became a popular vacation destination for those with means throughout the 1920s.

Unfortunately, the boom was not to last. Wages had been stagnant or decreasing for too long, and many workers could not even afford the products they made or crops they harvested. Coupled with the stock market crash of 1929, these conditions led to the **Great Depression**.

Many lost their jobs and livelihoods; some became homeless. Forced to live in camps with whatever shelter they could find, some Californians took up residence in large concrete pipes in Oakland in what would become known as "Pipe City." Others lived in tents and shanties throughout the state. Such misery exacerbated the anti-immigrant sentiment that was already present:

- The 1935 Filipino **Repatriation Act** sought to encourage Filipino laborers to return to the Philippines via government subsidies for transportation.

- Resentment toward Mexican Californians, often the result of xenophobia and fear over competition for scarce jobs, led to mass deportations, known as **repatriations**, throughout the 1930s.
    - The number of people forcibly deported during this period is debated, but some sources put the numbers at more than a million.
    - Many of these deportees, perhaps up to 60 percent, were American citizens.

Anger and outrage toward those viewed as "outsiders" extended to migrants to California from other states. Drought and unsustainable farming practices led to extreme erosion and dust storms in Nebraska, Kansas, Oklahoma, New Mexico, Colorado, and the Texas Panhandle in the 1930s. Seeking to escape the widespread environmental and economic degradation known as the **Dust Bowl** that was exacerbated by the Great Depression, some three hundred thousand people migrated to California, the largest mass movement to the state since the Gold Rush. These migrants, derogatorily referred to as **"Okies"** because many came from Oklahoma, chose California for several reasons:

- Family members who had already migrated to the state in previous decades encouraged them.

- Agricultural work and farm labor jobs were left vacant by the deportation and repatriation policies of the era.
    - These jobs often paid more in California than in other states, as large farms required a large labor force.

- Direct government unemployment aid, a hallmark of Depression-era policy, was higher in California than in other places.

Many Dust Bowl migrants, who frequently traveled via the iconic **Route 66**, sought employment on the farms of California's **San Joaquin Valley**. Here, they often found poor conditions, either in employer-run labor camps or on their own in tents or makeshift shelters. Communicable diseases spread in such conditions, and many became sick. As the population in valley communities swelled by as much as 50 percent, conditions for everyone, migrant and Californian alike, worsened.

The influx of labor depressed wages and overwhelmed public services, like schools and hospitals. As California's agricultural labor force grew exponentially, the once-abundant agricultural job market dried up. This led to intense competition for scarce employment. Desperate, many Dust Bowl migrants worked for lower wages than existing California residents and were often willing to cross picket lines. Some historians argue that the Dust Bowl migrants held back existing efforts at labor organization, particularly among the Filipino and Mexican workforce. Such a situation resulted in widespread hatred of "Okies," whom many Californians from all walks of life saw as threatening their communities and livelihood.

Though some of the Dust Bowl migrants returned to their homes after the Depression ended, many stayed in California and made new lives. Some even achieved significant economic success and eventually owned farms or businesses. They also contributed to the state's culture, particularly in the San Joaquin Valley, where their descendants today make up nearly half of the population.

Today, California is a diverse society, which includes immigrants, both documented and undocumented, and people from myriad cultural and ethnic backgrounds. While this diversity, especially in terms of foreign nationals and migrant workers, has been the subject of debate for much of American and California history, many view it today as a strength. Such diversity brings varied skills, languages, foods, music, and religions to California.

> **Did You Know?**
>
> Not all Dust Bowl migrants sought agricultural work. About one-third chased opportunity in Los Angeles, where skilled laborers could find work building planes and automobiles. However, most Dust Bowl migrants lacked such skills and struggled to find employment.

Practice Question

33) What event most directly led to the Dust Bowl crisis?
   A. US entry into World War II
   B. poor farming practices that caused erosion
   C. climate change that altered deposition patterns
   D. deportation and repatriation policies

Other Social Studies Topics

Geography

The study of geography is the study of spatial distribution. It stresses analyzing information based on the distribution, location, and interactions of different human and physical features of the earth. Geography is divided into two main areas:

- **Physical geography** explores the natural process of the earth.
- **Human geography** explores the impact of people on the physical world, such as how humans alter their environments.
    - It also looks at **social structures** as they relate to geography, such as how social events relate to places.
    - An example would be how immigration affected urban populations in the US during the nineteenth century.

Geography uses maps to determine spatial distributions, such as ethnic demographics in various **regions**, languages in a particular country, or even the number of volcanoes in a determined area. The main reason for creating a map or developing a geographic information system is to assess the **spatial relationships** between features. An example of a spatial relationship is the distance between residential areas and transportation stops.

All maps use **cardinal directions**: north, south, east, and west. Some maps also feature **intermediate directions** between each point. All of these are featured on a compass rose, which is used to determine locations and directions.

Absolute location describes a location identifiable by specific geographic coordinates. For example, latitude and longitude delineate specific coordinates, so the absolute location of New York City is 40°70'58" N, 74°11'81" W. Addresses are also absolute locations: for instance, the absolute location of the White House is 1600 Pennsylvania Avenue NW, Washington, DC 20500. **Relative location** describes where a place is situated in relation to another place or places. For example, the state of Illinois is located in the Midwest region of the United States; it borders Wisconsin to the north, Indiana to the east, Iowa and Missouri to the west, and Kentucky to the south.

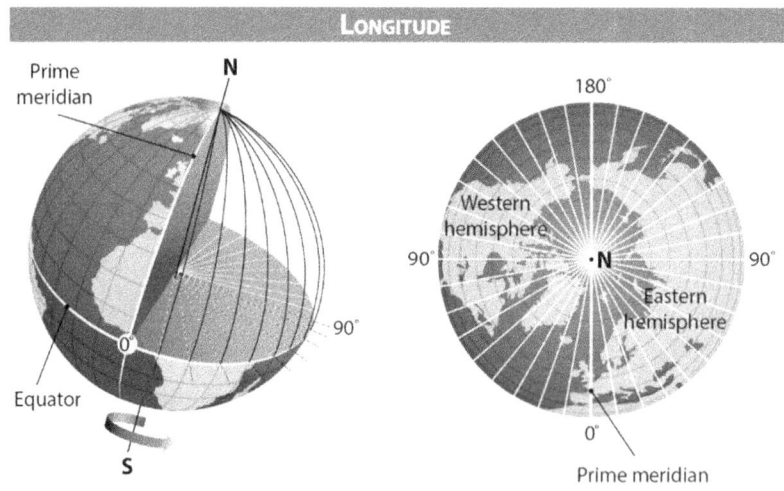

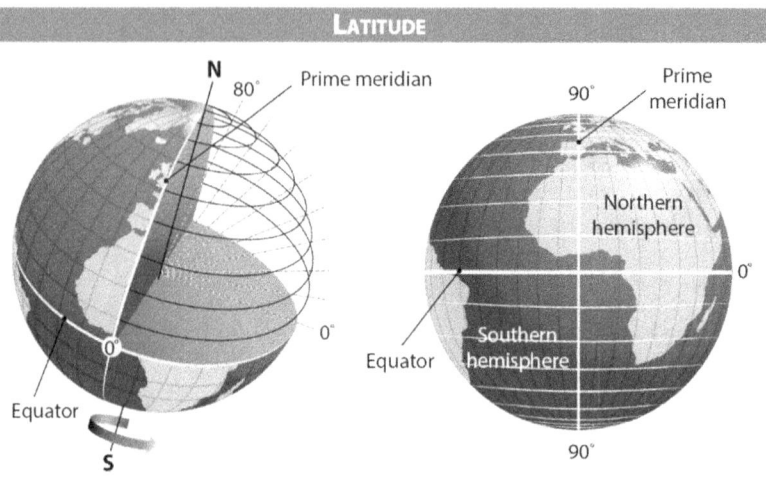

Figure 2.13. Longitude and Latitude

Maps display **geographic features**, the physical features of continents, bodies of water, plains, plateaus, mountains, and valleys. Raised elevations and bodies of water are indicated through shading or coloring; they are also labeled. In addition, maps show **political features** like towns and cities, and county, state, or national borders. They may also include significant bodies of water.

Despite their differences, physical and human geography are interconnected. For example, physical features can determine the feasibility of living in certain locations or practicing certain lifestyles. Physical features dictate the availability of **natural resources** such as fresh water, arable land, fuel, livestock, and game; they also affect climate patterns. Man-made resources also intersect with physical and human geography; for example, the Hoover Dam manages the Colorado River, a natural resource, in order to provide water and electricity to certain parts of the southwestern United States.

Physical regions of the world are broken down by distance from the equator. The **low latitudes**, from the equator to latitudes 23.5° north and south, have three distinct climates:

- **Tropical rainforests** can be found in the equatorial lowlands in Central Africa, Southeast Asia, and the Amazon basin.

- North and south of the rainforest is the **savannah**. The savannah is dry in the winter and wet in the summer, experiencing an average of 10 to 30 inches of rain.

- The **desert** lies beyond the savannah to the north and south. Deserts are the hottest and driest parts of the earth and receive less than 10 inches of rainfall a year. The best known deserts in the world are the Sahara Desert, the Australian Outback, and the Arabian Desert.

The **middle latitudes**, from latitudes 23.5° to 66.5° north and south, have a greater variety of climates, determined more by proximity to water than by the exact latitude. Three climates in the middle latitudes receive the most rain and therefore are the most fertile:

- The first is the **Mediterranean climate**, found in lands between latitudes 30° and 40° north and south that include land bordering the Mediterranean Sea, a small part of southwestern Africa, southern and southwestern Australia, a small part of Ukraine near the Black Sea, central Chile, and southern California.

- The **humid subtropical climate** is located on coastal areas north and south of the tropics. This climate receives warm ocean currents and warm winds year round, leading to a climate that is warm and moist. This is also the climate that supports the greatest percentage of the world's population. Japan, southeastern China, northeastern India, southeastern South Africa, the southeastern United States, and parts of South America all have subtropical climates.

- Finally, several areas that are near or surrounded by water experience the **marine climate**. Marine climates are warm and rainy, resulting in part from the warm ocean winds. Western Europe, the British Isles, the US and Canadian Pacific Northwest, southern Chile, southern New Zealand, and southeastern Australia all have marine climates.

The climate best for farming is the **humid continental climate**, the true four-season climate. This climate can be found in the northern and central United States, south-central and southeastern Canada, northern China, and the western and southeastern parts of the former Soviet bloc.

Those areas of continents far from the ocean are called **steppes**, or prairie. Flatlands with minimal rainfall, steppes can even become deserts if rainfall consistently dips below 10 inches per year.

The **high latitudes**, from latitudes 66.5° north and south to the poles, are home to two climates: tundra and taiga:

- The **tundra** features extremely cold and long winters; while the ground is frozen for most of the year, during the short summer the ground becomes mushy. With no arable land, it is home to few people.

- The **taiga** can be found south of the tundra in Northern Russia, Sweden, Norway, Finland, Canada, and Alaska. Home to the world's largest forestlands, the taiga also exhibits many swamps and marshes; importantly, it contains extreme mineral wealth. While there is a growing season, it is so short that meaningful agriculture is impossible; thus, the taiga is sparsely populated.

Students should understand that human activity, such as agriculture, ranching, logging, mining, and urban and suburban development impact the earth and the environment by interrupting ecosystems. Furthermore, they should also understand that **industrialization**, the process of manufacturing, creates byproducts that affect and can harm the environment.

Check Your Understanding
How does the climate of a location impact economic activity?

Our planet is divided into political divisions based on governmental jurisdiction. The largest units of these are sovereign states or nation-states that are generally referred to as **countries**. Within these countries are smaller units known as **states**, provinces, counties, parishes, districts, and cities or towns. The United States follows a pattern of states subdivided into counties or parishes and then cities or towns. It is important that, as developmentally appropriate, students understand that **borders** between both countries and states are human constructs. While the lines of demarcation may be based upon physical boundaries such as rivers or mountains, these are political borders created by humans that do not exist organically.

There are two primary types of communities based on population density. **Rural** communities, such as farms and villages, contain a smaller population of people, and they often participate in an agrarian, or **farming**, lifestyle. *Farming* is a somewhat general term often used to describe the use of land or water for the production or obtainment of food. This includes **ranching**, which uses land to produce livestock, and **fishing**, which extracts food from bodies of water or raises fish in tanks. **Urban** communities are cities and towns where the economy is driven by business and the **trade**, or exchange, of goods and services. Trade is one means of **cultural diffusion**, or the spread of one culture's practices to another's.

While both urban and rural areas may be important to the overall **economy**, or wealth of resources, of a country or region, urban areas tend to be centers of commerce and production. Cities originally developed around markets later grew around factories as industry developed. **Factories** are large buildings where products are made, originally by humans and increasingly by machines controlled by humans. Some cities are known for a particular type of factory, such as the automotive production factories in Detroit, Michigan. Additionally, most cities have elaborate transportation networks that move people and goods from one place to another. People living in cities often have many public transportation options such as trains, subways, and buses. These options are more limited in rural communities because of remoteness and lack of population density.

Rural areas, however, produce many raw materials and crops that must be transported to manufacturing centers and cities for production and sale to consumers. Since those who rely on ranching and fishing require land to produce or procure their foodstuffs, they, too, tend to be located in areas remote from urban centers. A railroad system that uses **trains** to ship important commodities, and a **highway** system that uses **trucks** to transport goods are very important to the **transportation** network of rural and remote communities. Without such networks, interdependent relationships between communities would not be possible. This interdependence is often marked by raw goods and commodities, such as cotton and soybeans, being produced in rural areas and then shipped to urban areas for transformation into processed foods and clothing. These finished goods are then shipped and sold both to urban and rural communities.

Though transporting goods over water does not require the same type of transportation network as transporting goods over land, this method does rely on the construction of ports and canals, which might be highly relevant to the economy of a given community. Although generally more expensive, **airplanes** can be used to transport people and goods. In some very remote areas, such as rural Alaska, airplane travel is the only method of transportation available because road and rail networks do not exist. Even in urban areas, the reliance on **shipping** direct to the consumer has become very popular as more and more people rely on the internet to buy consumer goods.

One trend in the United States has been increasing urbanization, or the shift in population from rural to urban areas. Recent data from the US Census Bureau reveals that over 80 percent of Americans live in urban areas. In some very fast-growing cities, the pace of **construction** of new homes, schools, and roads is often unable to accommodate population growth. This creates many urban problems like traffic, school overcrowding, and a lack of affordable housing.

Urbanization, or the development of cities, became a feature of human development at the advent of the nineteenth-century Industrial Revolution, when unskilled jobs in factories offered higher wages for workers than an agricultural lifestyle did. Urbanization and **suburbanization** continue today as cities develop and as urban dwellers move to growing suburbs. Development necessarily results in the destruction of the surrounding environment; however, new urban ecosystems result, and **urban planning** is itself a geographic specialty.

Another way to illustrate human and social behavior is by mapping **migration** patterns. This is the study of movement from one place to another, with the intention of settling permanently at the new location. As discussed above, urbanization is one type of migration. Some migration is internal—people moving from one place to another within the same region, like urbanization. Other migration involves people moving from one region of the world to another. Many immigrants have migrated to the United States from other countries. Push and pull factors cause people to migrate: economic, cultural, sociopolitical, or environmental reasons. Pull factors, like job opportunities or better living standards, attract people to new locations. Push factors, like famine, drought, war, lack of economic opportunities, and political persecution, drive people to leave their homes in search of relief.

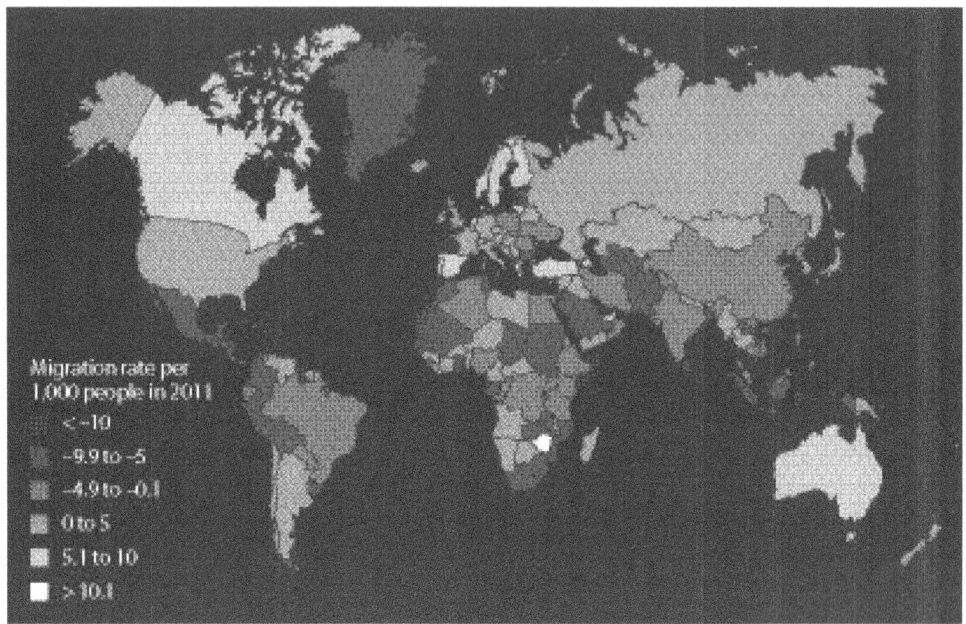

Figure 2.22. Migration Streams

Similar to the study of migration is the study of **demography**, which describes the statistical study of human populations. Demography often centers around the changing structures of human populations in a given location. Factors that impact demography include births, deaths, and migration.

Practice Questions

34) Which of the following are major physical regions in the continental United States?
   A. humid continental, humid subtropical, Mediterranean, marine, desert
   B. humid continental, humid subtropical, taiga, tundra, Mediterranean
   C. humid continental, Mediterranean, marine, taiga, tropical rainforest
   D. the Sun Belt, the Bible Belt, and the Coasts

35) Which of the following is NOT an example of human geography?
   A. studying the importance of trade among Central American countries
   B. examining regional differences in cuisine around the world
   C. studying the distribution of fauna and flora in North America
   D. deciding whether to build retail outlets based on local population

Civics, Anthropology, and Sociology

Civics

With citizenship comes responsibility. Today, US citizens maintain their government by **voting** for public officials at the local, state, and national levels. They also must pay **taxes** in order to provide the revenue the government requires to carry out its functions. The federal, state, and local governments all levy taxes of different kinds: income taxes, sales taxes, property taxes, and others. This money supports everything from installing stop signs to maintaining military aircraft.

US citizens are free to join **civic groups** that lobby government for legislation that works in their interest or that carry out public services in their communities. Some of these groups include the ACLU, which defends individual liberties, the NAACP, which works for African American rights, and the AARP, which supports the interests of older adults. Citizens can also join groups that carry out **community service**, such as the Boy Scouts and the Girl Scouts, or they may do such work through their churches, mosques, synagogues, or other places of worship. Some students may already be doing community service themselves.

Anthropology

Anthropology is the study of human culture and its development. Anthropology traces the evolution of modern human societies from their beginnings.

Figure 2.23. Early Tools

Early humans were **hunters and gatherers** who traveled around in small groups with few possessions that they often shared in common. Some anthropologists believe that in these small groups of a few dozen people, men and women were largely equal and worked together with little specialization.

Some ten to twelve thousand years ago, hunting and gathering societies gave way to **horticultural societies** that raised crops with simple tools and **pastoral societies** that raised domesticated animals, such as sheep. These two types of societies likely emerged at around the same time but had a key distinction in that pastoral societies were still largely nomadic as they moved their herds around to graze. In contrast, horticultural societies tended to be more sedentary.

Some 5,000 years ago, the plow was invented, and **agricultural societies** emerged. These societies marked a change in that much more food could be grown than in horticultural civilizations. This led to population growth and concentration in larger communities or cities as well as trade, which resulted from a surplus of agricultural products beyond the immediate needs of the community. As surplus increased and new tools, techniques, and ideas came via trade, the elements we typically associate with the notion of "culture," like art and music, began to

> **Did You Know?**
>
> While agriculture societies created more food, their impact on human health is largely believed by modern scholars to be negative. The remains of people from early agricultural societies reveal more health problems than those of hunters and gatherers.

become more sophisticated. Gender roles also became more pronounced as work in the fields required significant physical strength, and women were often pregnant in order to provide the large workforce needed to sustain such widespread agriculture

Practice Question

36) How did pastoral societies differ from horticultural societies?
   A. They moved from place to place.
   B. They relied on family units.
   C. They also hunted and gathered.
   D. They had new gender roles.

Sociology

As the word implies, sociology is the study of human society.

Socialization is a process where individuals learn skills, beliefs, values, and behavior patterns of society and how these can influence their own norms and customs. For example, family roles differ depending on age and gender, and there are norms that dictate how certain family members should act.

Primary socialization occurs when children learn the values, actions, and attitudes that are appropriate for members of their particular culture. For example, if a family eats dinner together every night, that child will likely assume that she must regularly communicate with the closest and most important people in her life.

Secondary socialization occurs when an individual learns the appropriate values, actions, attitudes, and behaviors as a member of a smaller group within a larger society. Secondary socialization generally occurs in adolescence or young adulthood; influences will be teachers, employers, and other authority figures.

Students learn that **institutions** are extensions of core social values and are created in response to varying individual and group needs. Institutions are formally structured groups that comprise society. At the macro level they include government, private enterprise, religious institutions, and academic institutions. At the micro level, they include local communities and the family unit. They are composed of a usually formal, often top-down structure with a small governing body in charge (either the executives in a government or private company or the parents in the family unit). For example, labor unions fight for better conditions for workers; governments maintain social stability; businesses provide goods, services, and profit; and religious organizations fulfill social and personal needs.

The study of institutions also includes understanding how they are maintained and changed, as well as how they exert influence among individuals. Studying communities helps clarify how individuals, families, and institutions socialize and come together to form values, beliefs, and behavior patterns, and how they may differ from those of other communities. Sociologists also study families and communities and the **interpersonal relationships**, or relationships between people, that make up a society.

Beyond these structures and relationships are broader social systems and structures. People may identify with a certain ethnic or racial group or a certain gender identity. These identities often impact life outcomes due to disparate access to health care, education, and employment opportunities. Such disparities also create **socioeconomic status** or class, which refers to a person's status in a society based on the combination of social and economic factors such as income, ethnicity, education status, job, and location.

More broadly, studying culture relates to understanding human and group behavior. Studying culture helps students understand that individuals develop culture and also adapt to it in changing circumstances (such as migration). Examining different belief systems and practices, such as celebrations, languages, and other norms, exposes students to multiple cultural perspectives on shared human experiences. Students may also explore the similarities and differences among cultures and how they evolve in various regions.

Practice Question

37) What are the three major forms of sociological interactions?
    A. culture, counterculture, and subculture
    B. celebrations, languages, and belief systems
    C. government, schools, and businesses
    D. cooperation, exchange, and conflict

Economics

The study of economics is the study of the production and consumption of products as well as how people produce and obtain these goods. It explains how people interact with the market; studying economics usually explains the behavior of people or the government.

Basic Economic Concepts

One of the most important concepts in economics is **supply and demand**. Supply refers to how much the market can actually offer, and demand is how much desire there is for a product or service. The demand is the relationship between price and quantity, which is how much people are willing to pay for the product. The supply simply means how much product producers are willing to supply at a certain price. This relationship between price and how much product is offered to the market is known as the supply relationship.

Price is used to show the relationship between supply and demand. When the demand is high for a product, the price generally goes up. When the demand is low, price falls; however, if the price is considered too high by the public, there may be excess supply because people will purchase less. Causes of excess supply include other price changes, including the price of alternative goods, and public preferences. Likewise, there might be excess demand if the price is set too low and many people want the product, but there may not be enough supply. This might happen if there is a government ban on the product, the government imposes a price ceiling, or suppliers decide to not raise prices.

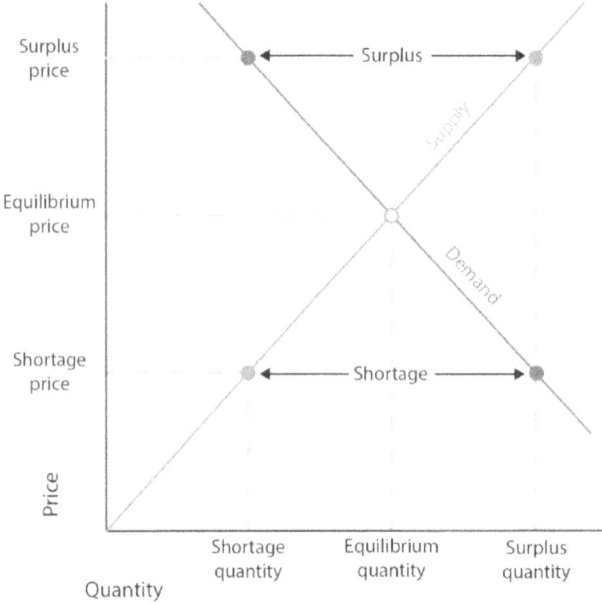

Figure 2.14. Equilibrium Price

For example, before Halloween, prices of Halloween candy are high because consumers are willing to pay high prices. They want to purchase enough candy to celebrate the holiday at parties and to distribute to trick-or-treaters, even if it is expensive. However, after Halloween, leftover candy is usually on sale. This is because demand for candy is low: the holiday is over and so people do not need it. That leftover candy represents excess supply. In order to get rid of it, suppliers drop prices to entice consumers with a sweet tooth to buy it even though Halloween has passed.

When supply and demand are equal, the economy is at equilibrium; however, that is not always the case. When there is insufficient supply to meet demand, the result is **scarcity**. People need to choose which want to satisfy. For example, if there is a low supply of chocolate, chocolate prices will be high. Consequently, a consumer must decide whether to spend more money than usual on chocolate or not to buy any at all.

Every choice has a value. **Opportunity cost** is when a consumer makes a choice at the cost of another choice or the value of an opportunity. For example, imagine that someone must choose between eating chocolate cake or apple pie. If that person chooses the chocolate cake, he gives up the opportunity to eat the apple pie. The opportunity cost is the apple pie. Decisions made by an individual or the government based on opportunity cost are driven by needs, wants, income, and time.

When making economic choices, both parts of the value (costs and benefits) should be considered. The ideal choice will have the greatest benefits at the lowest cost. For example, there are two stores that sell chocolate, but the first store sells it at $35 a box and the second store sells it at $40 a box. However, it takes an hour to drive to the first store and it will cost about $10 in gas to get there and back, while it takes 15 minutes and $2.50 in gas to reach the second store. Economically speaking, it is not worthwhile to drive to the first store. Choosing to pay more for the chocolate at the second store is the cost, and the benefit is the time and cost of gas saved by rejecting the first store.

> **Check Your Understanding**
>
> Which types of games or activities could be used with elementary-aged students to illustrate the concept of opportunity cost?

People use resources in order to create **wealth** and enhance their lives. These resources are either goods or services that people provide in exchange for money. People provide labor, creating goods and services available for purchase. Labor refers to people who work in almost any job—on farms, in factories, as computer programmers, and so forth. The goods and services produced enhance people's lives. For example, not everyone owns a farm or can grow a variety of produce, so consumers depend on farmers around the world to grow various agricultural products in order to obtain them. Those farmers use resources such as water and land in order to generate wealth. Likewise, not everyone can fix a computer, so a consumer can bring her computer to an expert to be repaired. The owner of a computer repair service would be compensated with cash, and he similarly builds wealth by using that cash to invest in the business, buy property, invest in the stock market, or for other purposes.

Technological innovation is also driven by the economy (and vice versa). For example, more efficient transportation has increased trade and the exchange of wealth. Railroads enabled US businesses to transport raw materials to their production facilities, thereby increasing the production of goods. These areas then will need more people to provide labor, helping companies and individuals generate more wealth and providing jobs and salaries to workers, who themselves were thus able to generate more wealth in cash.

One economic model examines the way in which money moves through a society. Known as the **circular flow model of economic exchanges**, this model maintains that money flows from producers or firms to workers or households as wages and then back to producers as workers purchase products with their wages.

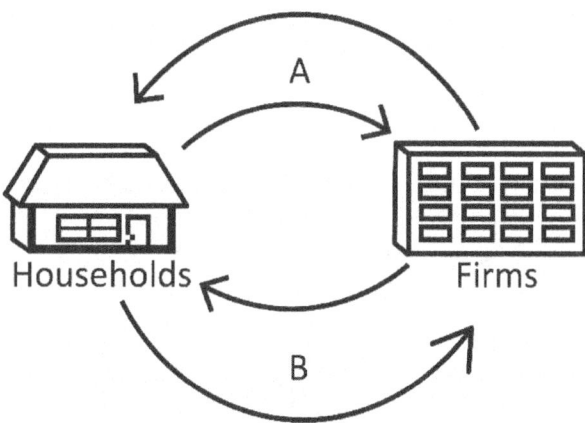

Figure 2.15. Circular Flow Model

Economic activity is also subject to the **business cycle**, or the ups and downs of the economy in terms of output, employment, income, and sales. The business cycle involved both the expansion of the economy, or **growth**, and the contraction of the economy, or **recession**.

Economic Regulation

The federal government helps to regulate the economy. **Government regulation** falls into either economic regulation or social regulation. Economic regulation controls prices directly or indirectly. The government works to prevent monopolies: the control of a market for a good or service by one company or group. For example, the government may prohibit utility companies from raising their prices beyond a certain point. Antitrust law is another type of economic regulation. It strengthens market forces to protect consumers from businesses and to eliminate or minimize the need for direct regulation. These laws are intended to ensure fair competition in the US economy.

The government also sets monetary and fiscal policies. **Monetary policy** dictates the actions of central banks to regulate the economy in terms of employment and price stability. **Fiscal policy** determines how and how much the government will tax and spend tax dollars. Government policies also govern **international trade**. Protective tariffs or taxes, quotas on imports, and laws that prohibit (embargo) or restrict trade with other nations are part of the regulatory practices of the government.

In spite of regulations, **economic globalization**, or the interdependence of global economies on each other, remains a central part of our world. That means that if one economy suffers, its biggest trade partners will also be impacted. Furthermore, some parts of the economy cannot be fully regulated in a global context. For example, sometimes counterfeit goods or substandard goods that may threaten consumer safety can still be purchased online from another country even if illegal in the country in which the consumer lives.

Social regulation encourages businesses to behave responsibly and prohibits harmful behavior. For example, the US Occupational Safety and Health Administration (OSHA) enforces workplace regulations to protect worker safety, and the Environmental Protection Agency (EPA) regulates industry by upholding environmental standards for emissions and waste.

Finally, the government collects **taxes** not only to cover its expenses but also to help fuel the economy. Federal taxes pay for costs like federal employee salaries and retirement programs, government programs, and the military. Other government programs that are financed through taxes include veterans' benefits and NASA. Payroll taxes help **finance** the Medicare and Social Security programs which provide assistance for the elderly and those with low incomes. Government spending helps to increase the wealth of businesses and individuals. For example, if the government spends money to build bridges and highways, construction businesses generate more income. If an individual is retired or cannot work for health reasons, Social Security will provide assistance.

The Economy of California

California's economy is the largest in the US and the fifth largest in the world (though some believe it will soon overtake Germany as the fourth largest economy). **Agriculture** is California's top economic activity, with milk, fruits, and vegetables as key products. Much of the agriculture takes place in the rich Central Valley region. **Mining** is also an important industry; mines are located throughout the state to extract gold and other precious metals, boron, and construction materials from the earth.

The **film industry** is another important part of the economy of the state. Many major motion picture studios are headquartered in Hollywood. This contributes to the **California tourism and entertainment industry**, another top industry. San Francisco, San Diego, and Los Angeles are all top tourist destinations. Tourism also supports many other industries, like food service and lodging.

Technology is also important to the economy of the state, with Silicon Valley and Stanford University near San Francisco continuing to be important players in the tech industry. Aerospace is another key industry; more aerospace engineers live in California than in any other state, which is no surprise as it has three NASA facilities: the Jet Propulsion Lab in Pasadena, Ames Research Center in Mountain View, and Dryden Flight Research Center in Edwards.

California produces much of its own energy and ranks fourth in **energy** production in the United States; however, it ranks second (behind Texas) in energy production from renewable resources, such as geothermal and solar energies. The state ranks seventh in the production of crude oil, much of which comes from the San Joaquin Basin. Because it is such a populous state, it also consumes more energy than any other state aside from Texas. Much of this consumption is gas for cars and jet fuel for its many busy air travelers. The California Energy Commission regulates energy and encourages the shift to sustainable energy use via policy recommendations, regulations, and enforcement.

California's large and diverse economy benefits not only the state and the country, but also the world. The state exports myriad agricultural products and manufactures; its top export is computer and electronics equipment, and its largest global markets are Mexico, Canada, and China.

California is a state rich in natural resources, but these resources are not infinite. One concern centers around the **water supply**. Most of California's fresh water in lakes and rivers is located in the northernmost part of the state, but the bulk of the demand for this water is in the southern region. To accommodate this, California devised an advanced and extensive system to transport water via aqueducts, dams, and reservoirs.

Still, water is not always plentiful, especially during droughts. There is competition surrounding water resources: large farms, urban residents, and environmental groups often have competing interests and priorities.

The vast network of dams and reservoirs brings water to the citizens of California, but it also brings broader environmental changes. Such changes have been criticized, particularly those affecting fish and other wildlife habitats and the plants that grow in these areas. Especially

> **Check Your Understanding**
>
> How is water availability connected with the economic activity of certain regions of California?

controversial is the **Sacramento–San Joaquin Delta**, the state's central water source. This estuary provides much of the state's drinking water and irrigates many acres of farmland; however, human-made structures and activities to remove water from the estuary have put local wildlife in peril, resulting in multiple lawsuits and countersuits on behalf of those seeking to use the water without restriction. While access to water is a serious concern, **water quality** is another problem, fueled by the large amount of land in California under agricultural cultivation:

- Pesticides and fertilizers help increase agricultural output, but they are washed away in irrigation and stormwater runoff.

- These pollutants often make their way to lakes and rivers and, ultimately, into the drinking water system.

- Nitrates from fertilizer are of particular concern and are being carefully monitored by the California State Water Resources Control Board's Nitrate Project.

Practice Questions

38) Which of the following terms BEST describes a situation in which the federal government prevents the only internet service company in a local community from raising its prices?
    A. economic regulation
    B. social regulation
    C. opportunity cost
    D. scarcity

39) Which of the following CANNOT shift a demand curve?
    A. changes in income
    B. the price of related goods
    C. production costs
    D. consumer tastes

Social Studies Skills

Social studies encourages students to investigate questions about people, their values, and the choices they make. In other words, students engage in **inquiry:** they seek information, knowledge, or the truth. Inquiry-based learning in social studies is a process in which students gather information by identifying relevant questions and uncovering sources in order to interpret information and report their findings.

Teachers can help students develop critical thinking skills by encouraging **questioning**. The more questions students ask, the more carefully they evaluate sources and actively research information that helps them to draw conclusions.

Using research and resource materials is a critical component in social studies processes. **Primary sources** are original records and information from a person who experienced the event firsthand. Primary sources include original documents like the US Constitution and Declaration of Independence, journals, speeches, physical artifacts, and some first-person accounts in places such as newspapers or historical documents.

Secondary sources are texts created by people who did not personally experience or witness the event. They are based on primary sources. Examples of secondary sources include books, research papers and analyses, and some reports or features in newspapers and magazines written by journalists and other writers.

Using a variety of sources is essential when conducting research. Analyzing the relationship between primary and secondary sources relating to the same subject matter gives students a deeper understanding of the topic being studied. Understanding the advantages and disadvantages of each source also helps students understand and actively engage in **data interpretation**—assessing whether the sources are valid or appropriate.

Using primary sources permits students to draw **conclusions** based on their own interpretations of those sources, rather than relying on secondary interpretations. Primary sources also allow students to address a topic more directly and usually provide information found nowhere else. However, certain primary sources may not have any objective information or accurate facts. Moreover, these types of sources can be difficult to find and analyze.

Secondary sources enrich study by providing different perspectives or points of view and expert conclusions. Furthermore, using reputable sources may be more efficient, more accessible, or easier to understand; however, secondary sources may focus on issues beyond the topic under study, be outdated, or be tainted by the author's bias.

Students must think critically when reading or using any social studies text. They should understand how to distinguish between **fact** and **opinion**. Facts are statements that can be proven, and opinions are statements that reflect someone's view; they cannot be proven. Understanding these differences helps students evaluate sources. If students can distinguish between fact and opinion, they can determine the validity of the source in question.

As access to information has increased with the Internet, students must also consider that not all social studies information sources present solely objective information. All information is influenced by the perspective or point of view of the recorder. Furthermore, social studies texts, particularly historical ones, have different ramifications for people of varying backgrounds. For example, a person who has experienced personal or familial trauma related to the immigration experience might feel differently about a text focusing on immigration. Similarly, a descendent of enslaved Americans will bring a personal perspective to a text about the history of slavery in America.

Practice Question

40) Which of the following are examples of primary sources?
    A. original photographs, first-hand newspaper reports, textbooks, and interviews
    B. memoirs, original photographs, first-hand newspaper reports, and diary entries
    C. speeches, newspaper reports, essays, and reviews
    D. essays, reviews, textbooks, and analytical papers

Answer Key

1) A: Confucius taught others to respect authority (filial piety) and encouraged group harmony.

2) D: During the *Pax Romana*, the Mediterranean region, was NOT under the control of a powerful senate. After Julius Caesar took power from the Senate, Rome was ruled by a powerful emperor.

3) B: Serfs were bonded to the land—they had to work it for the lord—however, the lord was obligated to protect them.

4) B: European powers controlled some areas in the Levant, but only temporarily.

5) C: Mali became wealthy due to gold and salt, which are valuable natural resources.

6) B: Russia expanded to the east, taking control of Siberia. Russia also moved westward, controlling parts of Eastern Europe.

7) D: All of the answer options are true. Byzantine scholars did leave Constantinople and bring classical learning to Europe, especially Rome. At its height under Suleiman the Magnificent, the Ottoman Empire stretched from Morocco through Anatolia and the Levant to Persia. The Ottomans represented a serious threat to Europe for centuries, as they controlled the Balkans.

8) D: Science and technology imported from the Middle East during the Crusades helped inspire the Renaissance.

9) D: Factories developed during the Industrial Revolution, and were therefore not present in the colonies while the slave trade was active.

10) C: Advanced transportation in high-altitude terrain enabled the Inca military to range widely throughout the Andes.

11) B: The Scientific Revolution, humanism, and logic undermined Church power by bringing into question Church teachings that were long regarded as fact.

12) B: Martin Luther and his followers opposed corruption in the Church and wanted changes.

13) C: Bolivar was a key leader in many independence movements in Latin America.

14) A: In *laissez-faire* (or free market) theory, the government lets the invisible hand of the market correct problems in the economy.

15) A: The colonists use of natural resources had little impact on the size of the Native American population.

16) C: Colonists relied on Native American communities for crucial knowledge and supplies, and Native Americans wanted to form alliances they believed would be helpful; however, conflict over encroachment by colonists also occurred.

17) A: In the southern colonies, larger groups of enslaved people lived on farms to provide forced agricultural labor.

18) C: The Alien and Sedition Acts were implemented during the administration of John Adams.

19) C: The colonial military had strong leaders and an intimate knowledge of the terrain, with many members of the military having been born in the colonies.

20) B: The Bill of Rights does not determine representation in Congress.

21) D: The Missouri Compromise prohibited slavery north of the thirty-sixth parallel in new US territories, permitting slavery in Missouri.

22) C: The Kansas-Nebraska Act allowed slavery, which the Missouri Compromise had previously forbidden, north of the thirty-sixth parallel throughout the plains and the Western territories.

23) C: The Confederacy had excellent military leaders, and much of the population strongly believed in the right of states to make decisions without federal interference.

24) D: The Emancipation Proclamation freed the slaves in the Confederacy.

25) C: Though African Americans could vote by law, Southern states worked vigorously to ensure that most African Americans could not vote in practice via restrictive laws, intimidation, and violence.

26) A: The Bessemer Process allowed steel to be manufactured more efficiently.

27) B: Before European arrival, California's Native American population was spread throughout the state and was organized into small tribal groups known as tribelets. The everyday lives of people in tribelets varied based on the regions in which they were located and the natural resources found in those regions.

28) C: The British asserted their power on the continent, which meant Spain needed to act quickly or risk loss of territory.

29) A: Gold was discovered in California in 1848, prompting interest in quickly making California a state.

30) D: More gold in circulation led to inflation, which increased the price of many consumer goods.

31) B: The transcontinental railroad gave California farmers a transportation system by which to ship their goods to new markets.

32) C: Recall allows California citizens to remove an elected official from office.

33) B: Farmers of the Midwest over-farmed the land, and a drought then led to extreme erosion.

34) A: Humid continental, humid subtropical, Mediterranean, marine, and desert are all major physical regions in North America.

35) C: Studying only flora and fauna is physical geography; the geographer is not studying human interactions with or impact on the earth.

36) A: As opposed to early horticultural societies that were more settled, pastoral societies still migrated to new places to allow their animals to graze.

37) D: Cooperation, exchange, and conflict are the primary forms of social interaction.

38) A: In this instance of economic regulation, the government is controlling prices by preventing a monopoly.

39) C: Production costs can impact the supply curve, but not the demand curve.

40) B: Memoirs, original photographs, first-hand newspaper reports, and diary entries are all examples of primary resources.

3. Science

Physical Science

Properties of Matter

The basic unit of all **matter** is the **atom**. Atoms are composed of three subatomic particles: protons, electrons, and neutrons:

- **Protons** have a positive charge and are found in the nucleus, or center, of the atom.
- **Neutrons**, which have no charge, are also located in the nucleus.
- Negatively charged **electrons** orbit the nucleus.

If an atom has the same number of protons and electrons, it will have no net charge. Charged atoms are called **ions**. Atoms that have more protons than electrons are positively charged and are called cations. Negatively charged atoms have more electrons than protons and are called anions.

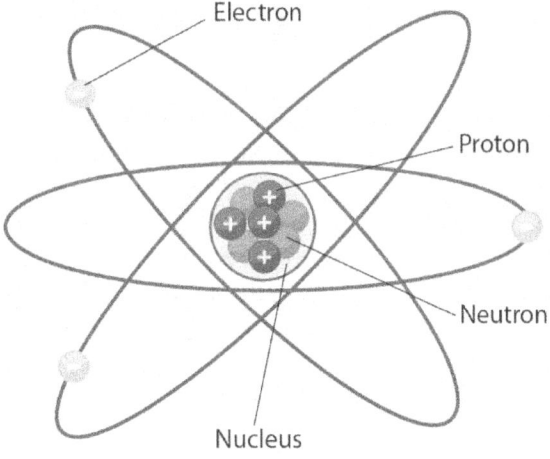

Figure 3.1. Atomic Structure

The mass of an atom is determined by adding the number of protons, neutrons, and electrons; however, electrons have very little mass, so the **atomic mass** is determined by adding just the mass of protons and neutrons.

> **Helpful Hint**
>
> The parts of an atom can be remembered using the abbreviation *PEN*: <u>p</u>rotons, <u>e</u>lectrons, <u>n</u>eutrons.

Elements, such as hydrogen and oxygen, are substances in their simplest forms that retain their unique characteristics. Each element has a distinct **atomic number** based on the number of protons in the nucleus. For example, hydrogen has one proton; oxygen has six. An element is defined by the number of protons it has, but variations of an element that have different numbers of neutrons are called **isotopes**. Some isotopes are unstable and emit radiation as they decay. These are called radioactive isotopes or radioisotopes. Others do not decay over time and are called stable isotopes.

A table of chemical elements arranged by atomic number is called **the periodic table**. The periodic table is organized in ascending order based on atomic number. Each of the seven rows on the table is known as a **period**. Every element within a period contains the same electron ground state. The eighteen columns are referred to as **groups**; each group has the same number of electros in its farthest electron shell. Because of this organization, a person can predict the properties of different elements based on their positions in the table.

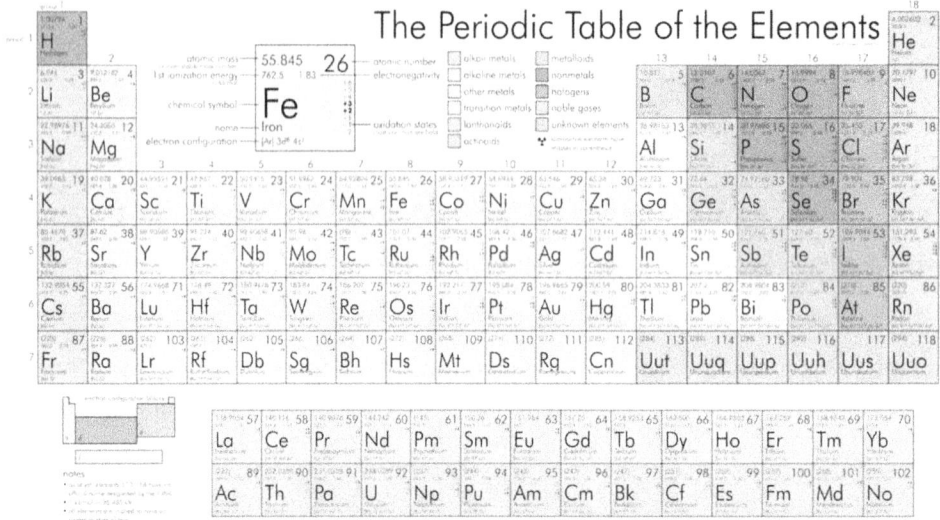

Figure 3.2. Periodic Table

When two or more atoms join together, they form a **molecule**. For example, O_3 (ozone) contains three oxygen atoms bound together, and H_2O (water) contains two hydrogen atoms and one oxygen atom. Water is a **compound** because it is made by combining two or more different elements. Atoms can be joined together by different types of bonds by sharing or exchanging valence electrons, which are electrons that can participate in chemical reactions with other elements. In a **covalent bond**, the atoms share one or more valence electrons. In an **ionic bond**, one or more electrons are transferred from one element to another to create two ions with opposite charges that are attracted to each other and bind together.

All matter exists in one of four **states**: solid, liquid, gas, or plasma:

- **Solid** matter has densely packed molecules and does not change volume or shape.
- **Liquids** have more loosely packed molecules and can change shape but not volume.
- **Gas** molecules are widely dispersed and can change both shape and volume.
  - **Plasma** is similar to gas but contains freely moving charged particles (although its overall charge is neutral).

Changes in temperature and pressure can cause matter to change states. Generally, adding energy (in the form of heat) changes a substance to a higher-energy state (e.g., solid to liquid). Transitions from a higher- to lower-energy state (e.g., liquid to solid) release energy. Each of these changes has a specific name:

- solid to liquid: melting
- liquid to solid: freezing
- liquid to gas: evaporation

- gas to liquid: condensation
- solid to gas: sublimation
- gas to solid: deposition

When the state of matter changes, it is an example of a **physical change**, which is a change that does not alter the chemical composition of a substance. In other words, the state of matter changes, but the underlying chemical nature of the substance itself does not change. Other examples of physical changes include cutting, heating, or changing the shape of a substance.

When substances are combined without a chemical reaction to bond them, the resulting substance is called a **mixture**. In a mixture, the components can be unevenly distributed, such as in trail mix or soil. Mixtures can be separated into their individual components:

- **Heterogenous mixtures** are those that can be easily separated because their elements lack uniformity.
    - A glass of water with ice in it is one example of a heterogenous mixture because the water is in two states—solid and liquid—and can be easily separated.
- **Homogenous mixtures** are those that are more difficult to separate because the composition is relatively uniform.
    - Sugar in coffee is a homogenous mixture that is harder to separate because the sugar is dissolved in the hot liquid.
- A **solution** is a mixture with uniform distribution.
    - The substance being dissolved is the **solute**, and the substance in which it is being dissolved is the **solvent**.

If a substance dissolves in a solvent, it is said to be **soluble**; if it does not dissolve, it is said to be **insoluble**. **Solubility** refers to the amount of a solute that will dissolve in a solvent. Solubility is impacted by many factors, such as the temperature, surface area, amount of solute, and degree of agitation (e.g., stirring). Solubility, and the factors that impact it, can be demonstrated for students with various methods, such as observing sugar in iced and hot tea or pouring oil into water.

Physical changes can be used to separate mixtures. For example, heating salt water until the water evaporates will separate a saltwater solution, leaving the salt behind. In contrast to physical changes, **chemical changes** occur when bonds between atoms are made or broken, resulting in a new substance or substances. Chemical changes are also called **chemical reactions**. Chemical reactions are either **exothermic**, meaning energy (heat) is released, or **endothermic**, meaning that energy is required for the reaction to take place.

Chemical reactions are represented by written mathematical equations. The **reactants**—the substances that are changing in the chemical reaction—are represented on the left side of the equation. The **products**, the new substances formed during the chemical reaction, are represented on the right side of the equation. The law of conservation of mass says that the amount of each element cannot change during a chemical reaction, so the same amount of each element must be represented on each side of the equation (i.e., the reactants and products must have the same amount of each element). This is called a **balanced equation**. For example, the

> **Helpful Hint**
>
> In both physical and chemical changes, matter is always conserved, meaning it can never be created or destroyed.

production of water from two molecules of hydrogen gas and one molecule of oxygen gas can be written as $2H_2 + O_2 \rightarrow 2H_2O$.

The substances on the left side of the equations are called the **reactants**. The + sign means "reacts with," and the arrow means "produces." The substances on the right side of the equations are called the **products**. The number in front of the substances tells how many molecules of the substance are used, although the number is only written if it is more than one. Common reactions include the following:

- **oxidation:** a chemical change in which a substance loses electrons, as when iron rusts when exposed to oxygen, forming iron oxide
- **combustion:** a chemical reaction that produces heat, carbon dioxide, and water, usually by burning a fuel
- **synthesis:** a chemical reaction in which two substances combine to form a single substance
- **decomposition:** a chemical reaction in which a single substance is broken down into two or more substances
- **neutralization:** a chemical reaction that occurs when an acid and a base react to produce a salt and water

Matter is classified by its **properties**, or characteristics. These properties include mass, weight, density, conductivity, solubility, and pH. **Mass** refers to the amount of matter in an object. Although the terms are often used interchangeably, mass is distinct from **weight**, which is the force of the gravitational pull on an object. Unlike weight, mass stays the same no matter where an object is located. When two objects of the same mass are on Earth and on the moon, the object on the moon will weigh less because the force of gravity on the moon is less than it is on Earth.

Density is the mass of the object divided by its volume, or the amount of space the object occupies. A denser object contains the same amount of mass in a smaller space than a less dense object. This is why a dense object, such as a bowling ball, feels heavier than a less dense object, like a soccer ball. The density of an object determines whether it will sink or float in a fluid. For example, the bowling ball will sink because it is denser than water, while the soccer ball will float.

Conductivity describes how well a material conducts heat or electricity. Silver, copper, aluminum, and iron are good conductors, while rubber, glass, and wood are poor conductors. Poor conductors are also called **insulators**.

Finally, the **pH scale** is used to describe the acidity of a substance or solution. **Acids** are compounds that contribute a hydrogen ion (H+) when in solution, and **bases** are compounds that contribute a hydroxide ion (OH−) in solution. The pH scale goes from 1 to 14, with 7 considered neutral. Acids (such as lemon juice and many carbonated soft drinks) have a pH lower than 7; bases (such as soap) have a pH greater than 7. Water is neutral with a pH of 7.

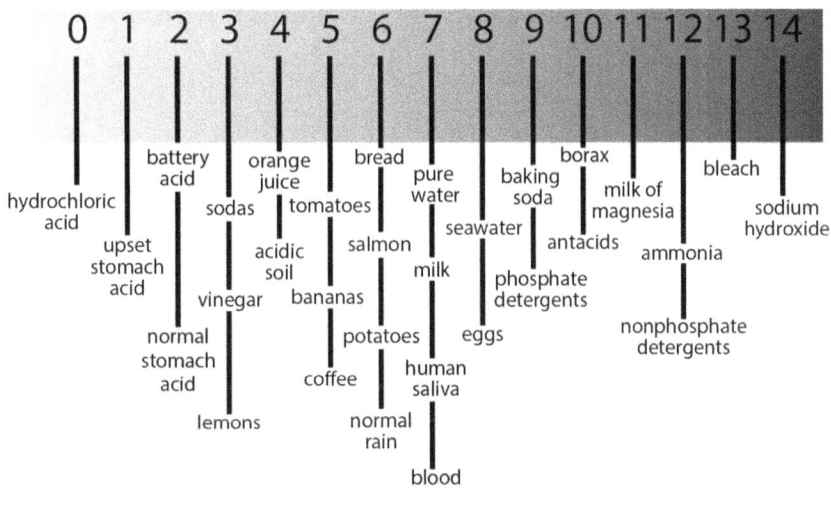

Figure 3.3. The pH Scale

Practice Questions

1) An atom has 5 electrons and 12 protons. What is the total charge of the atom?
    A. −17
    B. −7
    C. +7
    D. +17

2) Which type of chemical reaction takes place when kerosene reacts with oxygen to light a lamp?
    A. oxidation
    B. neutralization
    C. combustion
    D. convection

3) The state of matter at which particles are MOST loosely packed is
    A. liquid.
    B. gas.
    C. solid.
    D. plasma.

Force and Motion

The motion of objects can be measured using a number of different variables, including speed, displacement, velocity, and acceleration. These variables are either **vector** (magnitude and direction) or **scalar** (magnitude only) measurements.

Speed is a scalar measure that describes how quickly something moves using the following equation:

- speed = distance/time

Displacement is a vector measure of the shortest distance between the initial and final locations of a moving point as calculated using the following equation where v is the velocity, v^0 is the initial velocity, and t is the elapsed time.

- displacement = $\frac{1}{2}(v + v^0)t$

Velocity is a vector quantity that describes the rate at which an object changes position according to the following equation:

- velocity = displacement/time

An object that travels a certain distance and then returns to its starting point has a velocity of zero because its final position did not change. Its speed, however, can be found by dividing the total distance it traveled by the time it took to make the trip.

Acceleration is also a vector quantity and describes how quickly an object changes velocity. It is found using the following equation:

- acceleration = change in velocity/time

> **Helpful Hint**
>
> The normal force balances out gravity in resting objects. When a book rests on a table, gravity pulls down on it and the normal force pushes up, canceling each other out and holding the book still.

A push or pull that causes an object to move or change direction is called a **force**. Forces can arise from a number of different sources. **Gravity** is the attraction of one mass to another mass. For example, the earth's gravitational field pulls objects toward it, and the sun's gravitational field keeps planets in motion around it. Electrically charged objects create a field that causes other charged objects in that field to move. Other forces include **tension**, which is found in ropes pulling or holding up an object; **friction**, which is created by two objects moving against each other; and the **normal force**, which occurs when an object is resting on another object.

An object that is at rest or moving with a constant speed has a net force of zero, meaning all of the forces acting on it cancel each other out. Such an object is said to be at **equilibrium**. Isaac Newton proposed three **laws of motion** that govern forces:

- **Newton's first law:** An object at rest stays at rest and an object in motion stays in motion unless acted on by a force.
- **Newton's second law:** Force is equal to the mass of an object multiplied by its acceleration ($F = ma$).
- **Newton's third law:** For every action there is an equal and opposite reaction.

The laws of motion have made it possible to build **simple machines**, which take advantage of those laws to make work easier to perform. Simple machines include the inclined plane, wheel and axle, pulley, screw, wedge, and lever.

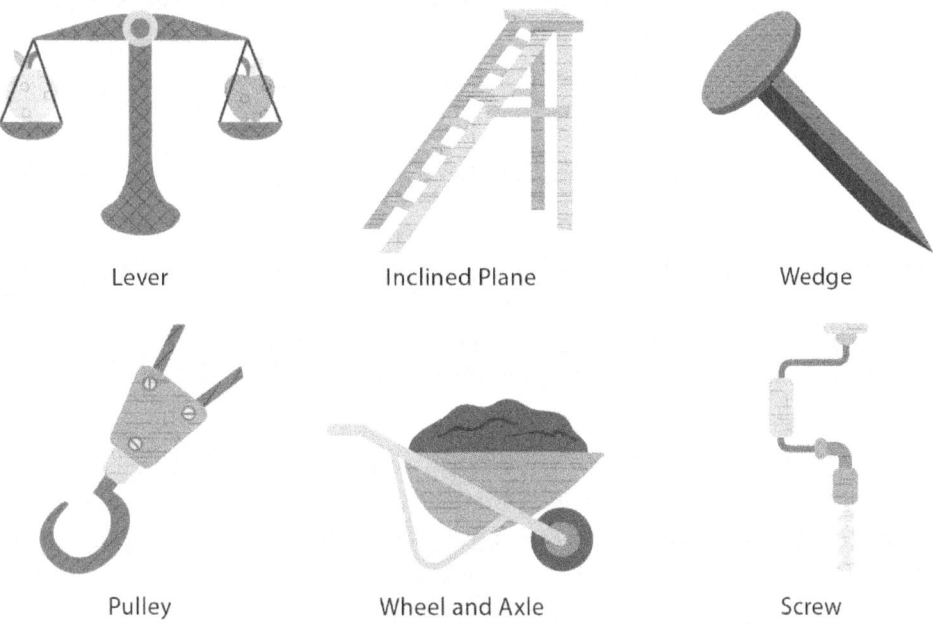

Figure 3.4. Simple Machine

Practice Questions

4) Which term describes the rate at which velocity changes?
   A. power.
   B. force.
   C. displacement.
   D. acceleration.

5) A box sliding down a ramp experiences all of the following forces EXCEPT
   A. tension.
   B. friction.
   C. gravity.
   D. normalcy.

Energy

Energy is the capacity of an object to do work, or, in other words, to cause some sort of movement or change. There are two kinds of energy: kinetic and potential. Objects in motion have **kinetic energy**, and objects that have the potential to be in motion due to their position have **potential energy**. Potential energy is defined in relation to a specific point. For example, a book held ten feet off the ground has more potential energy than a book held five feet off the ground because it has the potential to fall farther (i.e., to do more work).

Kinetic energy can be turned into potential energy and vice versa. In the example above, dropping one of the books turns its potential energy into kinetic energy. Conversely, picking up a book and placing it on a table turns kinetic energy into potential energy. In another example, a pendulum—an object with mass hanging from a fixed point—is able to swing indefinitely after an initial input of mechanical energy to start the motion by repeatedly converting potential energy to kinetic energy and back again.

> **Helpful Hint**
> Like matter, energy is always conserved. It can be changed from one form to another but never created or destroyed.

There are several types of potential energy. The energy stored in a book placed on a table is **gravitational potential energy** and is derived from the pull of the earth's gravity on the book. **Electric potential energy** is derived from the interaction between positive and negative charges. Because opposite charges attract each other, and like charges repel, energy can be stored when opposite charges are moved apart or when like charges are pushed together. Similarly, compressing a spring stores **elastic potential energy**, which is then converted to kinetic energy when the compressed spring is released. Energy is also stored in chemical bonds as **chemical potential energy**.

Temperature is the name given to the kinetic energy of all the atoms or molecules in a substance. While it might look like a substance is perfectly still, its atoms are actually constantly spinning and vibrating. The more energy the atoms have, the higher the substance's temperature. **Heat** is the movement of energy from one substance to another. Energy will spontaneously move from high energy (high temperature) substances to low energy (low temperature) substances.

The measurement of temperature is known as **thermometry**. Various scales are used to measure temperature. **Fahrenheit**, where water freezes at 32 degrees, is one such scale as is **Celsius**, where water freezes at zero degrees. **Kelvin** is another common scale, often used in scientific study. Zero degrees Celsius equals 273.15 K or kelvin.

This heat energy can be transferred by radiation, conduction, or convection. **Radiation** does not need a medium; the sun radiates energy to Earth through the vacuum of space. **Conduction** occurs when two substances are in contact with each other. When a pan is placed on a hot stove, the heat energy is conducted from the stove to the pan and then to the food in the pan. **Convection** transfers energy through circular movement of air or liquids. For example, a convection oven transfers heat through the circular movement caused by hot air rising and cold air sinking.

Energy in today's world comes from many sources. Energy sources are classified as **renewable**, or self-replenishing over time, and **nonrenewable**, or finite resources that will be used up completely at one point in time. Renewable energy sources include wind, solar, hydropower (water energy), geothermal energy, and biomass energy. Nonrenewable energy sources include oil, coal, natural gas, and nuclear energy.

Renewable energy sources are generally regarded as better for the earth and its people; however, renewable energy sources may present some disadvantages. Solar energy, for example, is an abundant and renewable source of energy that does not pollute water or air. It is, however, more expensive in its initial installation and requires a large space. Wind energy also requires a high up-front cost and may impact local wildlife, especially birds and bats. Like solar power, wind energy has low ongoing operating costs and may have great potential (like solar energy) for powering homes and businesses in the future.

Practice Questions

6) Which type of potential energy is stored in a compressed spring?
    A. chemical potential energy
    B. electric potential energy
    C. gravitational potential energy
    D. elastic potential energy

7) Which process allows the transfer of heat to occur from the contact between two substances?
    A. conduction
    B. convection
    C. radiation
    D. sublimation

Waves

Energy can also be transferred through **waves**, which are repeating pulses of energy. Waves that travel through a medium, like ripples on a pond or compressions in a Slinky, are called **mechanical waves**. Mechanical waves travel faster through denser mediums; for example, sound waves move faster through water than air. Waves that vibrate up and down (like the ripples on the pond) are **transverse waves**, and those that travel through compression (like the Slinky) are **longitudinal waves**.

Energy waves are described by properties such as amplitude, wavelength, frequency, period, speed, and phase. **Amplitude** is a measure of the wave's displacement from its rest position. **Wavelength** is the distance between two points on back-to-back wave cycles. **Frequency** describes the number of times per second the wave cycles. The time between wave crests is the **period** and the speed is how fast the wave is moving. The **phase** of a wave is the position on a wave cycle at a given point in time.

Longitudinal Wave

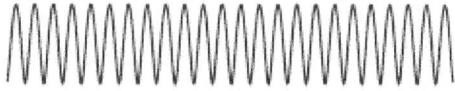
Transverse Wave

Figure 3.5. Types of Waves

Sound is a special type of longitudinal wave created by vibrations. Ears are able to interpret these waves as particular sounds. The frequency, or rate, of the vibration determines the sound's **pitch**. **Loudness** depends on the amplitude, or height, of a sound wave.

3. Science

The **Doppler effect** is the difference in perceived pitch caused by the motion of the object creating the wave. For example, as an ambulance approaches, the siren's pitch appears to increase to the observer and then to decrease as the ambulance moves away. This occurs because sound waves are compressed as the ambulance approaches an observer and spread out as the ambulance moves away from the observer.

Electromagnetic waves are composed of oscillating electric and magnetic fields and thus do not require a medium to travel through. The electromagnetic spectrum classifies the types of electromagnetic waves based on their frequency. These include radio waves, microwaves, X-rays, and visible light.

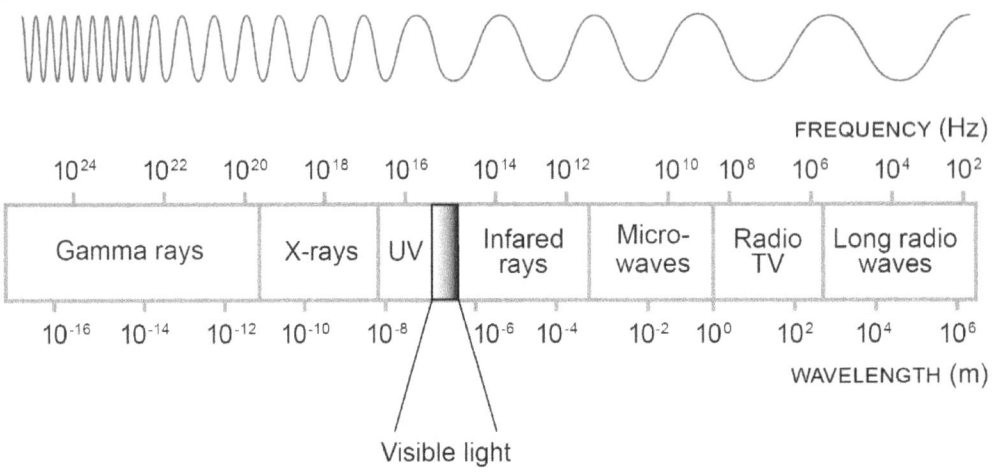

Figure 3.6. The Electromagnetic Spectrum

The study of light is called **optics**. Because visible light is a wave, it displays properties similar to other waves. It will **reflect**, or bounce off surfaces, which can be observed by shining a flashlight on a mirror. Light will also **refract**, or bend, when it travels between substances. This effect can be seen by holding a pencil upright in water and observing the apparent bend in the pencil.

Curved pieces of glass, called **lenses**, can be used to bend light in a way that affects how an image is perceived. Some microscopes, for example, use specific types of lenses to make objects appear larger. Eyeglasses also use lenses to correct poor vision.

> **Helpful Hint**
>
> The order of the colors in the spectrum of visible light can be remembered using the acronym *ROY G. BIV*: red, orange, yellow, green, blue, indigo, violet.

The frequency of a wave in the visible light spectrum is responsible for its **color**, with red/orange colors having a lower frequency than blue/violet colors. White light is a blend of all the frequencies of visible light. Passing white light through a prism will bend each frequency at a slightly different angle, separating the colors and creating a **rainbow**. Sunlight passing through raindrops can undergo this effect, creating rainbows in the sky.

There are many sources of light in our world that come from the sun, light bulbs, or even excited atoms (i.e. some neon lights). Students can be prompted to identify these light sources and determine how they work.

Practice Question

8) Which measurement describes the distance between crests in a wave?
    A. amplitude
    B. wavelength
    C. frequency
    D. period

Electricity and Magnetism

Electric charge is created by a difference in the balance of protons and electrons, which causes an object to have a positive or negative charge. Charged objects create an electric field that spreads outward from the object. Other charged objects in that field will experience a force: objects that have opposite charges will be **attracted** to each other, and objects with the same charge will be **repelled**, or pushed away, from each other.

Because protons cannot leave the nucleus, charge is created by the movement of electrons. Static electricity, or **electrostatic** charge, occurs when a surface has a buildup of charges. For example, when people rub a balloon on their head, the friction causes electrons to move from their hair to the balloon. This creates a negative charge on the balloon and positive charge on the hair; the resulting attraction causes the hair to move toward the balloon.

Electricity is the movement of electrons through a conductor, and an electric circuit is a closed loop through which electricity moves. Circuits include a **voltage** source, which powers the movement of electrons, known as **current**. Sources of voltage include batteries, **generators**, and wall outlets (which are in turn powered by electric power stations). Other items, such as lights, computers, or microwaves, can then be connected to the circuit to be powered by its electricity.

Magnets are created by the alignment of spinning electrons within a substance. This alignment occurs naturally in some substances, including iron, nickel, and cobalt, all of which can be used to produce **permanent magnets**. The alignment of electrons creates a **magnetic field** which, like an electric or gravitational field, can act on other objects. Magnetic fields have north and south **poles** that have properties similar to electric charges: opposite poles attract, and same poles repel each other. However, unlike an electric charge, which must be either positive or negative, a magnetic field always has two poles. If a magnet is cut in half, the result is two magnets that each have a north and south pole. Magnetic fields are depicted visually using **magnetic field lines**, which show the direction of the field at different points.

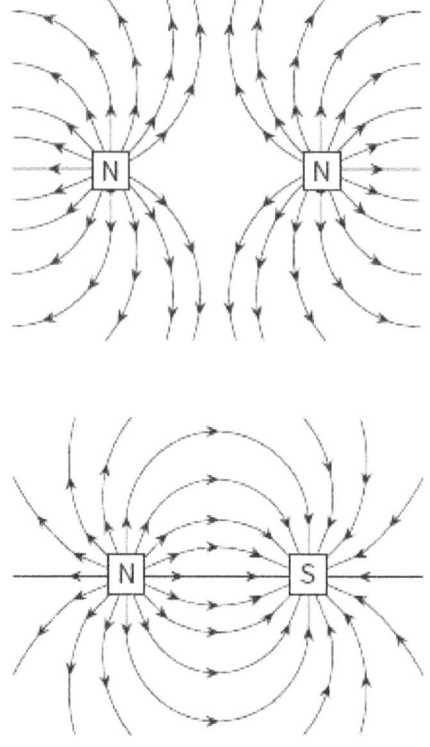

Figure 3.7. Magnetic Field Lines

Electricity and magnetism are closely related. A moving magnet creates an electric field, and a moving charged particle will create a magnetic field. A specific kind of **temporary magnet**, known as an electromagnet, can be made by coiling a wire around a metal object and running electricity through it. A magnetic field will be created when the wire contains a current but will disappear when the flow of electricity is stopped.

Practice Question

9) Two negative charges are held at a distance of 1 m from each other. When the charges are released, they will
   A. remain at rest.
   B. move closer together.
   C. move farther apart.
   D. move together in the same direction.

Life Science

Biomolecules

Life is made possible by a set of biological molecules that each serve a specific purpose. **Carbohydrates** are the sugars that act as sources of energy for all living things. **Lipids**, or fats, are a way for organisms to store energy, and they also help with cell functioning. **Proteins** serve a wide variety of biological functions, and are composed of building blocks called amino acids. **Enzymes** are a special type of protein that can cause or speed up a specific chemical reaction. Enzymes are important in the digestive system and help the body break down and extract energy from different kinds of foods.

Lastly, **nucleic acids**, such as DNA and RNA, store an organism's genetic code, which is all the information needed for the organism to function. Both DNA and RNA are made of small molecules called nucleotides. **DNA** has four types of nucleotides: adenine, cytosine, guanine, and thymine. **RNA** substitutes uracil for thymine. The nucleotides form pairs: adenine with thymine (or uracil) and cytosine with guanine. The pairs are linked by a backbone that forms a shape like two ropes twisted together, called a double helix. In some cells, nucleic acids are stored inside a special area called a **nucleus**. Within the nucleus, DNA is packed into units called **chromosomes**.

Practice Question

10) Enzymes are an example of which type of macromolecule?
    A. lipids
    B. nucleic acids
    C. carbohydrates
    D. proteins

Structure and Function of Organisms

Organisms are living things consisting of at least one **cell**, which is the smallest unit of life that can reproduce on its own. Unicellular organisms, such as amoebas, are made up of only one cell, while multicellular organisms are composed of many cells. The structure of any plant or animal organism can be viewed as a hierarchical relationship of systems. The largest structure is an organ system, like the human reproductive system, which contains individual organs (e.g., ovaries) that are made up of tissues, or groups of cells. The smallest units of an organism are subcellular organelles.

There are two basic types of cells: prokaryotic and eukaryotic:

- **Prokaryotic cells** do not have a nucleus, and some single-celled organisms, like bacteria, are prokaryotes.
- **Eukaryotic cells** contain a nucleus where the genetic material is stored; they are found in multicellular organisms.

A cell consists of cytoplasm and genetic material (DNA) inside a **cell membrane**, or protective covering. Separate from the cytoplasm in eukaryotic cells is the **nucleus**, which is the membrane-bound body that holds the cell's DNA. Within the cytoplasm of eukaryotic cells are a number of **organelles** that perform specific functions. These include **mitochondria**, which produce energy; **ribosomes**, which produce proteins; and **vacuoles**, which store water and other molecules.

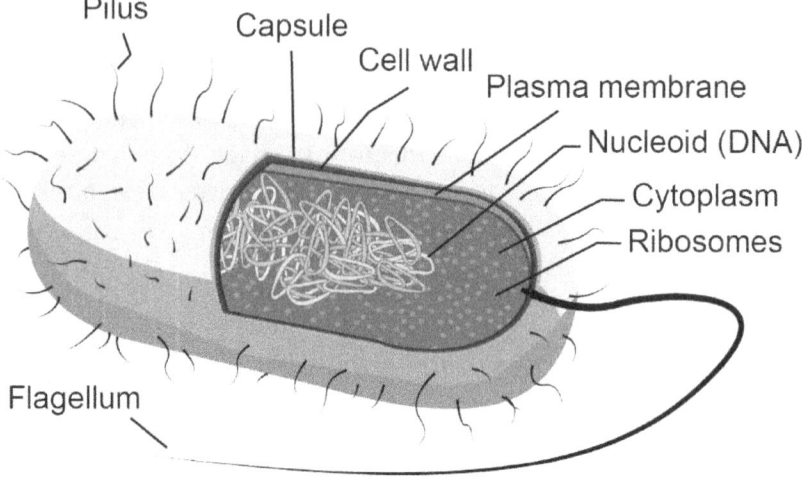

Figure 3.8. Prokaryotic Cell

Plant cells include a number of structures not found in animal cells. These include the **cell wall**, which provides the cell with a hard outer structure, and chloroplasts, where **photosynthesis** occurs. During photosynthesis, plants store energy from sunlight as sugars, which serve as the main source of energy for cell functions.

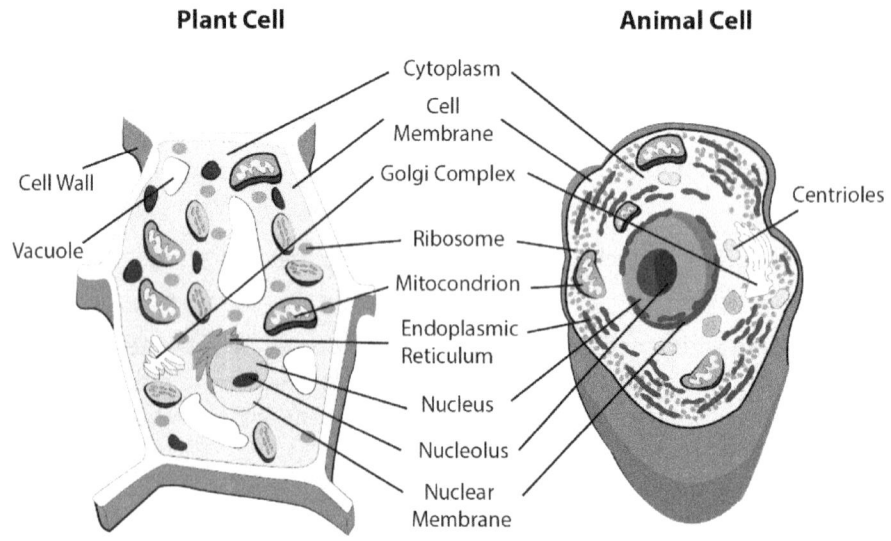

Figure 3.9. Animal Cell Versus Plant Cell

Cell division, or **mitosis**, produces two cells with the same DNA as the original cell. Mitosis has five steps: prophase, metaphase, anaphase, telophase, and interphase:

- **Prophase** is when the cell is getting ready to divide by duplicating its DNA.
- During **metaphase**, the chromosomes line up in pairs along the central axis of the cell.

- **Anaphase** is when the pairs begin to split, with one of the chromosomes moving toward one side of the cell and the other moving toward the opposite side.

- Once the chromosomes are at opposite sides of the cell, the cell moves into **telophase**: the cell membrane splits and two new cells are formed.

- After the division is completed, the two new cells return to a normal resting state, which is called **interphase**.

Meiosis is the formation of reproductive cells called gametes (eggs and sperm). Meiosis is a process that includes two cell divisions with phases similar to those of mitosis. In the first division, the chromosomes are duplicated and pairs of chromosomes align and exchange genetic material with one another during the prophase. The metaphase, anaphase, and telophase proceed much like those of mitosis. The interphase between the two division processes is very short and the DNA is not duplicated before the second division cycle. The cell divides again using the same process as described for mitosis; however, the chromosomes are not duplicated. Instead, each chromosome divides in half and each new cell receives only half of the genetic material contained in the original parent cell.

> **Helpful Hint**
>
> Phases of mitosis can be remembered using the phrase, "**I p**icked **m**y **a**pples **t**oday." The order is **i**nterphase, **p**rophase, **m**etaphase, **a**naphase, **t**elophase.

When an egg is fertilized by the sperm to form a zygote, half of the new organism's chromosomes come from the egg (mother) and half come from the sperm (father). In humans, reproductive cells have twenty-three chromosomes and body cells have forty-six (one set of twenty-three from each parent).

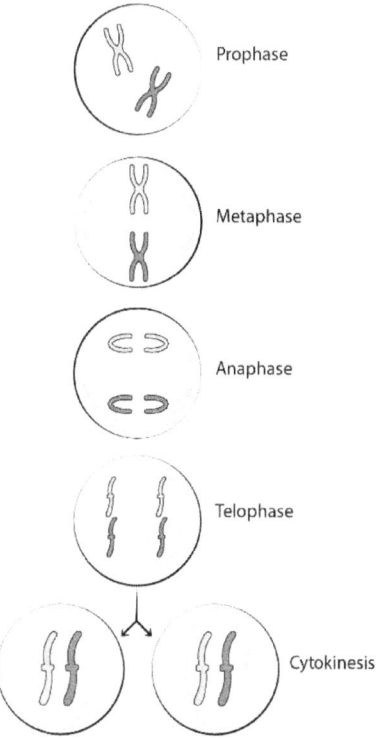

Figure 3.10. Phases of Mitosis

All organisms also have similarities, such as changes from birth to maturation, called a **life cycle**; an ability to reproduce; and a response to certain environmental stimuli. Environmental responses may vary, such as a tree losing its leaves when the days get shorter, or a wild horse running away from a loud noise. Additionally, all living organisms have similar basic needs, such as food, water, and space.

Living organisms must also change based on their environments. These changes may take the form of **adaptations** or **accommodations**, also known as acclimations. Adaptations are permanent changes in the chemical or physical make-up of the organism to cope with change. Acclimation or accommodations are temporary adjustments that organisms make when the environment changes. For example, a human in a cold environment may put on a coat, or a fish that is placed in an aquarium may be forced to adjust its diet.

Organisms are part of broader **systems**, defined as two or more parts that make a whole. There are many interconnected systems in our world, such as eco*systems*, the solar *system*, and even the human digestive *system*. Systems go through cycles of stability (where there are no observable changes) and cycles of change (which may create predictable patterns), such as day and night resulting from Earth's rotation. Cycles of change also include less predictable patterns, such as ecosystem destruction after a tornado or earthquake. Stable systems are often still changing, but at **dynamic equilibrium**, where physical movements or chemical reactions balance each other out. For example, a community that experiences out-migration of seventy people but in-migration of seventy people is stable due to dynamic equilibrium.

Practice Questions

11) The chromosomes of a eukaryotic organism are found in the
    A. chloroplast.
    B. nucleus.
    C. ribosome.
    D. cytoplasm.

12) A distinct difference between a plant cell and an animal cell is the presence of
    A. ribosomes.
    B. mitochondria.
    C. a cell wall.
    D. a nucleus.

Genetics and Evolution

When organisms reproduce, **genetic** information is passed to the next generation through deoxyribonucleic acid, or DNA. Within DNA are blocks of nucleotides called **genes**, each of which contains the code needed to produce a specific protein. Genes are responsible for **traits**, or characteristics, in organisms, such as eye color, height, and flower color. During sexual **reproduction**, the child receives two copies of each gene, one each from the mother and the father. Sexual reproduction is distinct from **asexual reproduction** in which the offspring have identical genes to a parent. Bacteria, fungi, many plants, and some animals use asexual reproduction.

In sexual reproduction, some of the genes will be **dominant**, meaning they are expressed, and some will be **recessive**, meaning they are not expressed. Each child will have a mix of its parents' traits. A special chart that shows all the possible genetic combinations from parents with given genotypes is called a **Punnett square**. A Punnett square is a grid with four squares, where the possible genes from one parent are written along the top and the possible genes from the other parent are written down the side. Each square is filled in with the corresponding letters from the top and side of the grid, with capital letters representing dominant genetic traits listed first, followed by lowercase letters representing recessive traits.

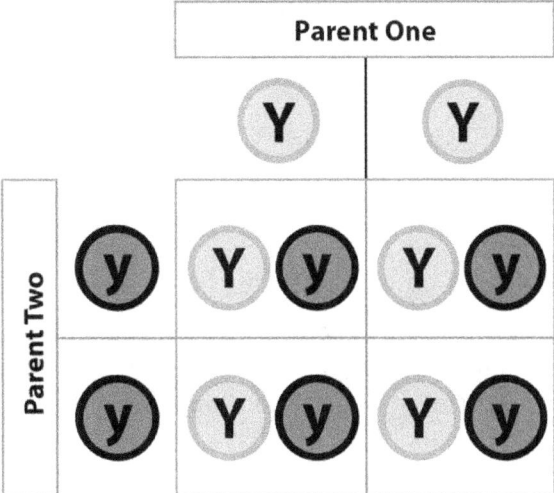

Figure 3.12. Punnett Square

Genes are not static. Over time, **mutations**—changes in the genetic code—occur that can affect an organism's ability to survive. Four common types of genetic mutations are substitution, insertion, deletion, and frameshift. Substitution mutations occur when one nucleotide is exchanged with another (such as switching the bases adenine and cytosine). Insertion mutations happen when extra nucleotide pairs are inserted into the DNA sequence. Removal of nucleotide pairs from the DNA sequence results in deletion mutations. Finally, frameshift mutations occur when the insertion or deletion of nucleotides causes the gene to be misread. Harmful mutations will appear less often in a population or be removed entirely because organisms with those mutations will be less likely to reproduce and thus will not pass on that trait.

Helpful Hint

Many of the rules of genetics were discovered by Gregor Mendel, a nineteenth-century abbot who used pea plants to show how traits are passed down through generations.

Beneficial mutations, called **adaptations**, may help an organism thrive in a particular environment. This means that the organism is more likely to reproduce, and thus that trait or adaptation will appear more often. Over time, this process, called **natural selection**, results in the **evolution** of new species. The theory of evolution was developed by naturalist Charles Darwin when he observed how finches on the Galapagos Islands had a variety of beak shapes and sizes that corresponded to different food sources, allowing the birds to coexist.

Consider This

Why might a harmful mutation continue to exist in a population?

Natural selection is distinct from **artificial selection**, in that artificial selection usually involves human interference and selective breeding for the most desirable traits. For example, humans have used artificial selection to create numerous breeds of dogs as well as plants with large, hardy fruits and vegetables.

While evolution is debated in some circles, the evidence supporting it is overwhelming. Examining the fossil record, studying comparative anatomy, and sequencing and comparing DNA are all methods by which to support Darwin's theory that life evolved over billions of years.

Practice Question

13) The process of organisms with advantageous traits surviving more often and producing more offspring than organisms without these advantageous traits describes which basic mechanism of evolution?
    A. gene flow
    B. genetic drift
    C. mutation
    D. natural selection

Human Body Systems

In a multicellular organism, cells are grouped together into **tissues**, and these tissues are grouped into **organs**, which perform specific **functions**. The heart, for example, is the organ that pumps blood throughout the body. Organs are further grouped into **organ systems**, such as the digestive or respiratory systems.

Anatomy is the study of the structure of organisms, and **physiology** is the study of how these structures function. Both disciplines study the systems that allow organisms to perform a number of crucial functions, including the exchange of energy, nutrients, and waste products with the environment. This exchange allows organisms to maintain **homeostasis**, or the stabilization of internal conditions.

> **Helpful Hint**
>
> Systems may be closed (i.e., nothing passes in or out of them) or open (i.e., they have inputs and outputs).

The human body has a number of systems that perform vital functions, including the digestive, excretory, respiratory, circulatory, skeletal, muscular, immune, nervous, endocrine, and reproductive systems.

The **digestive system** breaks food down into nutrients for use by the body's cells. Food enters through the **mouth** and moves through the **esophagus** to the **stomach**, where it is physically and chemically broken down. The food particles then move into the **small intestine**, where the majority of nutrients are absorbed. Finally, the remaining particles enter the **large intestine**, which mostly absorbs water, and waste exits through the **rectum** and **anus**. This system also includes other organs, such as the **liver**, **gallbladder**, and **pancreas**, that manufacture the substances needed for digestion.

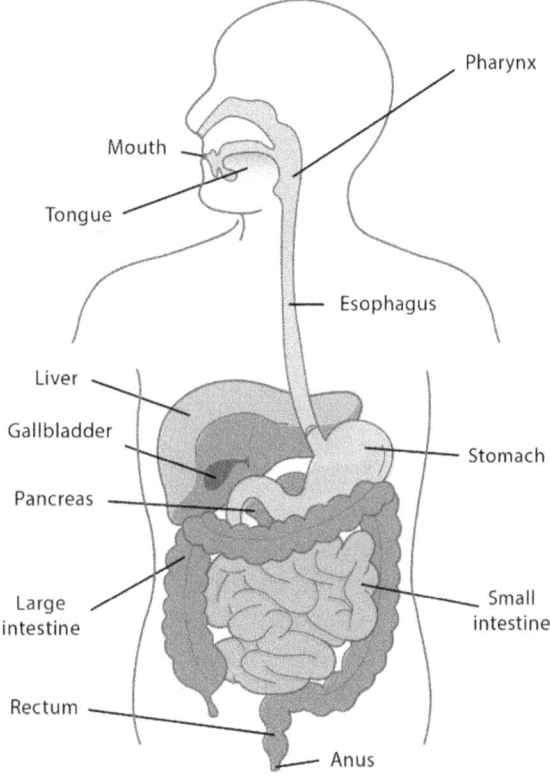

Figure 3.12. Digestive System

The **excretory system** removes waste products from the body. Its organs include the liver, which breaks down harmful substances, and the **kidneys**, which filter waste from the bloodstream. The excretory system also includes the **bladder** and **urinary tract**, which expel the waste filtered by the kidneys; the lungs, which expel the carbon dioxide created by cellular metabolism; and the skin, which secretes salt in the form of perspiration.

The **respiratory system** takes in oxygen (which is needed for cellular functioning) and expels carbon dioxide. Humans take in air primarily through the nose but also through the mouth. This air travels down the **trachea** and **bronchi** into the **lungs**, which are composed of millions of small structures, called alveoli, that allow for the exchange of gases between the blood and the air.

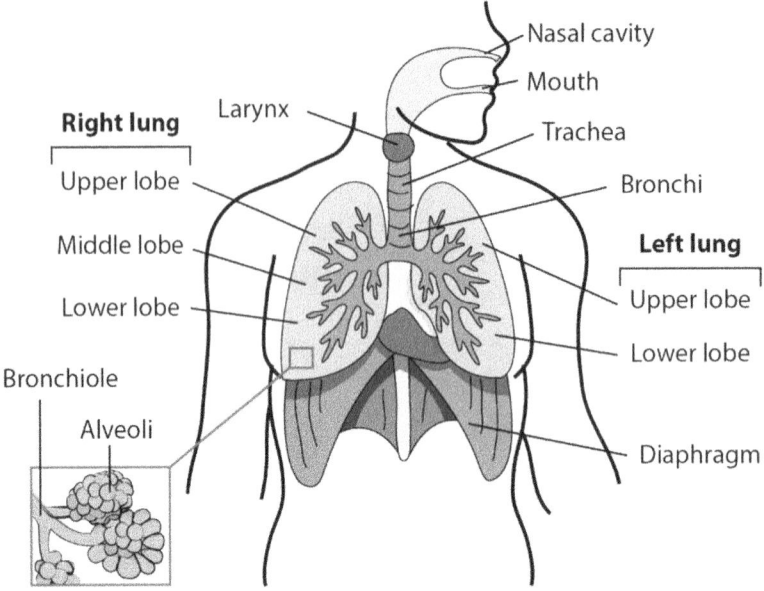

Figure 3.13. Respiratory System

The circulatory system carries oxygen, nutrients, and waste products in the blood to and from all the cells of the body. The **heart** is a four-chambered muscle that pumps blood throughout the body. The four chambers are the right atrium, right ventricle, left atrium, and left ventricle. Deoxygenated blood (blood from which all the oxygen has been extracted and used) enters the right atrium and then is sent from the right ventricle through the pulmonary artery to the lungs, where it collects oxygen. The oxygen-rich blood then returns to the left atrium of the heart and is pumped out of the left ventricle to the rest of the body.

Blood travels through a system of vessels. **Arteries** branch directly off the heart and carry blood away from it. The largest artery is the aorta, which carries blood from the heart to the rest of the body. **Veins** carry blood back to the heart from other parts of the body. Most veins carry deoxygenated blood, but the pulmonary veins carry oxygenated blood from the lungs back to the heart to then be pumped to the rest of the body. Arteries and veins branch into smaller and smaller vessels until they become **capillaries**, which are the smallest vessels and the site where gas exchange occurs.

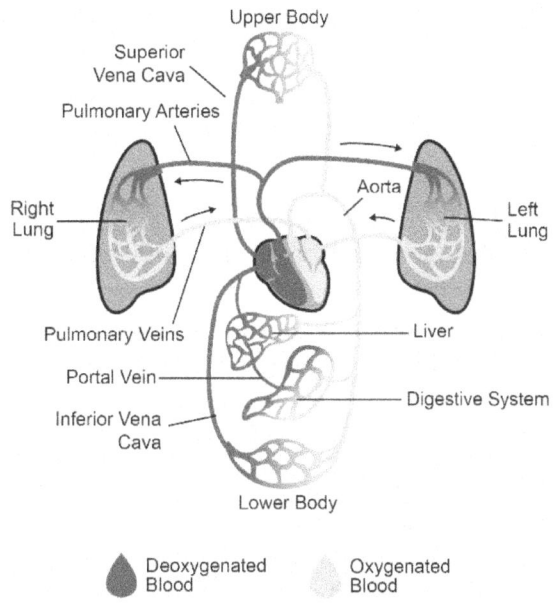

Figure 3.14. Circulatory System

The **skeletal system**, which is composed of the body's **bones** and **joints**, provides support for the body and helps with movement. Bones also store some of the body's nutrients and produce specific types of cells. Humans are born with 237 bones; however, many of these bones fuse during childhood, and adults have only 206 bones. Bones can have rough or smooth textures and come in four basic shapes: long, flat, short, and irregular.

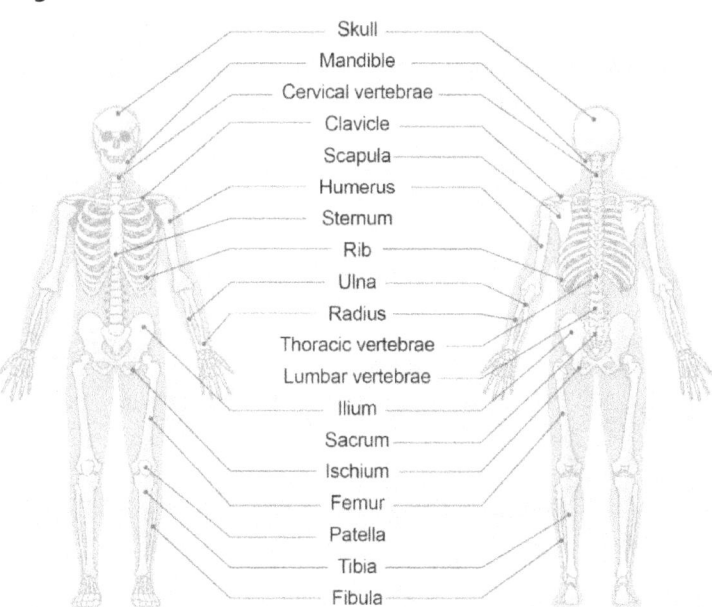

Figure 3.15. Important Bones of the Skeletal System

3. Science

The **muscular system** allows the body to move and also moves blood and other substances through the body. The human body has three types of muscles. Skeletal muscles are voluntary muscles (i.e., they can be controlled) that are attached to bones and move the body. Smooth muscles are involuntary muscles (i.e., they cannot be controlled) that create movement in parts of the digestive tract, blood vessels, and reproductive system. Finally, cardiac muscle is the involuntary muscle that contracts the heart, pumping blood throughout the body.

The **immune system** protects the body from infection by foreign particles and organisms. It includes the **skin** and mucous membranes, which act as physical barriers, and a number of specialized cells that destroy foreign substances in the body. The human body has an adaptive immune system, meaning it can recognize and respond to foreign substances once it has been exposed to them. This is the underlying mechanism behind vaccines.

The immune system is composed of **B-cells**, or B-lymphocytes, that produce special proteins called **antibodies** that bind to foreign substances, called **antigens**, and neutralize them. **T-cells**, or T-lymphocytes, remove body cells that have been infected by foreign invaders like bacteria or viruses. **Helper T-cells** coordinate production of antibodies by B-cells and the removal of infected cells by T-cells. **Killer T-cells** destroy body cells that have been infected by invaders after they are identified and removed by T-cells. Finally, **memory cells** remember antigens that have been removed so the immune system can respond more quickly if they enter the body again.

The **nervous system** processes external stimuli and sends signals throughout the body. It is made up of two parts. The central nervous system (CNS) includes the brain and spinal cord and is where information is processed and stored. The brain has three parts: the cerebrum, cerebellum, and medulla. The **cerebrum** is the biggest part of the brain, the wrinkly gray part at the front and top, and controls different functions like thinking, vision, hearing, touch, and smell. The **cerebellum** is located at the back and bottom of the brain and controls motor movements. The **medulla**, or brain stem, is where the brain connects to the spinal cord and controls automatic body functions, like breathing and heartbeat.

The peripheral nervous system (PNS) includes small cells called **neurons** that transmit information throughout the body using electrical signals. Neurons are made up of three basic parts: the cell body, dendrites, and axons. The cell body is the main part of the cell where the organelles are located. Dendrites are long arms that extend from the main cell body and communicate with dendrites from other cells through chemical messages passed across a space called a synapse. Axons are extensions from the cell body and transmit messages to the muscles.

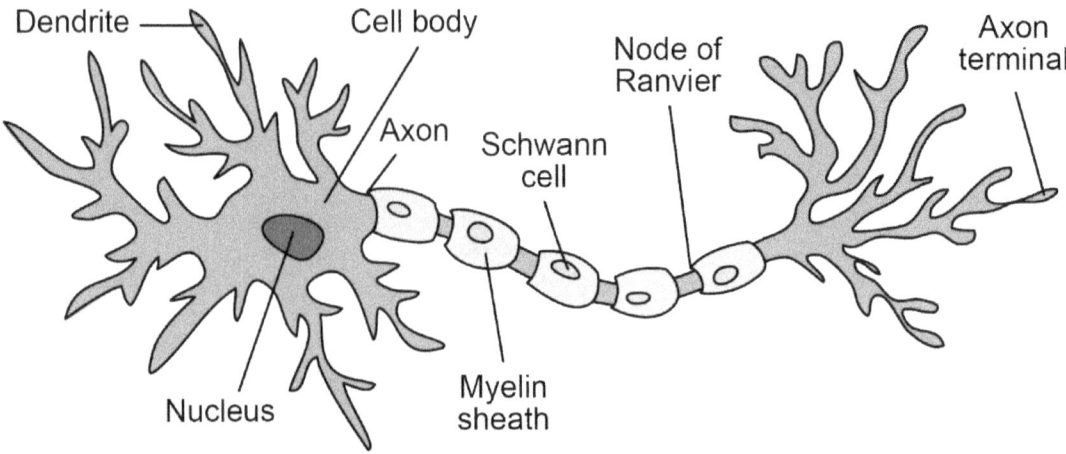

Figure 3.16. Neuron

The **endocrine system** is a collection of organs that produce **hormones**, which are chemicals that regulate bodily processes. These organs include the pituitary gland, hypothalamus, pineal gland, thyroid gland, parathyroid glands, adrenal glands, testes (in males), ovaries (in females), and the placenta (in pregnant females). Together, the hormones produced by these organs regulate a wide variety of bodily functions, including hunger, sleep, mood, reproduction, and temperature. Some organs that are part of other systems can also act as endocrine organs, including the pancreas and liver.

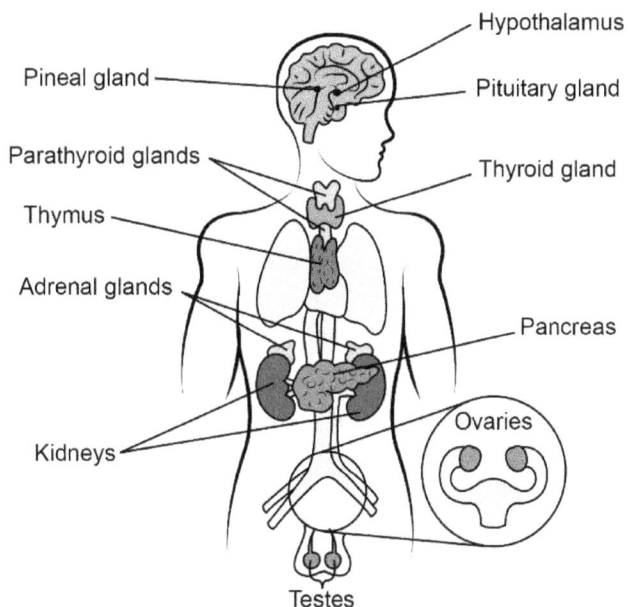

Figure 3.17. Endocrine System

The reproductive system includes the organs necessary for sexual reproduction. In males, sperm is produced in the **testes (also known as testicles)** and carried through a thin tube called the **vas deferens** to the **urethra**, which carries sperm through the **penis** and out of the body. The **prostate** is a muscular gland approximately the size of a walnut that is located between the male bladder and penis and produces a fluid that nourishes and protects sperm.

In the female reproductive system, eggs are produced in the **ovaries** and released roughly once a month to move through the **fallopian tubes** to the **uterus**. If an egg is fertilized, the new embryo implants in the lining of the **uterus** and develops over the course of about nine months. At the end of **gestation**, the baby leaves the uterus through the **cervix**, and exits the body through the **vagina**. If the egg is not fertilized, the uterus will shed its lining.

Practice Questions

14) What is the primary function of the respiratory system?
    A. to create sound and speech
    B. to take oxygen into the body while removing carbon dioxide
    C. to transport nutrients to the cells and tissue of the body
    D. to act as a barrier between the body's organs and foreign pathogens

15) Which muscular organ processes food material into smaller pieces and helps mix it with saliva?
   A. pharynx
   B. tongue
   C. diaphragm
   D. stomach

Plants

Plants are multicellular eukaryotic organisms that belong to the kingdom Plantae and produce energy primarily by photosynthesis. Photosynthesis is a process in which a chemical called **chlorophyll** uses energy from sunlight to convert water and carbon dioxide in the air into sugars. The chlorophyll is contained in special organelles called chloroplasts and is responsible for the green color of most plants' leaves.

One way plants are grouped is by how they transport water and nutrients throughout the plant. Some plants are vascular, which means that they have special tissues that transport water and nutrients, while others are nonvascular and distribute water and nutrients by passing them from cell to cell through osmosis or diffusion.

Vascular plants have three basic parts: leaves, a stem, and roots:

- **Leaves** are the organs where sunlight is captured and used by the chlorophyll to produce food for the plant through photosynthesis.
    - They come in many different shapes and sizes but are often broad and flat in order to capture as much sunlight as possible.
    - Most leaves are green because of the chlorophyll they contain.
- The **stem** is the part of the plant that provides structure and supports the weight of the plant.
    - The stem has special tissues that transport nutrients throughout the plant and is where plants store food.
    - The special tissue that plants use to transport water and minerals is called **xylem**.
    - **Phloem** is another special tissue that transports sugar and other nutrients throughout the plant.
- The **roots** anchor the plant and absorb water and nutrients from the soil.

> **Helpful Hint**
>
> The acronym *LAWN* represents the requirements for plants: **l**ight, **a**ir, **w**ater, **n**utrients.

Vascular plants are grouped as flowering or nonflowering based on how they reproduce. Flowering plants use flowers as their reproductive organs. Flowers are made from special brightly colored leaves called **petals** that together form the **corolla**. The petals are supported by other special leaves called **sepals** that together form the **calyx**. Inside the flower are both male and female reproductive organs. The male reproductive organ is called the **stamen** and has two parts, the **anther** and the **filament**. The male reproductive cells, called **pollen**, are produced in the stamen and stored in the anther. The anther is located at the end of a stalk, called the filament.

The female reproductive organ is called the **pistil**, and is usually located in the center of the flower. The pistil has two parts, the **carpel** and the **stigma**. The carpel is the ovary of the flower, where **ova** (eggs), the female reproductive cells, are produced. The stigma is where the pollen (the male reproductive cell) is received and is sometimes extended on a stalk called the **style**. Flowering plants are brightly colored to attract insects that move pollen from the anther to the stigma to fertilize the eggs.

After **fertilization** occurs, the flower forms a fruit that contains the seeds that grow from the fertilized eggs. **Seeds** are the plant embryo and come in a variety of shapes, sizes, and colors. The **fruit** provides nutrients and protects the seeds as they grow. It also attracts birds and animals that help distribute the seeds away from the plant. Seeds can also be distributed by air and water. The seeds are protected by a waxy layer called the seed coat.

Once the seed is distributed, it needs air, water, and soil to grow. When seeds begin to grow, it is called **germination**. The seed begins to form small roots and uses nutrients stored in a special organ called the **endosperm** for energy until it can form leaves and generate energy through photosynthesis. Flowering plants are also divided based on the number of embryos, or **cotyledons**, in their seeds. Plants with only one embryo in each seed, like corn or wheat, are called **monocots**. Those with two embryos in each seed, like beans, are called **dicots**. When the seed develops leaves, it is called a sprout or seedling. It continues to grow until it becomes a mature plant and can reproduce again by growing flowers.

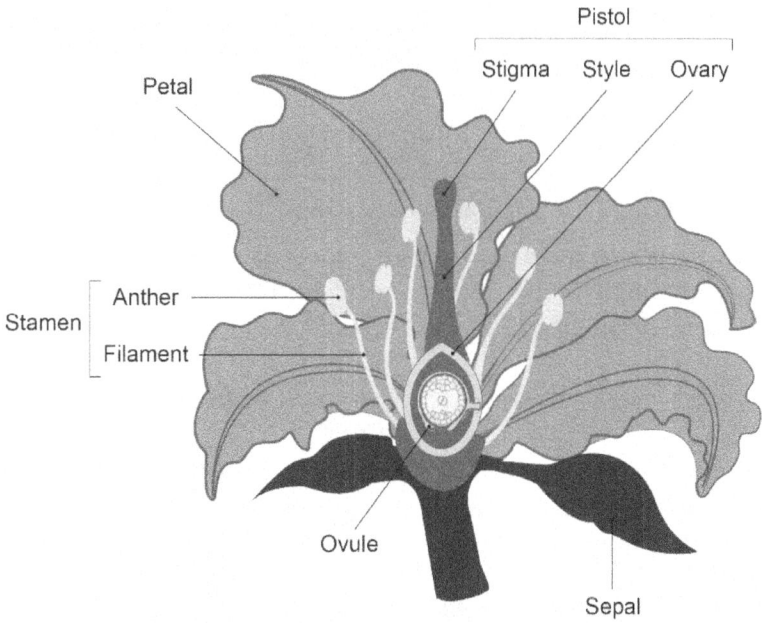

Figure 3.18. Flower with Male and Female Reproductive Structures

Nonflowering plants are divided into two groups: those that use seeds to reproduce and those that use spores to reproduce. Non-flowering plants that use seeds to reproduce are called **gymnosperms**, which literally means *naked seeds*. These plants produce seeds that do not have a covering like the fruits produced by flowering plants. **Conifers** are a major group of gymnosperm plants that use woody cones to protect their seeds. Most conifers are trees like pine, cedar, or redwood. Conifers produce male and female cones. The male cones produce pollen that is distributed by the wind, and if the pollen falls on a female cone, the female cone produces seeds that are protected by the cone. The seeds produced by conifers have winged structures on them that allow them to be carried by the wind. Once they reach the ground, the seeds germinate and grow.

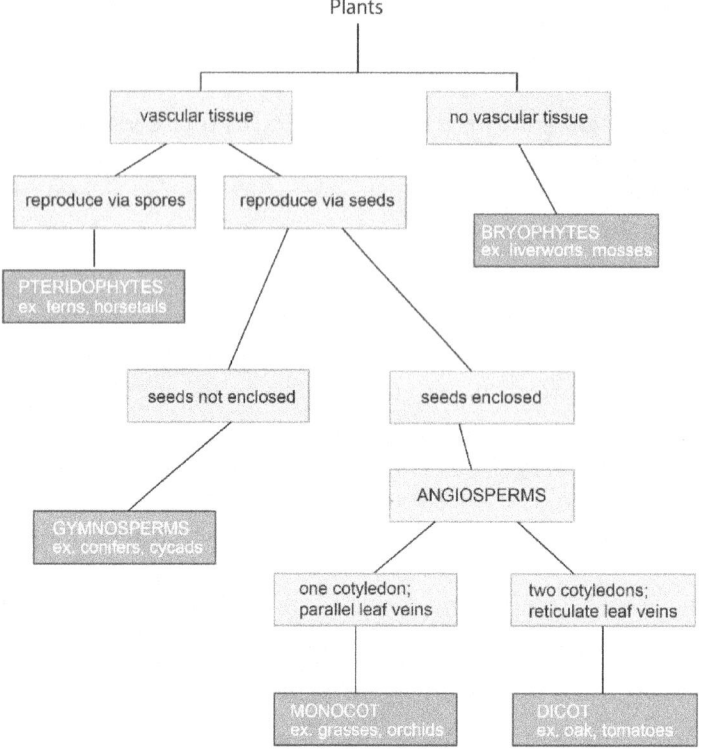

Figure 3.19. Plant Taxonomy

Plants that produce spores include ferns and mosses. **Spores** are usually a single cell and the plant produces them in large numbers. Because they are small and lightweight, they are distributed by the wind. Once the spores are distributed and land in a hospitable environment, they begin to divide and produce a new plant.

Practice Questions

16) The primary function of the root system is to
    A. anchor the plant.
    B. prevent water loss.
    C. deliver nutrients to all parts of the plant.
    D. absorb water and nutrients from the soil.

17) Which of the following is an evolutionary advantage of the angiosperms, giving them the competitive edge over other groups of plants?
    A. broad leaves that absorb more sunlight for photosynthesis
    B. the ability to be perennial, living and growing year after year
    C. fruit that nourishes the developing seed
    D. flowers that attract pollinators, ensuring more successful plant fertilization

Ecology

Ecology is the study of organisms' interactions with each other and the environment. As with the study of organisms, ecology includes a classification hierarchy. Groups of organisms of the same species living in the same geographic area are called **populations**. These organisms compete with each other for resources and mates and display characteristic patterns in growth related to their interactions with the environment. For example, many populations exhibit a **carrying capacity**, which is the highest number of individuals the resources in a given environment can support. Populations that outgrow their carrying capacity are likely to experience increased death rates until the population reaches a stable level again.

> **Helpful Hint**
>
> The five levels of ecology, from smallest to largest (**o**rganisms, **p**opulations, **c**ommunities, **e**cosystems, **b**iosphere), can be remembered using the phrase, "**O**ld **P**eople **C**atch **E**asy **B**reaks."

Populations of different species living together in the same geographic region are called **communities**. Within a community many different interactions among species occur. **Predators** consume **prey** for food, and some species are in **competition** for the same limited pool of resources. Two species may also have a **parasitic** relationship in which one organism benefits to the detriment of the other, such as ticks feeding off a dog. Organisms may also be involved in **symbiosis**, or a close relationship between two very different organisms. They may also engage in **mutualism**, which benefits both organisms, or **commensalism**, where only one organism benefits but leaves the other unharmed.

The lowest trophic level in the web is occupied by **producers**, which include plants and algae that produce energy directly from the sun. The next level are **primary consumers** (herbivores), which consume plant matter. The next trophic level includes **secondary consumers** (carnivores), which consume herbivores. A food web may also contain another level of **tertiary consumers** (carnivores that consume other carnivores). In a real community, these webs can be extremely complex, with species existing on multiple trophic levels. Communities also include **decomposers**, which are organisms that break down dead matter.

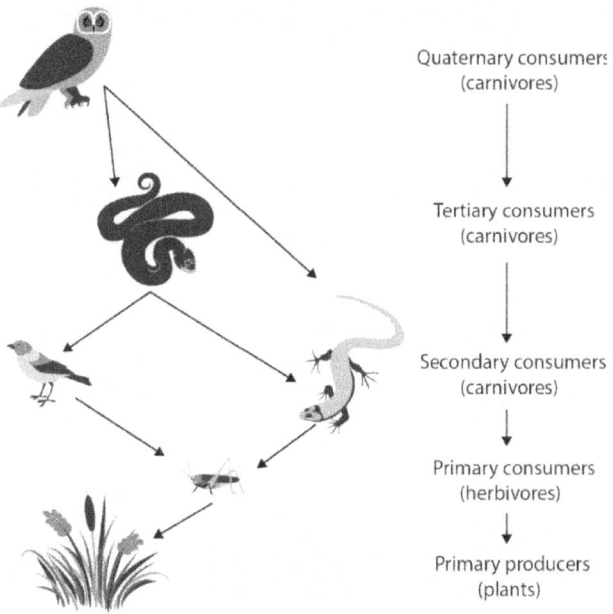

Figure 3.19. Food Web

The collection of biotic (living) and abiotic (nonliving) features in a geographic area is called an **ecosystem**. In a forest, for example, the ecosystem consists of all the organisms—animals, plants, fungi, bacteria, and so on—in addition to the soil, groundwater, rocks, and other abiotic features. Ecosystems are constantly developing and changing through a process called **ecological succession**. There are two types of ecological succession: primary and secondary. **Primary succession** describes the development and changes that occur during colonization of a new habitat, such as newly exposed rock. **Secondary succession** describes changes to previously colonized habitats that have been disrupted by events such as forest fires.

> **Check Your Understanding**
>
> What would happen if all of the decomposers disappeared from an ecosystem?

Ecosystems contain the resources that life within them rely on, such as water, soil, and temperatures conducive to survival of the organisms that live there. One crucial part of any ecosystem and of all life on Earth is carbon. Plants take carbon from their environment; this carbon is found and moved between plants, the soil, the ocean, and the atmosphere in what is known as the **carbon cycle**. Carbon is often referred to as the foundation for all life because of its central role in photosynthesis and its presence in DNA.

Biomes are collections of plant and animal communities that exist within specific climates. They are similar to ecosystems, but they do not include abiotic components and can exist within and across continents. For example, the Amazon rainforest is a specific ecosystem, while tropical rainforests in general are considered a biome that includes a set of similar communities across the world. Together, all the living and nonliving parts of the earth are known as the **biosphere**.

Terrestrial biomes are usually defined by distinctive patterns in temperature and rainfall, and aquatic biomes are defined by the type of water and organisms found there. Examples of biomes include the following:

- **desert:** a biome with extreme temperatures, very low rainfall, and specialized vegetation and small mammals
- **tropical rainforest:** a hot and wet biome with an extremely high diversity of species
- **temperate grassland:** a biome with moderate precipitation, distinct seasons, and grasses and shrubs that dominate
- **savanna:** tropical grassland with nutrient-poor soil
- **temperate broadleaf forest:** a biome with moderate precipitation and temperatures; dominated by deciduous trees
- **tundra:** a biome with extremely low temperatures, short growing seasons, and little or no tree growth
- **coral reef:** a marine (saltwater) system with high levels of diversity

- **wetland:** an area of land saturated with water; includes five types—ocean, estuary, river, lake, and marsh

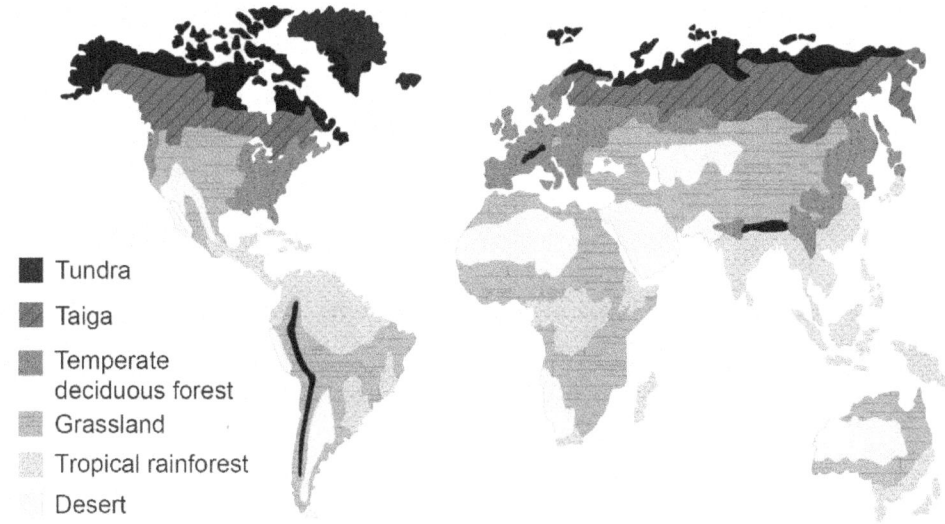

Figure 3.20. The World's Biomes

Ecosystems are not static environments but rather sites of constant change. The organisms within an ecosystem must therefore constantly shift and change as temperature, water, and soil change over time. For example, some organisms migrate with seasonal temperature shifts or when water in one area becomes scarce.

If the delicate balance of an ecosystem is disrupted, the system may not function properly. For example, if all of the secondary consumers disappear, the population of primary consumers would increase, causing the primary consumers to overeat the producers and eventually starve. Species called **keystone species** are especially important in a particular community, and removing them decreases the overall diversity of the ecosystem.

A major contemporary concern for virtually every ecosystem on Earth is **climate change**. Most scholars define climate change as long-term shifts or changes in weather patterns. Climate change can have impacts on local ecosystems, such as a group of apes living in a small area, or on far broader groups of organisms. For example, climate change in an island area, such as Indonesia, could impact every organism in that area.

Climate change has both natural and human causes. Natural causes of climate change include changes in Earth's orbit and axis of rotation, changes in the sun's energy, volcanic activity, and natural changes in Earth's surface and carbon dioxide concentrations. However, natural causes do not explain all climate change. Human activities, like the burning of fossil fuels and agricultural and industrial processes, have increased greenhouse gases in what is known as the **greenhouse effect**. Increased levels of carbon dioxide, methane, nitrous oxide, and chlorofluorocarbons contribute to the greenhouse effect.

To impact climate change, experts advise two paths: mitigation and adaptation. **Mitigation** involves reducing or eliminating the release of greenhouse gases into the atmosphere. **Adaptation** is more about adapting to the changing climate. Mitigation strategies might include eliminating the use of fossil fuels and increasing the use of renewable resources, shifting to more sustainable agricultural practices, and improving energy efficiency in homes and businesses. Adaptation strategies might include shifting the growing season or growing location of certain crops due to changes in climate and reducing risks to populations from extreme weather events by building barriers and reinforcing buildings.

Practice Questions

18) Which organism is a primary consumer?
    A. mushroom
    B. corn
    C. cow
    D. lion

19) Which of the following terrestrial biomes is tropical, dominated by grasses, and has poor soil?
    A. taiga
    B. estuary
    C. chaparral
    D. savanna

Earth and Space Science

Astronomy

Astronomy is the study of space. Earth is just one of a group of **planets** that orbit the **sun**, which is the star at the center of Earth's **solar system**. The planets in the solar system are Mercury, Venus, Earth, Mars, Jupiter, Saturn, Uranus, and Neptune. Every planet, except Mercury and Venus, has **moons**, or naturally occurring satellites that orbit a planet. The solar system also includes **asteroids** and **comets**, small rocky or icy objects that orbit the sun. Many of these are clustered in the asteroid belt, which is located between the orbits of Mars and Jupiter.

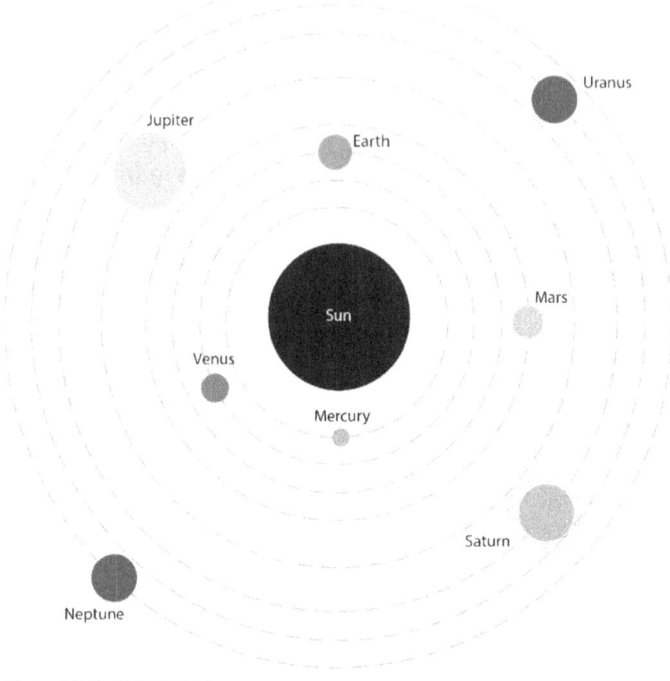

Figure 1.6. The Solar System

Figure 3.21. Solar System

The solar system is a small part of a bigger star system called a galaxy. (The galaxy that is home to Earth is called the Milky Way.) **Galaxies** consist of gas, dust, and hundreds of billions of **stars**, which are hot balls of plasma and gases, all held together by gravity. The universe has many types of stars, including supergiants, giants, white dwarfs, and neutron stars.

> **Helpful Hint**
>
> The phrase "**M**y **V**ery **E**ducated **M**other **J**ust **S**erved **U**s **N**oodles" can help students remember the order of the planets: **M**ercury, **V**enus, **E**arth, **M**ars, **J**upiter, **S**aturn, **U**ranus, **N**eptune.

The closer and larger the star is to Earth, the brighter it will appear. Generally stars are only apparent in the night sky when a person's portion of the earth is pointed away from the sun. This phenomenon also makes the Moon visible at night and the sun visible during the day. Additionally, because Earth orbits the sun through the course of a year, we see different parts of the night sky during different seasons. This is why different constellations are visible at different times.

Stars form in nebulas, which are large clouds of dust and gas. When very large stars collapse, they create **black holes**, which have a gravitational force so strong that even light cannot escape.

Earth, the moon, and the sun interact in a number of ways that impact the planet. The moon reflects sunlight in what are called **lunar phases**. A **new moon** occurs when sunlight is hitting the far side of the moon that cannot be seen from Earth; sunlight reflecting off the near side we can see is called a **full moon**. During the other lunar phases (waxing crescent, first quarter, waxing gibbous, waning gibbous, third quarter, and waning crescent), people on Earth see only a portion of the moon.

The cycles of day, night, and the seasons are determined by Earth's motion around the sun. It takes approximately 365 days, or one year, for Earth to revolve around the sun. While Earth is revolving around the sun, it is also rotating on its axis, which takes approximately 24 hours, or one day. As the planet rotates, different areas alternately face toward the sun and away from the sun, creating night and day.

Earth's axis is not directly perpendicular to its orbit, meaning the planet is tilted. The seasons are caused by this tilt. When the Northern Hemisphere is tilted toward the sun, it receives more sunlight and experiences summer. At the same time that the Northern Hemisphere experiences summer, the Southern Hemisphere, which receives less direct sunlight, experiences winter. As the earth revolves, the Northern Hemisphere tilts away from the sun and moves into winter, while the Southern Hemisphere tilts toward the sun and moves into summer.

Earth's rotation means people at different places on the planet will see the sun in a different place in the sky at the same time. In order to better standardize this experience with a time label, **time zones** were created. Time zones are based on **longitude**, defined as the distance east or west of the prime meridian, or the line that runs through Greenwich, England. This line serves as the starting point of time zones, known as Greenwich mean time (GMT). Locations east of this line have a later time, while locations to the west have an earlier time. Time zones help all people on earth experience sunrise in the morning hours, sunset in the evening hours, and the sun at its highest at noon.

Practice Question

20) What term is used when the moon moves between Earth and the sun?
    A. aurora
    B. lunar eclipse
    C. black hole
    D. solar eclipse

Geology

> **Helpful Hint**
>
> Luster describes how light reflects off the surface of a mineral. Terms to describe luster include *dull*, *metallic*, *pearly*, and *waxy*.

Geology is the study of the minerals and rocks that make up the earth. A **mineral** is a naturally occurring, solid, inorganic substance with a crystalline structure. There are several properties that help identify a mineral, including color, luster, hardness, and density. Examples of minerals include talc, diamonds, and topaz. Although a **rock** is also a naturally occurring solid, it can be either organic or inorganic and is composed of one or more minerals. Rocks are classified based on how they were formed. The three types of rocks are igneous, sedimentary, and metamorphic. **Igneous rocks** are the result of tectonic processes that bring **magma**, or melted rock, to the earth's surface; they can form either above or below the surface. **Sedimentary rocks** are formed when rock fragments are compacted as a result of weathering and erosion. Lastly, **metamorphic rocks** form when extreme temperatures and pressure change the structure of preexisting rocks.

The rock cycle describes how rocks form and break down. Typically, the cooling and solidification of magma as it rises to the surface creates igneous rocks. These rocks are then subject to **weathering**, the mechanical and/or chemical processes by which rocks break down. During **erosion**, the resulting sediment is deposited in a new location. This **deposition** creates new sedimentary rocks. As new layers are added, rocks and minerals are forced closer to the earth's core where they are subject to heat and pressure, resulting in metamorphic rock. Eventually, they will reach their melting point and return to magma, starting the cycle over again. This process takes place over hundreds of thousands or even millions of years.

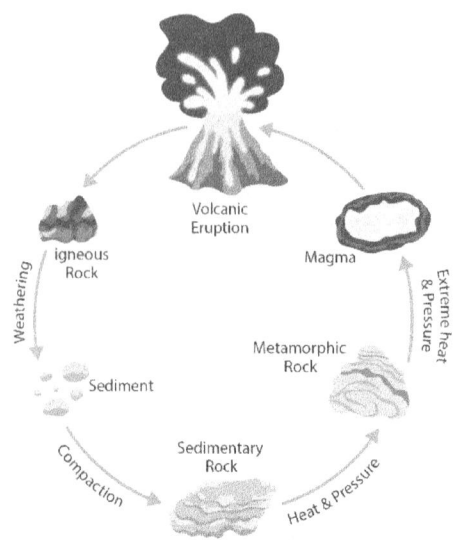

Figure 3.29. The Rock Cycle

The outermost layer of Earth is called the **crust**, a very thin and broken surface layer. Beneath the crust is the **mantle**, a dense layer of rock. The mantle has an upper layer that is cooler and more rigid, and a deep mantle that is hotter and more liquid. Under the mantle is the **core**, which also includes two parts: a liquid outer core and an inner core composed of solid iron. Scientists believe the inner core spins at a rate slightly different from the rest of the planet, which creates Earth's magnetic field.

Figure 3.30. Earth's Layers

The crust and upper layer of the mantle make up the **lithosphere**, the planet's surface layer. Under the lithosphere is a hot, semisolid part of the mantle called the **asthenosphere**. The lithosphere includes **tectonic plates**, which are the broken pieces of Earth's solid outer crust. The tectonic plates float on top of the more liquid asthenosphere that flows very slowly beneath them.

Earth's surface is divided into seven large land masses called **continents**, which are often separated by oceans. Scientists believe that over 200 million years ago the continents were joined together in one giant landmass called Pangaea. Due to **continental drift**, the slow movement of the tectonic plates, the continents gradually shifted to their current positions—and are still moving.

Many geologic features and events are located along the boundaries where Earth's tectonic plates meet. There are three types of plate boundaries: divergent, convergent, and transform:

- A **divergent plate boundary** occurs when tectonic plates are moving away from one another and can form new ridges or ocean basins.

- A **convergent plate boundary** is where two tectonic plates collide and one plate is pushed upward on top of the other, forming mountains, or one is pushed downward, forming a trench.

- A **transform plate boundary** is formed when plates move in opposite directions along a boundary.

Plate tectonics theory explains the creation of landforms as plates move. The theory is supported by evidence such as the fact that earthquakes, volcanoes, and mountains typically occur at the boundaries of moving plates. Mid-ocean ridges caused by seafloor spreading, where magma that rises to the earth's surface causes tectonic plates to move away, is also commonly cited evidence for this theory.

Earthquakes happen along plate boundaries as the tectonic plates crash into each other or scrape together when they move and cause the ground to shake violently. **Volcanoes**, which are vents in the earth's crust that allow molten rock to reach the surface, frequently occur along the edges of tectonic plates. However, they can also occur at hotspots located far from plate boundaries. There are three types of volcanoes: composite, shield, and cinder cone:

- A **composite volcano**, or stratovolcano, is cone-shaped, with steep sides, and is made of layers of solid lava, ash, and rock.

- A **shield volcano** is more dome-shaped, with gently sloping sides, and is made mostly of fluid lava flows.

- A **cinder cone volcano** is a small, steep hill formed by ash and debris surrounding a single lava vent and often has a crater at the top.

Plate tectonics influences organisms in many ways. Shifting plates can cause land to be uplifted or to sink, which can lead to rising sea levels. This can change ecosystems and the organisms that rely on them. Volcanoes can release sulfates and ash into the air, causing problems for organisms in the vicinity. Earthquakes move sediment on both land and the seafloor, which can bury organisms or the plants upon which they feed.

Earthquakes can also be highly dangerous to human populations. Soil type, geology, fault location, and earthquake **magnitude** can all impact the severity of the impact on humans. The magnitude of an earthquake is measured on an instrument called a seismometer. An earthquake with a magnitude of less than 2.5 is minor and usually not even felt, while a magnitude 7.0 or greater earthquake is generally a major event.

> **Check Your Understanding**
>
> How do earthquakes cause changes in the earth's systems?

Though most earthquakes are natural occurrences, human-induced earthquakes such as mining, wastewater disposal, or reservoir impounding have been proven to cause quakes. Thus, one way to prevent earthquakes is to limit these activities. Natural earthquakes cannot be prevented but people can prepare for them by examining fault maps, building structures to withstand most earthquakes, and creating a family or community earthquake response plan.

Paleontology, the study of the history of life on Earth, is sometimes also considered part of geology. Paleontologists study the **rock record**, which retains biological history in the form of **fossils**, the preserved remains and traces of ancient life. Fossils can be used to learn about the evolution of life on the planet, including bacteria, plants, and animals that have gone extinct. Throughout Earth's history, there have been five documented catastrophic events that caused major extinctions. For each mass extinction, there are several theories about the cause but no definitive answers. Theories about what triggered mass extinctions include climate change, ice ages, asteroid and comet impacts, and volcanic activity.

Scientists believe that Earth is about 4.5 billion years old. They have divided Earth's history into stages based on geological or paleontological events that happened during each time period. There are four major time periods: the Precambrian era, the Paleozoic era, the Mesozoic era, and the Cenozoic era:

- The **Precambrian** era is the period from Earth's formation until life began to appear.
- Plants and animals developed during the **Paleozoic** era, but about 95 percent of all life on Earth became extinct at the end of this period.
- The **Mesozoic** era was the age of the dinosaurs, but their extinction by the end of this period is believed to have been caused by a large asteroid that hit the earth.
- The **Cenozoic** era began after the dinosaurs became extinct and is the current time period. Birds, flowering plants, and mammals—including humans—developed during this period.

Practice Questions

21) Which process within the rock cycle creates metamorphic rock?
    A. compaction
    B. heat and pressure
    C. crystallization
    D. weathering

22) Which of the following is NOT a characteristic of a mineral?
    A. naturally occurring
    B. organic
    C. solid
    D. a crystalline structure

23) The magnitude of an earthquake refers to its
    A. power.
    B. energy release.
    C. destructive ability.
    D. depth.

Meteorology

Above the surface of Earth is the mass of gases called the **atmosphere**. The atmosphere includes the troposphere, which is closest to Earth, followed by the stratosphere, mesosphere, and thermosphere. The outermost layer of the atmosphere is the exosphere, which extends to 6,200 miles above Earth's surface. Generally, temperature in the atmosphere decreases with altitude. The **ozone layer**, which captures harmful radiation from the sun, is located in the stratosphere.

> **Helpful Hint**
>
> Between each layer is a boundary where conditions change. This boundary takes the first part of the name of the lower layer followed by the suffix *–pause*. For example, the boundary between the troposphere and stratosphere is called the tropopause.

The humidity, or amount of water vapor in the air, and temperature are two major atmospheric conditions that determine **weather**, the day-to-day changes in atmospheric conditions. The study of weather is known as **meteorology**. A warm front occurs when warm air moves over and replaces a cold air mass, causing the air at the front to feel warmer and more humid. A cold front occurs when cold air moves under and replaces a warm air mass, causing a drop in temperature.

As warm air rises, the water vapor in it condenses around tiny pieces of dust, forming a water droplet or ice crystal. A **cloud** is made up of billions of these tiny water droplets or ice crystals. Clouds are defined by their locations in the sky and their shapes:

- Clouds that appear highest in the sky are called **cirrus clouds**; they are usually thin and wispy and do not produce precipitation.
- **Stratus clouds** are flat, wispy, white or gray clouds found in the lower level of the sky.
- **Cumulus clouds** are tall, puffy clouds that are often dark at the bottom and whiter toward the top.
- Clouds with the prefix *alto–* (altocumulus, altostratus) are located in the middle level of the sky and produce precipitation that does not reach the ground.
- **Nimbus clouds**, such as nimbostratus and cumulonimbus, have a lot of water vapor in them and are likely to produce precipitation.

Weather is also impacted by the world's oceans. Oceans absorb radiation from the sun in tropical locations. As hot ocean waters evaporate, the temperature of the surrounding air increases, forming rain, which then moves to land with wind. In areas further away from the equator, ocean currents bring warm water and rain toward the poles and cold water from the poles back toward the center. This system is somewhat self-regulating and keeps much of the earth at a temperature that is habitable.

Ocean currents are also part of what is known as the **ENSO cycle**, or the **El Niño/Southern Oscillation cycle**. El Niño refers to above-average ocean surface temperatures in the Pacific, which decreases rainfall in the northwestern US and increase rainfall in the southeastern US during the winter months. In contrast, La Niña cycles involve cooler surface temperatures in the Pacific, which make for cooler winter temperatures in the northwest and warmer temperatures in the southeast.

Sometimes, weather turns violent. Tropical cyclones, or **hurricanes**, originate over warm ocean water. Hurricanes have destructive winds of 74 miles per hour or more and create large storm surges—when sea water rises above the normal tide level—that can cause extensive damage along coastlines. Hurricanes, typhoons, and cyclones are all the same type of storm; they just have different names based on where the storm is located. Hurricanes originate in the Atlantic or Eastern Pacific Ocean, typhoons in the Western Pacific Ocean, and cyclones in the Indian Ocean. **Tornadoes** occur when unstable warm and cold air masses collide and a rotation is created by fast-moving winds.

Severe weather has many unfortunate impacts, but technological tools can help predict such events so that people can prepare. **Doppler radar**, which detects wind strength, direction, and precipitation, is one such tool. Satellite imagery also helps meteorologists study and predict weather. **Weather balloons**, or radiosondes, collect data from the upper stratosphere. **Automated surface-observing systems** (ASOS) also monitor and track weather on Earth's surface. Computers help analyze all of this data and make predictions based on mathematical models.

The long-term weather conditions in a geographic location are called **climate**. A **climate zone** is a large area that experiences similar average temperature and precipitation. The three major climate zones, based on temperature, are the polar, temperate, and tropical zones. Each climate zone is divided into subclimates that have unique characteristics. The tropical climate zone (warm temperatures) can be divided into tropical wet, tropical wet and dry, semiarid, and arid. The temperate climate zones (moderate temperatures) include Mediterranean, humid subtropical, marine West Coast, humid continental, and subarctic. The polar climate zones (cold temperatures) include tundra, highlands, nonpermanent ice, and ice cap. Polar climates are cold and experience prolonged, dark winters due to the tilt of Earth's axis.

Practice Questions

24) Which characteristic generally increases as altitude increases in the troposphere?
    A. temperature
    B. pressure
    C. density
    D. none of the above

25) Which layer of the atmosphere absorbs harmful ultraviolet radiation from the sun?
    A. the mesosphere
    B. the stratosphere
    C. the troposphere
    D. the thermosphere

Earth's Water

Earth's surface includes many bodies of water that together form the **hydrosphere**; the study of water on Earth is called **hydrology**. The hydrosphere is distinct but interconnected with other Earth systems, like the **atmosphere** (the air or blanket of gases that surrounds Earth), **biosphere** (life on Earth), and **lithosphere** (ground). These spheres work together in myriad ways. For example, animals drink water on the ground, which connects hydrosphere, lithosphere, and biosphere.

The largest bodies in the hydrosphere are salt water **oceans**. There are five oceans: the Arctic, Atlantic, Indian, Pacific, and Southern. Together, the oceans account for 71 percent of Earth's surface and 97 percent of Earth's water.

Oceans are subject to **tides**, cyclic rising and falling water levels at shorelines, which are the result of the gravitational pull of the moon and sun. **Currents** are movements of the ocean water caused by differences in salt content or temperature and winds. **Waves** carry energy through the water and are caused by wind blowing across the surface of the ocean. Tides shape coastal topography as they cause erosion, which may create new landforms like platforms or notches.

Other bodies of water include **lakes**, usually fresh water, and **seas**, mainly salt water. Rain that falls on the land flows into **rivers** and **streams**, which are moving bodies of water that flow into lakes, seas, and oceans. The areas where rivers and streams meet salt water are called **estuaries**. Estuaries often contain brackish water, or the mix between salt and fresh water; estuaries often boast ecosystems full of unique organisms specially adapted to this salinity.

When all the rain that falls on a given area of land flows into a single body of water, that land area is called a **watershed** or **drainage basin**. The earth also contains **groundwater**, or water that is stored underground in rock formations called **aquifers**. Groundwater is key to the exchange of water between the land and subsurface. Water from the surface moves into the subsurface and fills aquifers. The water stored in these aquifers eventually makes its way back to the surface.

Much of Earth's water is stored as ice. The North and South Poles are usually covered in large sheets of ice called **polar ice**. **Glaciers** are large masses of ice and snow that move. Over long periods of time, they scour Earth's surface, creating features such as lakes and valleys. Large chunks of ice that break off from glaciers are called **icebergs**.

The **water cycle** is the circulation of water throughout the earth's surface, atmosphere, and hydrosphere. Water on the earth's surface **evaporates**, or changes from a liquid to a gas, and becomes water vapor. Water vapor in the air then comes together to form **clouds**. When it cools, this water vapor condenses into a liquid and falls from the sky as **precipitation**, which includes rain, sleet, snow, and hail. Precipitation replenishes groundwater and the water found in features such as lakes and rivers, starting the cycle over again.

Practice Question

26) The rhythmic movements of water caused by the gravitational pull of the moon and sun are called what?
   A. tides
   B. currents
   C. glaciers
   D. waves

Science Skills and Processes

Scientific Inquiry

Investigation, or **inquiry-based** science, provides the strongest foundation for scientific thinking. Inquiry-based science is guided by the **scientific method**, which provides a framework for observing, measuring, and drawing conclusions about the world.

The first step in the scientific method is **observation**. From observations, scientists develop questions and research the currently available information about a particular topic. This research helps them formulate a reasonable and testable explanation for their observations, a statement known as a **hypothesis**. Scientists then design and conduct an **experiment** in which they collect data that will demonstrate whether their hypothesis is false or not. It is important to note that a hypothesis can never be proven true—it can be confirmed as false, or enough data can be collected to *infer* that it is true. In order for data to support a hypothesis, it must be consistent and reproducible.

> **Helpful Hint**
>
> The phrase, "**Q**ueen **R**achel **h**opes **e**very **c**oward **g**ains **c**ourage" can help students remember the scientific method: **q**uestion, **r**esearch, **h**ypothesis, **e**xperiment, **c**ollect data, **g**raph/analyze data, **c**onclusion.

When scientists have repeatedly tested a hypothesis, and that hypothesis has become widely accepted, it becomes known as a **theory**. Theories provide a widely accepted explanation for a natural phenomenon. The theory of evolution, for example, states that natural selection is the mechanism that led to the current diversity of species found on Earth. A scientific **law** is a description of a natural phenomenon. However, unlike a theory, it does not explain how something happens. For example, Newton's law of universal gravitation states that the gravitational force between two objects depends on their distance and mass.

> **Consider This**
>
> What are the limitations of adhering rigidly to the scientific method?

Science, while grounded in observation and data, is not perfect, and scientific knowledge is always growing and changing. Scientists must be able to react to new observations and adjust their hypotheses as needed to address new evidence. By constantly observing, asking questions, and rigorously testing hypotheses, scientists are able to slowly build on the collective pool of scientific knowledge.

Practice Questions

27) Which step should students take BEFORE making a hypothesis in a scientific experiment?
    A. interpret data
    B. make a graph
    C. research
    D. do the experiment

28) Evolution is an example of which of the following?
    A. theory
    B. law
    C. hypothesis
    D. fact

Experimental Design

Scientists use a rigorous set of rules to design experiments. The protocols of **experimental design** are meant to ensure that scientists are actually testing what they set out to test. A well-designed experiment will measure the impact of a single factor on a system, thus allowing the experimenter to draw conclusions about that factor. Such an experiment typically begins with a **testable question**, such as *Which type of fertilizer has the greatest effect on plant growth?* This question is testable because it can be answered via scientific investigation.

Every experiment includes variables, which are the factors or treatments that may affect the outcome of the experiment. **Independent variables** (also called controlled variables or controlled parameters) are controlled by the experimenter. They are usually the factors that the experimenter has hypothesized will have an effect on the system. Often, a design will include a treatment group and a **control group**, which does not receive the treatment. The **dependent variables** are factors that are influenced by the independent variable.

For example, in an experiment investigating which type of fertilizer has the greatest effect on plant growth, the independent variable is the type of fertilizer used. The scientist is controlling, or manipulating, the type of fertilizer. The dependent variable is plant growth because the amount of plant growth depends on the type of fertilizer. The type of plant, the amount of water, and the amount of sunlight the plants receive are controls because those variables of the experiment are kept the same for each plant.

When designing an experiment, scientists must identify possible sources of **experimental error**. These can be **confounding variables**, which are factors that act much like the independent variable and thus can make it appear that the independent variable has a greater effect than it actually does. The design may also include unknown variables that are not controlled by the scientists. Finally, scientists must be aware of human error, particularly in collecting data and making observations, and of possible equipment errors.

Extraneous, or confounding variables, and human error contribute to the overall **accuracy** of results. Accuracy refers to how close the results or measurements are to known values. So, if the experiment sought to determine at what temperature water freezes into ice and determined the temperature was 40 degrees Fahrenheit, that experiment would lack accuracy. Similar to accuracy is **replicability**, which refers to the ability of other researchers to get similar results under the same conditions. Quality scientific research is both accurate and replicable.

During the experiment, scientists collect data, which must then be analyzed and presented appropriately. This can mean running a statistical analysis on the data (e.g., finding the mean) or putting the data in graph form. An analysis allows scientists to see trends in the data and determine if those trends are statistically significant. From the data and its analysis, scientists can draw a **conclusion** about the experiment.

Scientists also sometimes use **models** in their research. These models are a simplified representation of a system. For example, a mathematical equation that describes fluctuations in a population might be used to test how a certain variable is likely to affect that population. Or scientists might use a greenhouse to model a particular ecosystem so they can more closely control the variables in the environment.

Scientists must describe their data in a way that others can understand but must be cognizant of various factors that may impact results and color the data. **Scale** is one important factor to consider. For example, if the researcher only uses two different fertilizers in the plant experiment, the results may not be **generalizable**, or applicable to a broader population (i.e. all fertilizers). Similarly, the **proportion**, or ratio, of fertilizer to water may change results.

Furthermore, scientists cannot always establish a **cause-and-effect** relationship as the result of a study or experiment. Often results are reported as **correlations** versus causations, meaning that if there is a strong positive correlation between two variables (e.g.one type of fertilizer is correlated with more plant growth), then *maybe* the variable (fertilizer type) was the cause, but maybe not. Other factors, like confounding variables such as soil type and individual plant health, may be responsible for the difference in plant growth. Sometimes correlations are most appropriate when the relationship between variables is unclear. For example, though scientists know that low vitamin D levels are linked with depression, it is not known if less vitamin D causes depression or if depression decreases vitamin D levels.

> **Check Your Understanding**
>
> How could the difference between causation and correlation be demonstrated to young students?

Scientists often present research results using charts and graphs. (See Chapter 4 for information on the use of data displays). Like other phases of the process of scientific inquiry, care should be taken in how data is represented in charts and graphs. The scale of the axes, the type of graphic chosen, and even the units used can all have a tremendous impact on data presentation and can make data displays effective or misleading.

Practice Question

29) Which of the following is the variable in a scientific investigation that is manipulated by the researcher in order to test the hypothesis?
   A. control
   B. experimental
   C. dependent
   D. hypothetical

Equipment and Safety Procedures

When choosing and setting up a lab, teachers need to remember that they are liable for any accidents or hazardous incidents that occur under their supervision. For many classrooms, **standard laboratory equipment** includes flat top tables with stools so students can view experiments from several angles.

Safety gear, microscopes, beakers, **measurement tools**, test tubes, eyedroppers, weights, magnets, and timers should be some of the available equipment. Measurement tools for length include metric rulers and tape measures. Beakers and graduated cylinders are used to measure volume. Balance scales measure mass.

Standard safety equipment like goggles, aprons, protective gloves, and a fire extinguisher must be available. In addition to using standard safety equipment, students should be instructed on appropriate **apparel**. For example, long hair should be tied back and loose clothing and jewelry should be secured. Closed-toe shoes should be worn.

Student **behavior** guidelines are important, but they take on even more significance when students are working in potentially dangerous situations. Adults should model safety practices, such as wearing goggles. Parents and students should be required to sign a document that outlines safety procedures. Students should be warned about potential dangers as they arise in each experiment. Students must be diligently supervised, and those who do not comply with safety standards should be removed from the lab. At the end of an experiment, students must know how to properly clean up equipment and dispose of waste.

Emergency procedures should include proactively monitoring students and equipment and wearing safety gear. Plans for emergency first aid for electric shock, poisoning, burns, fire, evacuations, spills, and animal bites should be established.

Practice Question

30) Which tool measures the volume of an object?
   A. thermometer
   B. graduated cylinder
   C. balance
   D. barometer

Answer Key

1) C: An atom with 5 electrons and 12 protons has a total charge of –5e + 12e = +7e.

2) C: Combustion is a chemical reaction that produces carbon dioxide and water. Burning lamp oil (fuel) is combustion.

3) B: Gas is the state of matter in which atomic particles are most loosely packed and the greatest amount of space exists among atoms.

4) D: Acceleration is the rate at which velocity changes.

5) A: Tension is the force that results from objects being pulled or hung.

6) D: A compressed spring is an example of elastic potential energy.

7) A: Conduction is the transfer of heat from the contact of a solid or liquid to another solid or liquid.

8) B: Wavelength is the length of each cycle of the wave, which can be found by measuring between crests.

9) C: The two charges are both negative, so they will repel each other and move apart.

10) D: An enzyme is a protein that catalyzes a reaction.

11) B: The nucleus is the organelle that carries the DNA of eukaryotic organisms.

12) C: A plant cell is enveloped by a cell wall, but animal cells do not possess cell walls.

13) D: The mechanism of natural selection is rooted in the idea that there is variation in inherited traits among a population of organisms and that there is differential reproduction as a result.

14) B: Oxygen intake and carbon dioxide disposal are the primary functions of the respiratory system.

15) B: The tongue is the muscle that helps break apart food, mix it with saliva, and direct it toward the esophagus.

16) D: The roots primarily exist to continually grow towards water and absorb it and other nutrients.

17) D: The attractive nature of the flower encourages animals to pollinate the plant.

18) C: Cows eat plants but do not eat other animals; therefore, cows are primary consumers.

19) D: The savanna is tropical grassland with nutrient-poor soil.

20) D: When the moon moves between Earth and the sun, a solar eclipse occurs, blocking sunlight from the planet.

21) B: Heat and pressure change the composition of sedimentary rock to create metamorphic rock.

22) B: A mineral is inorganic; only a rock may be composed of organic material.

23) B: The magnitude of an earthquake refers to the energy released during the earthquake.

24) D: Temperature, pressure, and density all decrease as altitude increases.

25) B: The stratosphere contains a sublayer called the ozone layer, which absorbs harmful ultraviolet radiation from the sun.

26) A: Tides, the rise and fall of the ocean level at shorelines, are caused by the moon and sun.

27) C: Students (and scientists) need to conduct research before making a reasonable and testable hypothesis.

28) A: Evolution is a scientific theory, which is a set of explanatory ideas substantiated by evidence through repeated experiments and observations.

29) B: Experimental variables, also known as independent variables, are the variables that are changed by the scientist.

30) B: A graduated cylinder measures volume.

4. Math

Number Sense

Number Theory

A basic foundation in numeracy is vital for establishing the groundwork for understanding advanced mathematical concepts. Students begin working with **natural numbers**, which are used when counting (e.g., 1, 2, 3). Once a basic understanding of natural numbers is achieved, more advanced concepts, such as whole numbers and integers, can be introduced. **Whole numbers** are similar to natural numbers, except that whole numbers include zero. **Fractions** are parts of whole numbers. Fractions can be expressed as such (e.g., 1/2) or as a **percent** (i.e., a part out of 100, such as 50%). Mixed numbers contain both numbers and fractions, such as $3\frac{1}{4}$. **Integers** are positive or negative whole numbers—not fractions or decimals.

> **Check Your Understanding**
>
> What are some examples of concrete objects that could be used to teach numeracy in the classroom?

Rational numbers are numbers that can be made by dividing two integers. Rational numbers must be expressed as a terminating or a repeating decimal, such as 0.125 or $0.\underline{66}$. Pi (π) would not be a rational number because it does not terminate or repeat (π = 3.14159265…); instead, pi goes on forever with no repeating pattern. Integers are rational numbers because they can be written as a fraction with a denominator of 1.

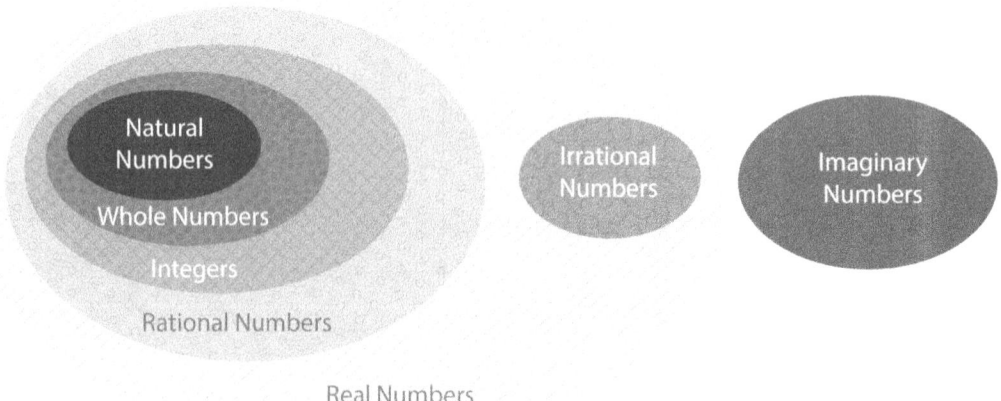

Figure 4.1. Types of Numbers

The set of rational and irrational numbers make up the set of **real numbers**. Real numbers can be represented on a **number line**, where 0 is in the middle, positive numbers are to the right, and negative numbers are to the left. An example of a number line is shown in Figure 4.2; remember that fractions and decimals are between the integers.

Figure 4.2. Number Line

The **opposite** of a number is the negative version of that number (or positive version if the number is negative). Remember that the distance between a number and 0 on the number line is the same as the distance between the opposite of that number and 0.

As opposed to real numbers, **imaginary numbers** are not real but rather are represented by the imaginary unit i. Imaginary numbers, when squared, will produce a negative result. There are many rules for imaginary numbers, including the following:

- $i = \sqrt{-1}$
- $i^2 = -1$

Negative numbers with larger opposites are actually smaller than negative numbers with smaller opposites. For example:

$$-40 < -2.4 < 0 < .1 < 20$$

The **absolute value** (| |) of a number is the positive value of a number or its opposite; for example, |−3| = 3 and |3| = 3.

Every whole number (except 1) is either a prime number or a composite number. A **prime number** is a natural number greater than 1 that can be divided evenly by only 1 and itself. For example, 7 is a prime number because it can only be divided by the numbers 1 and 7.

On the other hand, a **composite number** is a natural number greater than 1 that can be evenly divided by at least one other number besides 1 and itself. For example, 6 is a composite number because it can be divided by 1, 2, 3, and 6.

Practice Questions

1) To which of the following number sets does 3 NOT belong?
   A. irrational
   B. rational
   C. whole
   D. integer

2) Classify the number $\frac{13}{14}$.
   A. irrational
   B. imaginary
   C. rational
   D. integer

4. Math

Place Value

While historically some civilizations have used other numbering systems, today most of the world uses the base-10 system. In the **base-10** system, each **digit** (the numeric symbols 0 – 9) in a number is worth ten times as much as the number to the right of it (see Table 4.1.).

Table 4.1. Place Value Chart									
1,000,000	100,000	10,000	1,000	100	10	1	•	1/10	1/100
10^6	10^5	10^4	10^3	10^2	10^1	10^0		10^{-1}	10^{-2}
millions	hundred thousands	ten thousands	Thousands	hundreds	tens	ones	decimal	tenths	Hundredth

For example, in the number 321, each digit has a different value based on its location. This is called **place value.** Knowing the place value of each digit allows students to write a number in expanded form. **Expanded form** is breaking up a number by the value of each digit. For example, the expanded form of 321 is written as 300 + 20 + 1.

Check Your Understanding

How does learning expanded notation deepen a student's understanding of the concept of a number?

Practice Question

3) Which digit is in the hundredths place when 1.3208 is divided by 5.2?
   A. 0
   B. 4
   C. 5
   D. 8

Operations with Positive and Negative Numbers

When adding or subtracting negative numbers, look at a number line. When adding two numbers, whether they are positive or negative, count to the right; when subtracting, count to the left. Note that adding a negative value is the same as subtracting. Subtracting a negative value is the same as adding.

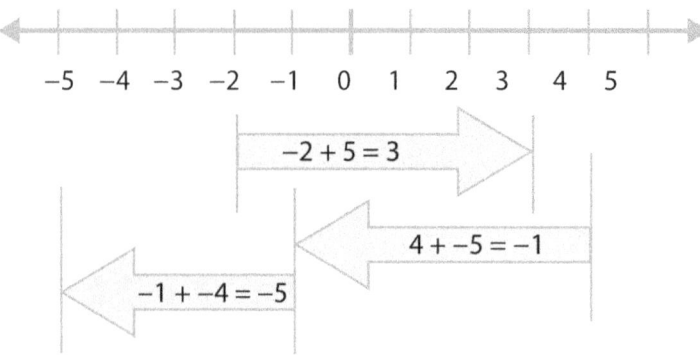

Figure 4.3. Adding Positive and Negative Numbers

Helpful Hint	Multiplying and dividing with negative and positive numbers is somewhat easier. Multiplying two numbers with the same sign gives a positive result, and multiplying two numbers with different signs gives a negative result. The same rules apply to division.
Subtracting a negative number is the same as adding a positive number: $5 - (-10) = 5 + (+10)$	

4.2. Operations with Positive and Negative Numbers

Addition and Subtraction	Multiplication and Division
Positive + Positive = Positive $4 + 5 = 9$	Positive × Positive = Positive $5 \times 3 = 15$
Negative + Negative = Negative $-4 + -5 = -9$ $-4 - 5 = -9$	Negative × Negative = Positive $-6 \times -5 = 30$
Negative + Positive = Depends When adding a positive number and negative number, subtract the absolute values of the two numbers (larger – smaller absolute values) and make the sign the same sign of the largest absolute value of the numbers. $-15 + 9 = -6$	Negative × Positive = Negative $-5 \times 4 = -20$ $3 \times -6 = -18$

Practice Question

4) Which of the following has the greatest value?
    A. $-4(3)(-2)$
    B. $-16 - 17 + 31$
    C. $18 - 15 + 27$
    D. $-20 + 10 + 10$

Algorithms

An **algorithm** is a set of steps to follow when performing mathematical operations. Even the simplest of computations has an algorithm. Algorithms can be thought of as **standard** or **nonstandard**. Standard algorithms are the most typical ways of solving problems, such as "carrying" for addition or "borrowing" for subtraction. Nonstandard, or alternative, algorithms were popularized in the text *Everyday Mathematics* and include the area or box method of multiplication, the grid or array method, partial products method and partial sums algorithm. Nonstandard algorithms may be easier for some students to learn or understand.

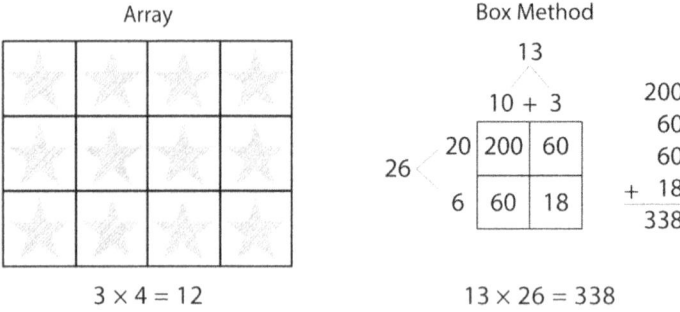

Figure 4.4. Teaching Multiplication

As problems become more complicated, there are rules, or properties, that guide the problem-solver. These are described in Table 4.2.

Table 4.2. Mathematical Properties

Name	Description	Applies to	Example
Commutative property	The order of the operation does not matter.	addition	$a + b = b + a$
		multiplication	$ab = ba$
Associative property	Grouping of numbers does not matter.	addition	$(a + b) + c = a + (b + c)$
		multiplication	$(a \times b) \times c = a \times (b \times c)$
Distributive property	Multiply a value by all the values inside brackets, and then add.	multiplication	$a(b + c) = ab + ac$
Identity property	Adding zero or multiplying by one will not change the original value.	addition	$a + 0 = a$
		multiplication	$a \times 1 = a$
Zero property	Multiplying any value by zero yields a result of zero.	multiplication	$a \times 0 = 0$

When solving a multi-step equation, the **order of operations** must be used to get the correct answer. Generally speaking, the problem should be worked in the following order: (1) parentheses and brackets, (2) exponents and square roots, (3) multiplication and division, and (4) addition and subtraction. The acronym *PEMDAS*, which stands for "**P**lease **e**xcuse **m**y **d**ear **A**unt **S**ally," can be used to remember the order of operations:

P – parentheses

E – exponents

M – multiplication

D – division

A – addition

S – subtraction

The steps "Multiplication–Division" and "Addition–Subtraction" go in order from left to right. In other words, divide before multiplying if the division problem is on the left. For example, the expression $(3^2 - 2)^2 + (4)5^3$ is simplified using the following steps:

1. Parentheses: Because the parentheses in this problem contain two operations (exponents and subtraction), use the order of operations within the parentheses. (Exponents come before subtraction.)

$$(3^2 - 2)^2 + (4)5^3 = (9 - 2)^2 + (4)5^3 = (7)^2 + (4)5^3$$

2. Exponents:

$$(7)^2 + (4)5^3 = 49 + (4)125$$

3. Multiplication and division:

$$49 + (4)125 = 49 + 500$$

4. Addition and subtraction:

$$49 + 500 = 549$$

Practice Questions

5) Which expression is equivalent to dividing 400 by 16?
   A. 2(200 – 8)
   B. (400 ÷ 4) ÷ 12
   C. (216 ÷ 8) + (184 ÷ 8)
   D. (216 ÷ 16) + (184 ÷ 16)

6) Which number is equal to $(5^2 + 1)^2 + 3^3$?
   A. 703
   B. 694
   C. 30
   D. 53

Operations with Fractions and Decimals

Fractions use two numbers separated by a horizontal bar to show as parts of a whole. Fractions include a **numerator** (the number on the top of a fraction) and a **denominator** (the number on the bottom of a fraction). The denominator is the "whole," and the numerator is the "part." For example, if there are 12 students on the chess team, and 5 of the students are selected to represent the school in a tournament, the fraction of the chess team going to the tournament is $\frac{5}{12}$.

If the numerator of a fraction is 1, it is called a **unit fraction**. In the chess team example, $\frac{1}{12}$ is the unit fraction. Five $\frac{1}{12}$ units represent the part of the team that is going to the tournament. As the "whole" gets larger, one "part" becomes smaller and smaller. Think of cutting a cake: cutting 8 slices creates smaller slices than cutting the same cake into 4 slices. So, as the denominator of unit fractions increases, the value of the fraction itself decreases.

The same basic operations that can be performed with whole numbers can also be performed on fractions, with a few modifications. When adding and subtracting fractions, each fraction must have a **common denominator**. The operation is performed in the numerator, and the denominator remains

4. Math

the same. For example, if 3/12 of the chess team described above is eliminated in the second round of the tournament, the total fraction of the team remaining will be $\frac{5}{12} - \frac{3}{12} = \frac{5-3}{12} = \frac{2}{12}$.

In 2/12, both the numerator and the denominator are divisible by 2, meaning the fraction is not in its simplest form. To simplify the fraction, reduce the numerator and denominator by dividing both by the same value: $\frac{2}{12} = \frac{2 \div 2}{12 \div 2} = \frac{1}{6}$.

If the fractions to be added or subtracted do not have a common denominator, the **least common multiple** of the denominators (also known as the **least common denominator**) must be found. In the operation $\frac{2}{3} - \frac{1}{2}$, the common denominator will be a **multiple** of both 3 and 2. Multiples are found by multiplying the denominator by whole numbers until a common multiple is found:

- multiples of 3 are **3** (3 × 1), **6** (3 × 2), **9** (3 × 3), ...
- multiples of 2 are **2** (2 × 1), **4** (2 × 2), **6** (2 × 3), ...

Since 6 is the smallest multiple of both 3 and 2, it is the least common multiple and can be used as the common denominator. Both the numerator and denominator of each fraction should be multiplied by the appropriate whole number: $\frac{2}{3}\left(\frac{2}{2}\right) - \frac{1}{2}\left(\frac{3}{3}\right) = \frac{4}{6} - \frac{3}{6} = \frac{1}{6}$.

When multiplying fractions, simply multiply each numerator together and each denominator together. To divide two fractions, invert the second fraction (swap the numerator and denominator) then multiply normally. Note that multiplying fractions creates a value smaller than either original value:

- $\frac{5}{6} \times \frac{2}{3} = \frac{10}{18} = \frac{5}{9}$
- $\frac{5}{6} \div \frac{2}{3} = \frac{5}{6} \times \frac{3}{2} = \frac{15}{12} = \frac{5}{4}$

Testing Tip

The acronym **SMURF** is used for dividing fractions: **s**ame, **m**ultiply, **u**pside down, **r**ename, and **f**raction.

Another way to represent parts of a whole is by using decimals. A **decimal** is any real number in the base-10 system, but it often refers to numbers with digits to the right of the decimal point.

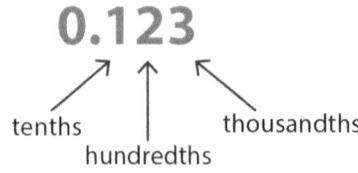

Figure 4.5. Decimals and Place Value

Fractions can be converted to decimals by simply dividing the denominator by the numerator. To convert a decimal to a fraction, place the numbers to the right of the decimal over the appropriate base-10 power and simplify the fraction. To convert a decimal to a percentage, multiply the decimal by

100, or move the decimal point two digits to the right. To convert a percentage to a decimal, divide by 100, or move the decimal point two digits to the left:

- $\frac{1}{2} = 1 \div 2 = 0.5$

- $0.375 = \frac{375}{1,000} = \frac{3}{8}$

- $0.375 = 37.5\%$

- $50\% = 0.50 = 0.5$

When working with fractions and decimals, skills like **rounding** and **estimation** can be useful to help students evaluate the accuracy of their answers. Rounding refers to simplification of a number to a certain place value. For example, the number 36.83 could be rounded to the nearest tenths place to become 36.8, rounded to the nearest ones place to become 37, or rounded to the nearest tens place to become 40.

Estimation is similar to rounding but refers to a prediction of or calculation of a rough answer. For example, if the problem is 84 + 23, a student might estimate that 80 + 20 = 100, so the answer will be close to 100. If the student comes up with an answer of 1,234, for example, she will know that there is a mistake in the calculation.

Practice Questions

7) Simplify: $\left(1\frac{1}{2}\right)\left(2\frac{2}{3}\right) \div 1\frac{1}{4}$

  A. $3\frac{1}{12}$

  B. $3\frac{1}{5}$

  C. 4

  D. 5

8) Allison used $2\frac{1}{2}$ cups of flour to make a cake and $\frac{3}{4}$ of a cup of flour to make a pie. If she started with 4 cups of flour, how many cups of flour does she have left?

  A. $\frac{3}{4}$

  B. 1

  C. $\frac{5}{2}$

  D. $\frac{13}{4}$

Scientific Notation

Scientific notation is a notation that can be used with very small and very large numbers that are difficult to work with. It is relatively easy to go back and forth between standard notation (i.e., "regular") numbers and scientific notation numbers, which are numbers that are multiplied by powers of 10.

For scientific notation, use a number between 1 and 10 (not including 10; for example, 9.99 would work) and multiply it by 10 raised to a number. To turn a number greater than 10 into scientific notation, move the decimal point to the left and use a positive exponent. To turn a number less than 1 into scientific notation, move the decimal point to the right and use a negative exponent. Count left or right either from the decimal point—if there is one—or from the end of the number (at the right), if there is not one.

Helpful Hint

When converting a decimal to scientific notation, if the number between 1 and 10 is larger than the number you started with, the power of 10 will be negative. If the number between 1 and 10 is smaller than the number you started with, the power of 10 will be positive.

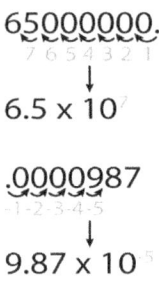

Figure 4.7. Scientific Notation

Scientific notation is used by simplifying numbers with numbers between 1 and 10. These numbers are then multiplied by **10** raised to an exponent. For example, the number 870,000,000, can be abbreviated to 8.7×10^8. Also, $0.000045 = 4.5 \times 10^{-5}$.

Table 4.3. Scientific Notation

Math	Explanation
$8,500 = 8.5 \times 10^3$	Since 8.5 is between 1 and 10; to go from a *larger number to smaller number*, move the decimal to the left 3 places, and use a *positive exponent* (3).
$0.0012 = 1.2 \times 10^{-3}$	Since 1.2 is between 1 and 10; to go from a *smaller number to larger number*, move the decimal to the right 3 places, and use a *negative exponent* (–3).
$3.4 \times 10^5 = 340,000$	Because of the *positive exponent*, move the decimal 5 places *to the right* (adding zeros) to end up with a larger number.
$6.6 \times 10^{-4} = 0.00066$	Because of the *negative exponent*, move the decimal 4 places *to the left* (adding zeros from the decimal point) to end up with a *smaller number*.

Practice Question

9) Which of the following is the correct scientific notation for the number 34,500,000?
   A. 3.45×10^{-7}
   B. 3.45×10^{6}
   C. 34.5×10^{6}
   D. 3.45×10^{7}

Algebraic Thinking

Algebraic Expressions

Algebraic expressions contain numbers, variables, and at least one mathematical operation. Each group of numbers and variables in an expression is called a **term** (e.g., 3x or 16y). A **binomial** is an algebraic expression with two terms (e.g., 3x + 16y), a **trinomial** has three terms, and a **polynomial** has more than three terms. Algebraic expressions can be evaluated for a specific value by plugging that value into the expression and simplifying.

To add or subtract linear algebraic expressions, add the variables and numbers (constants) separately. For example, $(5x - 3) + (3x - 2) = (5x + 3x) + (-3 - 2) = 8x - 5$. Now subtract, making sure that the minus sign is distributed through the parentheses, and remember that two negatives in a row is the same as a positive:

$$(13x - 5y + 2) - (8x - y - 3) = (13x - 8x) + (-5y - -y) + (2 - -3)$$
$$= (13x - 8x) + (-5y + y) + (2 + 3) = 5x - 4y + 5$$

To **evaluate** an algebraic expression for a certain value, simply "plug in" that value into the variable wherever it appears. For example, evaluate $3x + 5y - z^2 + x^2$ when $x = 2, y = -4,$ and $z = -1$:

$$3(2) + 5(-4) - (-1)^2 + 2^2 = 6 - 20 - 1 + 4 = -11$$

> **Helpful Hint**
>
> To multiply binomials, use the acronym **FOIL**: **f**irst, **o**uter, **i**nner, **l**ast. For example, $(a + b)(c + d) = ac + ad + bc + bd$.

Simplifying expressions may require distributing and factoring, which are opposite processes based on the distributive property. These are ways to create **equivalent expressions**, which are algebraic expressions that are equal to one another but expressed in a different format.

To **distribute**, multiply the term outside the parentheses by each term inside the parentheses. For each term, coefficients are multiplied, and exponents are added (following the rules of exponents):

> **Helpful Hint**
>
> You can check your factoring by redistributing the term outside the parentheses.

$$2x(3x_2 + 7) = 6x_3 + 14x$$

Factoring is the reverse process: taking a polynomial and writing it as a product of two or more factors. The first step in factoring a polynomial is always to "undistribute," or factor out, the greatest common factor (GCF) among the terms. The remaining terms are placed in parentheses:

$$14a_2 + 7a = 7a(2a + 1)$$

To multiply **binomials** (expressions with two terms), remember the FOIL acronym: <u>f</u>irst, <u>o</u>uter, <u>i</u>nner, and <u>l</u>ast. Multiple the first term in each expression, the outer terms, the inner terms, and the last term in each expression. Then simplify the expression:

$$(2x + 3)(x - 4)$$
$$= (2x)(x) + (2x)(-4) + (3)(x) + 3(-4)$$
$$= 2x^2 - 8x + 3x - 12$$
$$= 2x^2 - 5x - 12$$

Practice Questions

10) If $x = 5$, what is the value of the algebraic expression $2x - x$?
   A. 5
   B. 10
   C. 15
   D. 20

11) $(3x + 2)2 =$
   A. $9x2 + 4$
   B. $9x2 + 6x + 4$
   C. $9x2 + 10x + 4$
   D. $9x2 + 12x + 4$

Linear Equations

In an **equation**, two expressions are joined by an equal sign, which indicates that the two expressions are equal to each other. The two sides of an equation act like a balanced scale: operations can be performed on equations as long as the same operation is performed on both sides to maintain the balance.

This property can be used to solve the equation by performing operations that isolate the variable on one side. For example, the equation $4x + 12 = 2x + 48$ can be solved for x using the following steps:

1. Subtract 12 from both sides of the equation:

$$(4x + 12) - 12 = (2x + 48) - 12 \rightarrow 4x = 2x + 36$$

2. Subtract 2x from both sides of the equation:

$$(4x) - 2x = (2x + 36) - 2x \rightarrow 2x = 36$$

3. Divide both sides by 2:

$$\frac{2x}{2} = \frac{36}{2} \rightarrow x = 18$$

Linear equations follow a specific pattern that results in a straight line when graphed. The most common way to write a linear equation is **slope-intercept form**, $y = mx + b$. In this equation, b is the y-intercept, which is the point where the line crosses the y-axis, or where x equals zero. Slope is

> **Helpful Hint**
>
> **Linear** equations with the same slope are parallel. When two slopes are reciprocal negatives (such as 2 and $-\frac{1}{2}$), the lines are perpendicular.

represented by the letter *m* and describes how steep the line is. Slope is often described as "rise over run" because it is calculated as the difference in *y*-values (rise) over the difference in *x*-values (run):

$$m = \frac{y_2 - y_1}{x_2 - x_1}$$

A **coordinate plane** is a plane containing the *x*- and *y*-axes. The **x-axis** is the horizontal line on a graph, where *y* = 0. The **y-axis** is the vertical line on a graph, where *x* = 0.

The *x*-axis and *y*-axis intersect to create four **quadrants**. The first quadrant is in the upper right, and the other quadrants are labeled counterclockwise using the Roman numerals I, II, III, and IV. **Points**, or locations, on the graph are written as **ordered pairs**, (*x*, *y*), with the point (0, 0) called the **origin**. Points are plotted by counting over *x* places from the origin horizontally and *y* places from the origin vertically.

To graph a linear equation, identify the *y*-intercept and place that point on the *y*-axis. Then, starting at the *y*-intercept, use the slope to go "up and over" and place the next point. The numerator of the slope is the number of units to go up (or down if the slope is negative). The denominator of the slope is the number of units to go right. Repeat the process to plot additional points. These points can then be connected to draw the line.

To find the equation of a line, identify the *y*-intercept, if possible, on the graph and use two easily identifiable points to find the slope.

Another way to express a linear equation is in **standard form**: *Ax* + *By* = *C*. To graph such an equation, it can be converted to slope-intercept form, or the slope and intercepts can be found from the standard form:

- $m = -\frac{A}{B}$
- x-intercept = $\frac{C}{A}$
- y-intercept = $\frac{C}{B}$

> **Helpful Hint**
>
> The **point-slope equation** can be used to find the equation of a line using the slope and one point (x_1, y_1): $y - y_1 = m(x - x_1)$.

It is easy to find the *x*- and *y*-intercepts from this form. To find the *x*-intercept, simply set *y* = 0 and solve for *x*. Similarly, to find the *y*-intercept, set *x* = 0 and solve for *y*. Once these two points are known, a line can be drawn through them.

Systems of equations are sets of equations that include two or more variables. These systems can only be solved when there are at least as many equations as there are variables. The solution to the system is the set of values for each variable that satisfies every equation in the system. Graphically, this will be the values where lines intersect:

- If the lines intersect at one point, there is **one solution**.
- If the lines are parallel (hence, they do not intersect), the system will have **no solution**.
    - If the lines are multiples of each other, meaning they share all coordinates, then the system has **an infinite number of solutions** because every point on the line is a solution.

There are three common methods for solving systems of equations: graphing, substitution, and elimination. To solve by graphing, rewrite each equation in slope-intercept form and graph each line individually. The graph will show if the system of equations has one solution, no solution, or infinitely many solutions.

To perform **substitution**, solve one equation for one variable and then substitute the resulting expression for that variable into the second equation and solve for the variable:

Solve the system of equations:
$$2x - 4y = 28$$
$$4x - 12y = 36$$

Solve one equation for one variable:
$$2x - 4y = 28$$
$$x = 2y + 14$$

Substitute the resulting expression for x in the second equation, and solve for y:
$$4x - 12y = 36$$
$$4(2y + 14) - 12y = 36$$
$$-4y = -20$$
$$y = 5$$

Substitute y = 5 into either equation to find the value of x:
$$2x - 4y = 28$$
$$2x - 4(5) = 28$$
$$x = 24$$

The solution is $(24, 5)$.

To solve using **elimination**, add or subtract two equations so that one or more variables are eliminated. It's often necessary to multiply one or both equations by a scalar (constant) to allow the variables to cancel. Equations can be added or subtracted as many times as necessary to solve for each variable.

Solve the system of equations:
$$6x + 10y = 18$$
$$4x + 15y = 37$$

Multiply each equation so that the x variables have opposite coefficients:
$$-2(6x + 10y = 18) \rightarrow -12x - 20y = -36$$
$$3(4x + 15y = 37) \rightarrow 12x + 45y = 111$$

Add the two equations to eliminate the x terms and solve for y:
$$25y = 75$$
$$y = 3$$

Replace y with 3 in either of the original equations:
$$6x + 10(3) = 18$$
$$6x = -12$$
$$x = -2$$

The solution is $(-2, 3)$.

Practice Questions

12) Solve for x: $5x - 4 = 3(8 + 3x)$
   A. -7
   B. $-\frac{3}{4}$
   C. $\frac{3}{4}$
   D. 7

13) Which of the following is an equation of the line that passes through the points $(4, -3)$ and $(-2, 9)$ in the xy-plane?
   A. $y = -2x + 5$
   B. $y = -\frac{1}{2}x - 1$
   C. $y = \frac{1}{2}x - 5$
   D. $y = 2x - 11$

Quadratic Equations

Quadratic equations are second-degree polynomials; the highest power on the dependent variable is 2. The graph of a quadratic function is a **parabola**, which is U-shaped and has three important components:

- The **vertex** is where the graph changes direction.
- The **axis of symmetry** is the vertical line that cuts the graph into two equal halves.
- The axis of symmetry always passes through the vertex.

The **zeros** or **roots** of the quadratic are the *x*-intercepts of the graph.

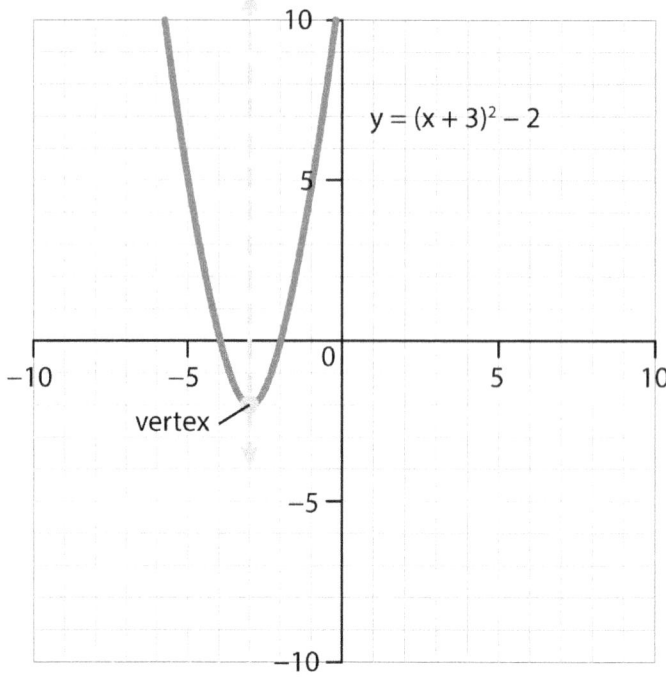

Figure 4.8. Parabola

Quadratic equations can be expressed in standard form or vertex form:

Standard form: $y = ax^2 + bx + c$ **Vertex form:** $y = a(x - h)^2 + k$

Axis of symmetry: $x = -\dfrac{b}{2a}$ Vertex: (h, k)

Vertex: $\left(-\dfrac{b}{2a}, f\left(-\dfrac{b}{2a}\right)\right)$ Axis of symmetry: $x = h$

Equations in vertex form can be converted to standard form by squaring $(x - h)$ using FOIL, distributing the *a*, adding *k*, and simplifying the result:

Write $y = 2(x - 6)^2 - 14$ in standard form.

Square the $(x - h)$ component.

$$y = 2(x - 6)^2 - 14$$
$$y = 2(x - 6)(x - 6) - 14$$
$$y = 2(x^2 - 12x + 36) - 14$$

Distribute the *a* and simplify.

$$y = 2x^2 - 24x + 72 - 14$$
$$y = 2x^2 - 24x + 58$$

Equations can be converted from standard form to vertex form by **completing the square**.

For the standard form of $y = ax^2 + bx + c$

1. move c to the left side of the equation by subtracting it from both sides;
2. divide the entire equation by a (so the coefficient of x^2 is 1);
3. take half of the coefficient of x, square it, and add the quantity to both sides of the equation;
4. convert the right side of the equation to a perfect binomial squared, $(x + m)^2$; and
5. isolate y to put the equation in proper vertex form.

> **Helpful Hint**
>
> In both equations, the sign of a determines which direction the parabola opens: if a is positive, it opens upward; if a is negative, it opens downward.

Write $y = -3x^2 + 24x - 27$ in vertex form.

Move c to the other side of the equation:

$$y = -3x^2 + 24x - 27$$
$$y + 27 = -3x^2 + 24x$$

Divide by $a = -3$:

$$-\frac{y}{3} - 9 = x^2 - 8x$$

Take half of the new b, square it, and add that quantity to both sides:

$$\tfrac{1}{2}(-8) = -4 \text{ and } (-4)^2 = 16$$

$$-\frac{y}{3} - 9 + 16 = x^2 - 8x + 16$$

Write the right side as a squared binomial and simplify:

$$-\frac{y}{3} + 7 = (x - 4)^2$$

Rewrite the equation in vertex form:

$$y = -3(x - 4)^2 + 21$$

Solving the quadratic equation $ax^2 + bx + c = 0$ determines the x-intercepts of the parabola (by making $y = 0$). These are also called the **roots** (or **zeros**) of the quadratic function. A quadratic equation may have zero, one, or two real solutions.

There are several ways to find the roots. One method is to look at the graph of the quadratic. If the graph lies above the x-axis, the quadratic equation has zero roots. If the graph of the vertex is on the x-axis, the quadratic has one root, and if the graph crosses the x-axis at two points, the quadratic has two roots.

Another way to find the roots is to factor the quadratic as a product of two binomials, and then use the zero-product property. (If $m \times n = 0$, then either $m = 0$ or $n = 0$). This can only be used for quadratic equations that can be factored.

Find the root(s) of $z^2 - 4z = -4$.

Factor as a binomial:

$$z^2 - 4z = -4$$

$$z^2 - 4z + 4 = 0$$

$$(z - 2)(z - 2) = 0$$

Set each factor equal to zero and solve for z:

$$(z - 2) = 0$$

$$z = 2$$

All quadratic equations can be solved using the **quadratic formula:**

$$x = \frac{-b \pm \sqrt{b^2 - 4ac}}{2a}$$

The a, b, and c are from the standard form of quadratic equations. (Note: to use the quadratic equation, the right-hand side of the equation must be equal to zero, $ax^2 + bx + c = 0$.)

The part of the formula under the radical ($b^2 - 4ac$) is known as the **discriminant**. The discriminant tells how many and what type of roots will result without calculating the roots.

The Discriminant		
If $b^2 - 4ac$ is	there will be	and the parabola
zero	only one real root	has its vertex on the x-axis (**one** x-intercept since the quadratic equation simplifies to $x = \frac{-b}{2a}$).
positive	two real roots	has **two** x-intercepts.
negative	zero real roots (but two complex roots)	has **no** x-intercepts (never touches the x-axis).

Solve: $3x2 + 16x = -5$

Write the equation in standard form:

$$3x2 + 16 + 5 = 0$$

Solve using the quadratic formula:

$$a = 3, b = 16, c = 5$$

$$x = \frac{-b \pm \sqrt{b^2 - 4ac}}{2a}$$

$$= \frac{-16 \pm \sqrt{16^2 - 4(3)(5)}}{2(3)}$$

$$= -16 \pm \frac{\sqrt{256-60}}{6}$$

$$= \frac{16 \pm \sqrt{196}}{6}$$

$$= \frac{16 \pm 14}{6}$$

$$x = \frac{-16+14}{6} = -\frac{1}{3} \text{ or } x = \frac{-16-14}{6} = -5$$

The solutions are -5 and $-\frac{1}{3}$.

Practice Question

14) What is the vertex form of the equation $y = x^2 + 6x - 8$?
    A. $y = (x+3)^2 - 17$
    B. $y = (x+3)^2 + 1$
    C. $y = (x+6)^2 - 14$
    D. $y = (x+6)^2 - 11$

Functions

Functions demonstrate a relationship between sets of values, called the inputs and outputs. Functions are distinct from **relations** because relations have more than one output for one input, while functions have only one output for every input. All ordered pairs are relations, but only certain relations are functions. To test whether a relation is a function, plug in values to see if outputs are the same:

Relation (more than one output per the same input):

X	Y
-4	-2, 16
0	4
2	12, -6
6	18

Function (only one output per each input):

X	Y
-4	-2
0	4
2	12
6	18

The input is the **independent variable**, and the output is called the **dependent variable** because it depends on the input. Usually (but not always) x is the independent variable, and y is the dependent variable. The coordinates found in the function table can then be plotted on a set of axes to find the corresponding graph.

Table 4.4. Function Table

\multicolumn{3}{c}{$3x + y = 12$}
x	y	
1	9	$3(1) + y = 12$ $3 + y = 12$ $y = 9$
2	6	$3(2) + y = 12$ $6 + y = 12$ $y = 6$
3	3	$3(3) + y = 12$ $9 + y = 12$ $y = 3$

Tables may be used to connect the y-value (dependent variable) to the x-value (independent variable) in an equation. The values may be plotted to see whether the relationship is linear, and if it is, to identify a slope and y-intercept. Table 4.5. shows values to be evaluated.

Helpful Hint

If the difference between x values and the difference between y values are constant, then the function is linear.

Table 4.5. Table of Values to be Evaluated

x	2	3	4	5
y	8	11	14	17

Plotting the points shows that the relationship is linear with a slope of 3. Another way to determine the relationship is to notice a pattern where the difference between each x-value is 1, and the difference between each y-value is 3. Since these differences are the same for all x- and y-values, the data can be modeled as a linear equation. The slope is: $\frac{change\ in\ y}{change\ in\ x} = \frac{3}{1} = 3$. To get the y-intercept, when $x = 2$, add 2 more to 3x to get 8, the y-value. Thus, the equation is $y = 3x + 2$. Table 4.6. shows an example of a table with **non-linear** values.

Table 4.6. Table of Non-linear Values

x	1	2	3	4
f(x)	2	5	10	17

Note that each value for f(x)—equivalent of the y-value above—is the x-value squared, plus 1. This quadratic pattern can be modeled by $f(x) = x^2 + 1$.

Practice Question

15) Which equation describes the relationship between x and y shown in the table below?

x	Y
3	11
5	15
7	19

A. $y = -2x - 5$
B. $y = 2x + 5$
C. $y = 4x + 2$
D. $y = x2 + 2$

Inequalities

Inequalities are similar to equations, but both sides of the problem are not equal (≠). Inequalities may be represented as follows:

- greater than (>)
- greater than or equal to (≥)
- less than (<)
- less than or equal to (≤)

Inequalities may be represented on a number line, as shown below. A circle is placed on the end point with a filled circle representing ≤ and ≥ and an empty circle representing < and >. An arrow is then drawn to show either all the values greater than or less than.

Inequalities can be solved by manipulating them much like equations; however, the solution to an inequality is a set of numbers, not a single value. For example, simplifying 4x + 2 ≤ 14 gives the inequality x ≤ 3, meaning every number less than 3 would also be included in the set of correct answers.

Additionally, the direction of the inequality sign must be reversed when the inequality is divided by a negative number:

$$10 - 2x > 40$$
$$-2x > 4$$
$$x < -2$$

Compound inequalities have more than one inequality expression:

$$5 < x < 12 \rightarrow x > 5 \text{ and } x < 12$$

Inequalities joined by *and* are **intersections**. The solution to these compound inequalities will be all the values that make <u>both</u> inequalities true.

Inequalities joined by *or* are **unions**. The solution to a union will be all the values that make <u>either</u> inequality true.

Solve the inequality:

$$-1 \leq 3(x+2) - 1 \leq x + 3$$

$$\begin{aligned} -1 &\leq 3(x+2) - 1 \\ -2 &\leq x \end{aligned} \qquad \begin{aligned} 3(x+2) - 1 &\leq x + 3 \\ x &\leq -1 \end{aligned}$$

$$-2 \leq x \leq -1$$

Inequalities with one variable may be represented on a number line, as shown in Figure 4.9. A circle is placed on the end point with a filled circle representing ≥ and ≤, and an empty circle representing < and >. An arrow is then drawn to show either all of the values greater than or less than the value circled.

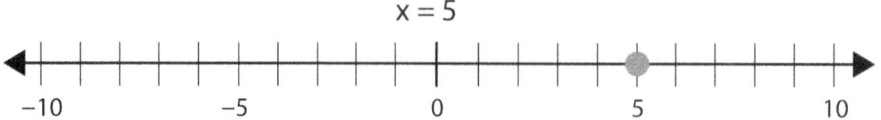

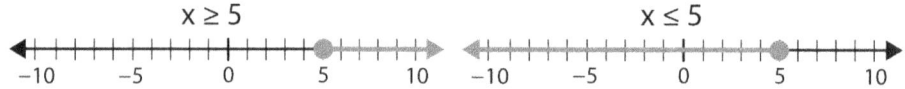

Figure 4.9. Inequality Line Graph

> **Helpful Hint**
>
> A dashed line is used for "greater/less than" because the solution may approach that line, but the coordinates on the line can never be a solution.

Linear inequalities in two variables can be graphed the same way as linear equations. Start by graphing the corresponding equation of a line (temporarily replace the inequality with an equal sign, and then graph). If the inequality is a "greater/less than," a dashed line is used; a solid line is used to indicate "greater/less than or equal to."

One side of the boundary line is the set of all points (x, y) that make the inequality true. This side is shaded to indicate that all of these values are solutions.

The simplest method to determine which side should be shaded is to choose a point (x, y) on one side of the boundary and evaluate the inequality, substituting these x- and y-values. If the point makes the inequality true, that side is shaded; if it does not, it is not a solution, so the other side is shaded.

Systems of linear equalities contain two variables. To solve systems of inequalities, use the following steps:

- Solve for y.

- Graph the line (y=....).

- Shade the region that satisfies the inequality.

- Repeat steps 1 – 3 for each inequality in the system.

- The answer is the overlapping shaded region.

Figure 4.10. Graphing Systems of Linear Equations

Practice Question

16) Which of the following is a solution to the inequality $2x + y \leq -10$?
    A. (0, 0)
    B. (10, 2)
    C. (10, 10)
    D. (-10, -10)

Algebra Word Problems

Math word problems involve translations (almost word-for-word, like a language) from English to math; they also take a lot of practice.

Table 4.7. Translating Word Problems

English Word(s)	Math Translation
is, will be, yields	=
what number, how much	"n" (or any variable)
in addition to, increased by, added to	+
sum of x and y	$x + y$
difference of x and y	$x - y$
product of x and y	$x \times y$
quotient of x and y	$x \div y$ or $\frac{x}{y}$
opposite of x	$-x$
ratio of x to y	$x \div y$ or $\frac{x}{y}$
a number n less 2	$n - 2$
a number n less than 2	$2 - n$
a number n reduced by 2	$n - 2$
Of	times
p percent	$\frac{p}{100}$, or move decimal left 2 places
half, twice	$\frac{x}{2}$, $2x$
average of x, y, and z (and so on)	$\frac{x + y + z + \ldots}{\text{how many numbers are on top}}$

Table 4.7. Translating Word Problems

English Word(s)	Math Translation
y increased by x%	$y + (y \times \frac{x}{100})$
y decreased by x%	$y - (y \times \frac{x}{100})$
y is at least (or no less than) x	$y \geq x$
y is at most (or no more than) x	$y \leq x$

- Usually, the question in the problem is a key for what the variable(s) should be.

- For consecutive integers, use n, n + 1, n + 2, and so on.

- For even or odd consecutive integers, use n, n + 2, n + 4, and so on.

- Use easier numbers to figure the problem out (such as the number 100 in percent problems) before using the actual numbers.

- If the problem asks for a **unit rate**, determine the ratio of the y-value (sometimes a dollar amount) to the x-value, when the x-value is 1. This is basically the slope of the linear functions. Some examples of unit rates are feet per second, miles per hour, and costs per unit.

Age Problem:

Twice a man's age is no more than 5 years less than his father's age. If m represents the man's age, and f his father's age, what is the inequality that would represent this situation?

Solution:

Translate almost word-for-word from English to math: $2m \leq f - 5$

Unit Rate Problem:

A shopper buys 6 pounds of apples for $4.80. What is the unit rate of a pound of apples?

Solution:

To get the unit rate, find the amount for one pound of apples; this is when x apples equals 1. Set up a ratio: $\frac{4.8}{6} = \frac{x}{1}$; $x = \$0.80$.

Multi-variable Problem:

If b books cost d dollars each and each student must buy 2 books, how much will each student pay for his or her books?

Solution:

Make it into an easier problem. If 100 books cost $2,000, each student would have to pay $\frac{2,000}{100} \times 2$, or $40. This is the same as $\frac{d}{b} \times 2$, or $\frac{2d}{b}$.

Distance Problem:

If a car is going 57 miles per hour, how many hours does it take the car to go 228 miles?

Solution:

Since Distance = Rate × Time, solve for Time: Time = $\frac{Distance}{Rate} = \frac{228}{57} = 4$ hours.

Percentage Problem:

In a clothing store, the manager earns $\frac{1}{4}$ more than her salesperson. What percentage of the manager's salary is the salesperson's salary?

Solution:

Translate: $m = s + 0.25s$; $m = 1.25s$; $s = \frac{m}{1.25} = \frac{1}{1.25} \times m = 0.8m = 80\%$.

The salesperson's salary is 80% of the manager's salary.

Practice Question

17) Valerie receives a base salary of $740 a week for working 40 hours. For every extra hour she works, she is paid at a rate of $27.75 per hour. If Valerie works *t* hours in a week, which of the following equations represents the amount of money, *A*, that she will receive?
    A. $A = 740 + 27.75(t - 40)$
    B. $A = 740 + 27.75(40 - t)$
    C. $A = 27.75t - 740$
    D. $A = 27.75t + 740$

Geometry and Measurement

Units and Measurement

The United States uses *customary units*, sometimes called *standard units*. In this system, several different units can be used to describe the same variable. These units and the relationships between them are shown in Table 4.8.

Table 4.8. US Customary Units		
Variable Measured	Unit	Conversions
Length	inches, foot, yard, mile	12 inches = 1 foot 3 feet = 1 yard 5,280 feet = 1 mile

Table 4.8. US Customary Units

Weight	ounces, pound, ton	16 ounces = 1 pound
		2,000 pounds = 1 ton
Volume	fluid ounces, cup, pint, quart, gallon	8 fluid ounces = 1 cup
		2 cups = 1 pint
		2 pints = 1 quart
		4 quarts = 1 gallon
Time	second, minute, hour, day	60 seconds = 1 minute
		60 minutes = 1 hour
		24 hours = 1 day
Area	square inch, square foot, square yard	144 square inches = 1 square foot
		9 square feet = 1 square yard

Most other countries use the metric system, which has its own set of units for variables like length, weight, and volume. These units are modified by prefixes that make large and small numbers easier to handle. These units and prefixes are shown in Table 4.9.

Table 4.9. Metric Units and Prefixes

Variable Measured	Base Unit
Length	Meter
Weight	Gram
Volume	Liter

Metric Prefix	Conversion
Kilo	base unit × 1,000
Hecto	base unit × 100
Deka	base unit × 10
Deci	base unit × 0.1
Centi	base unit × 0.01
Milli	base unit × 0.001

Conversion factors are used to convert one unit to another (either within the same system or between different systems). A conversion factor is simply a fraction built from two equivalent values. For example, there are 12 inches in 1 foot, so the conversion factor is $\frac{12\ in}{1\ ft}$ or $\frac{1\ ft}{12\ in}$.

To convert from one unit to another, multiply the original value by a conversion factor. Choose a conversion factor that will eliminate the unwanted unit with the desired unit:

How many inches are in 6 feet?

$$6\ ft \times \frac{12\ in}{1\ ft} = \frac{6\ ft \times 12\ in}{1\ ft} = 72\ in$$

Practice Question

18) Convert the following measurements:

   A. 4.25 kilometers to meters
   B. 8 m² to mm²
   C. 12 feet to inches
   D. 23 meters to feet

Classifying Geometric Figures

Geometric figures are shapes comprised of points, lines, or planes. A **point** is simply a location in space; it does not have any dimensional properties such as length, area, or volume. A collection of points that extends infinitely in both directions is a **line**, and one that extends infinitely in only one direction is a **ray**. A section of a line with a beginning and end is a **line segment**. A **straightedge** is a helpful tool for creating geometric figures because it allows for straight line segments to be drawn.

Lines, rays, and line segments are examples of **one-dimensional** objects because they can only be measured in one dimension (length).

Lines, rays, and line segments can intersect to create **angles**, which are measured in degrees or radians. Angles between 0 and 90 degrees are **acute**, and angles between 90 and 180 degrees are **obtuse**. An angle of exactly 90 degrees is a **right angle**, and two lines that form right angles are **perpendicular**. Lines that do not intersect are described as **parallel**. Parallel lines have many properties:

- They have an equal distance between them.
- They never intersect.
- If a **transversal**, or intersecting line, cuts through two parallel lines, it will form 4 angles.
- The angles formed by a transversal are equal.
- Pairs of internal and external angles made by a transversal are equal.
- Vertically opposite angles made by a transversal are equal.

Two angles with measurements that add up to 90 degrees are **complementary**, and two angles with measurements that add up to 180 degrees are **supplementary**. Two adjacent (touching) angles are called a **linear pair**, and they are supplementary. The **sum of angles in a triangle** is 180 degrees.

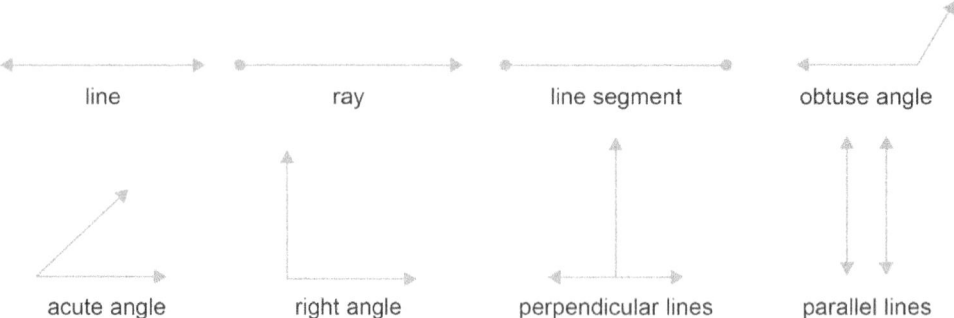

Figure 4.11. Lines and Angles

Two-dimensional objects can be measured in two dimensions (length and width). A **plane** is a two-dimensional object that extends infinitely in both dimensions. **Polygons** are two-dimensional shapes, such as triangles and squares, that have three or more straight sides. **Regular polygons** are polygons with sides that are all the same length. The sum of all the interior angle measurements in a polygon with n sides is $(n - 2) \times 180$ degrees, and the sum of all the exterior angles is 360 degrees for any polygon.

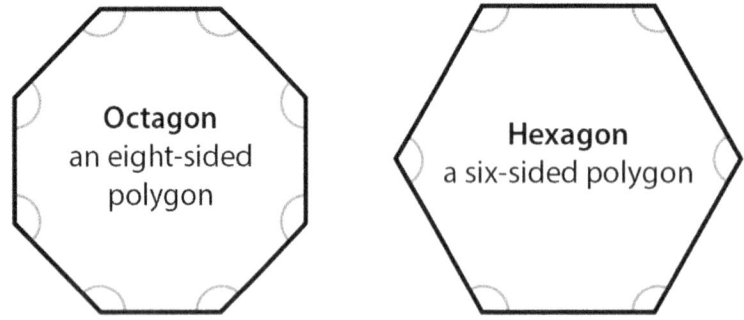

Figure 4.12. Polygons

Three-dimensional objects (Figure 4.13.), such as cubes, can be measured in three dimensions—length, width, and height. Three-dimensional objects are also called **solids**, and the shape of a flattened solid is called a **net** (Figure 4.14.).

Figure 4.13. Three-Dimensional Object

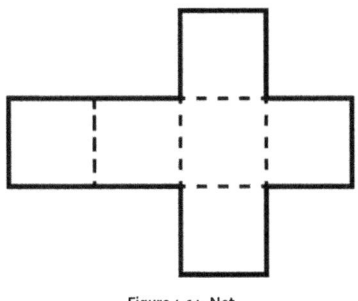

Figure 4.14. Net

Practice Question

19) What is the measure of each exterior angle of a regular 300-gon?
   A. 1.2°
   B. 2.4°
   C. 178.8°
   D. 360°

Properties of Shapes

The **length**, or distance from one point to another on an object, can be determined using a tape measure or a ruler. The size of the surface of a two-dimensional object is its **area**. The area of an object is its length times its width and is measured in square units. For example, if a wall is 3 feet long and 2 feet wide, its area would be 6 square feet. The distance around a two-dimensional figure is its **perimeter**, which can be found by adding the lengths of all the sides.

Table 4.10. Area and Perimeter of Basic Shapes		
Shape	**Areas**	**Perimeter**
Triangle	$A = \frac{1}{2}bh$	$P = s_1 + s_2 + s_3$
Square	$A = s^2$	$P = 4s$
Rectangle	$A = l \times w$	$P = 2l + 2w$
Circle	$A = \pi r^2$	$C = 2\pi r$ (Circumference)

For the rectangle shown in Figure 4.15., the area would be 8 m² because $2\,m \times 4\,m = 8\,m^2$. The perimeter of the rectangle would be 12 meters because the sum of the length of all sides is 2 m + 4 m + 2 m + 4 m = 12 m.

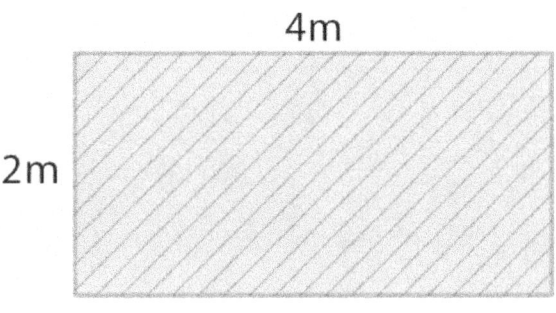

Figure 4.15. Fencing

The **surface area** of a three-dimensional object can be figured by adding the areas of all the sides. For example, the box in Figure 4.16. is 4 feet long, 3 feet wide, and 1 foot deep. The surface area is found by adding the areas of each face:

- top: 4 ft. × 3 ft. = 12 ft2
- bottom: 4 ft. × 3 ft. = 12 ft2
- front: 4 ft. × 1 ft. = 4 ft2
- back: 4 ft. × 1 ft. = 4 ft2
- right: 1 ft. × 1 ft. = 1 ft2
- left: 1 ft. × 1 ft. = 1 ft2

> **Check Your Understanding**
>
> When would someone need to be able to calculate the surface area of a three-dimensional object in the real world?

Figure 4.16. Surface Area

A **net** (flattened out three-dimensional solid) can also be used to find the surface area of solids. For example, for a square pyramid with a base with side 6 m and a slant height (height in the middle of the triangular faces) of 8 m, the surface area can be calculated with a square and four triangles:

Surface Area = Area of Square Base + Area of 4 Triangles = $6^2 + 4\left[\frac{1}{2}(6 \times 8)\right] = 36 + 96 = 132\ m$.

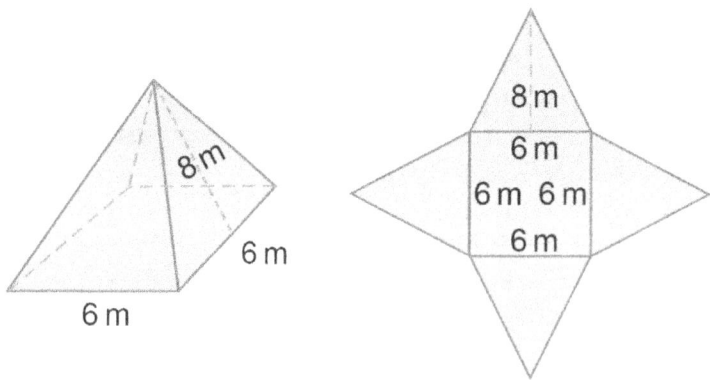

Figure 4.17. Surface Area of a Pyramid

Volume is the amount of space that a three-dimensional object takes up. Volume is measured in cubic units (e.g., ft^3 or mm^3). The volume of a solid can be determined by multiplying length times width times height. In the rectangular prism shown in Figure 4.18., the volume is 3 in. × 1 in. × 1 in. = 3 in³:

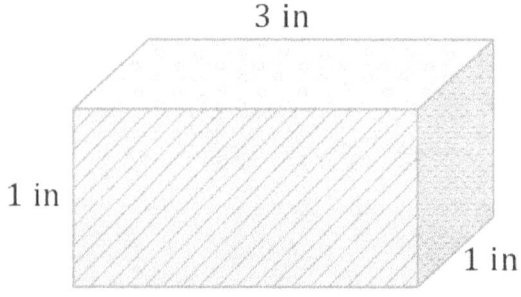

Figure 4.18. Volume

Table 4.11. shows formulas for the surface area and volume of basic solids. Note that lateral area (LA) is the surface area of the solids without the bases, which are the two parallel faces between the height.

Table 4.11. Area and Volume of Basic Solids

Solid	Volume	Surface Area
Sphere (r is radius)	$V = \frac{4}{3}\pi r^3$	$SA = 4\pi r^2$
Cube (s is side)	$V = s^3$	$SA = 6s^2$
Cylinder (r is radius of base; B is area of base)	$V = \pi r^2 h$	$SA = LA + 2B = 2\pi rh + 2\pi r^2$
Right rectangular prism (LA, or lateral area, is the perimeter of base times height; B is area of base)	$V = Bh$	$SA = LA + 2B$
Cone (h is height [distance from center to tip]; r is radius [distance from center of circle to tip of cone]; s is slant [length of the edge of the circle to the tip of the cone])	$V = \frac{1}{3}\pi r^2 h$	$SA = \pi rs + \pi r^2$

Figure 4.19. shows an example of finding the volume and surface area of a **right rectangular prism** with a height of 8 cm and square bases with sides of 2 cm. Remember that the bases are the two squares that are on either side of the height.

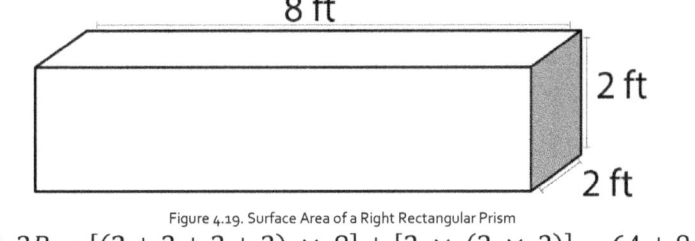

Figure 4.19. Surface Area of a Right Rectangular Prism

$$SA = LA + 2B = [(2 + 2 + 2 + 2) \times 8] + [2 \times (2 \times 2)] = 64 + 8 = 72\ cm$$

Note that the SA can also be found by adding the areas of all the sides:

$$SA = (2 \times 8) + (2 \times 8) + (2 \times 8) + (2 \times 8) + (2 \times 2) + (2 \times 2) = 64 + 8 = 72\ cm$$

Practice Question

20) What is the perimeter of the regular polygon?

A. 4 in.
B. 8 in.
C. 10 in.
D. 32 in.

Circles

Circles are a fundamental shape in geometry. A **compass** is a tool with a needle, hinge, and pencil that can be used to draw circles or arcs.

A **circle** is the set of all the points in a plane that are the same distance from a fixed point (called the center). The distance from the center to any point on the circle is the **radius** of the circle. The distance around the circle (the perimeter) is called the **circumference**.

The ratio of a circle's circumference to its diameter is a constant value called pi (π), an irrational number which is commonly rounded to 3.14. The formula to find a circle's circumference is $C = 2\pi r$. The formula to find the enclosed area of a circle is $A = \pi r^2$.

Circles have a number of unique parts:

- The **diameter** is the largest measurement across a circle. It passes through the circle's center, extending from one side of the circle to the other. The measure of the diameter is twice the measure of the radius.

- A line that cuts across a circle and touches it twice is called a **secant** line.

- The part of a secant line that lies within a circle is called a **chord**.

- A line that touches a circle or any curve at one point is **tangent** to the circle or the curve. A line tangent to a circle and a radius drawn to the point of tangency meet at a right angle (90°).

- An **arc** is any portion of a circle between two points on the circle. The measure of an arc is in degrees, whereas the length of the arc will be in linear measurement (such as centimeters or inches).

- An angle with its vertex at the center of a circle is called a **central angle**.

> **Helpful Hint**
>
> "Trying to square a circle" means attempting to create a square that has the same area as a circle. Because the area of a circle depends on π, which is an irrational number, this task is impossible. The phrase is often used to describe trying to do something that cannot be done.

- A **sector** is the part of a circle that is inside the rays of a central angle (it is shape is like a slice of pie).

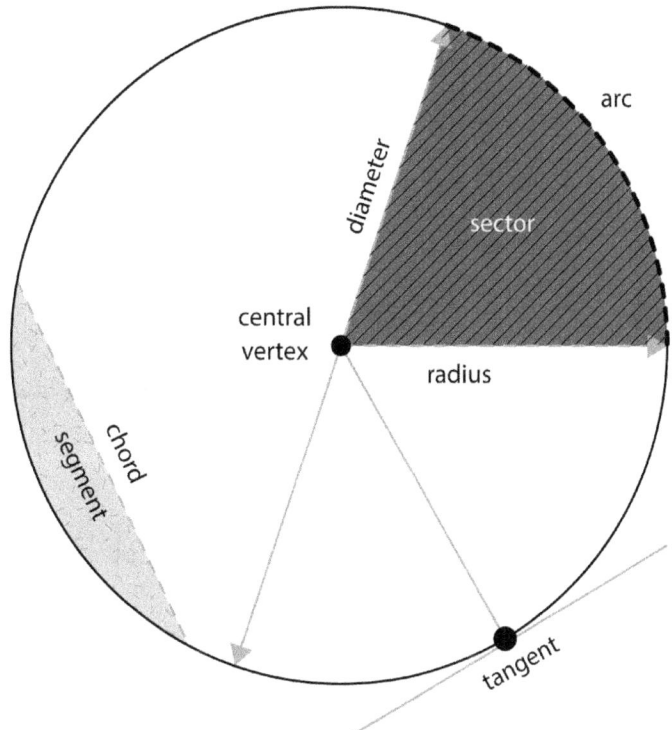

Figure 4.20. Parts of a Circle

Practice Question

21) *W*, *X*, *Y*, and *Z* lie on a circle with center *A*. If the diameter of the circle is 75, what is the sum of *AW*, *AX*, *AY*, and *AZ*?
    A. 75
    B. 300
    C. 150
    D. 106.5

Triangles

Triangles have three sides, and the three interior angles always sum to 180°. The formula for the area of a triangle is $A = \frac{1}{2}bh$ or one-half the product of the base and height (or altitude) of the triangle.

Triangles can be classified in two ways: by sides and by angles:

- A **scalene triangle** has no equal sides or angles.

- An **isosceles triangle** has two equal sides and two equal angles (often called base angles).

- In an **equilateral triangle**, all three sides are equal as are all three angles. Moreover, because he sum of the angles of a triangle is always 180°, each angle of an equilateral triangle must be 60°.

A **right triangle** has one right angle (90°) and two acute angles. An **acute triangle** has three acute angles (all angles are less than 90°). An **obtuse triangle** has one obtuse angle (more than 90°) and two acute angles

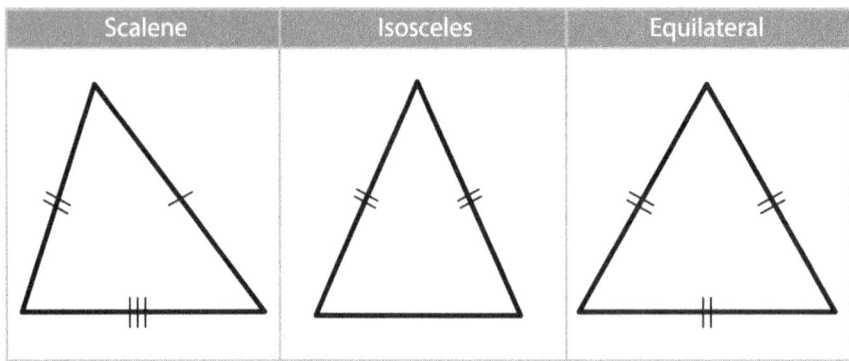

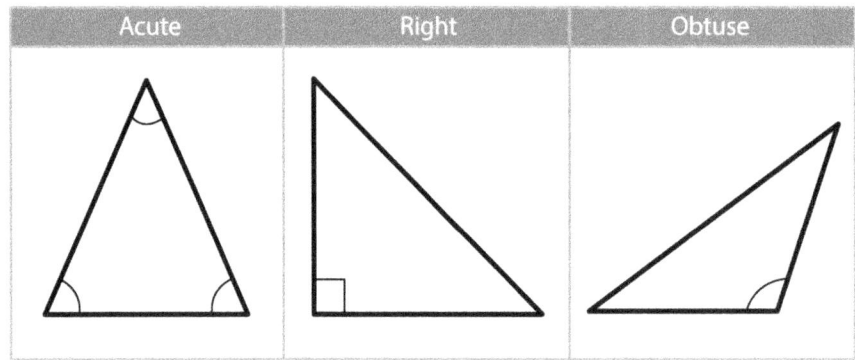

Figure 4.21. Types of Triangles

For any triangle, the side opposite the largest angle will have the longest length, while the side opposite the smallest angle will have the shortest length. The **triangle inequality theorem** states that the sum of any two sides of a triangle must be greater than the third side. This leads to the **third-side rule**: if b and c are two sides of a triangle, then the measure of the third side a must be between the sum of the other two sides and the difference of the other two sides: $c - b < a < c + b$.

Solving for missing angles or sides of a triangle is a common type of triangle problem. Often a right triangle will come up on its own or within another triangle. The relationship among a right triangle's sides is known as the **Pythagorean theorem**: $a^2 + b^2 = c^2$, where c is the hypotenuse and is across from the 90° angle.

> **Did You Know?**
>
> The Pythagorean theorem is usually credited to Greek philosopher and mathematician Pythagoras; however, many scholars believe it was actually developed by one of his followers after his death.

Practice Question

22) Which of the following could be the perimeter of a triangle with two sides that measure 13 and 5?
    A. 24.5
    B. 26.5
    C. 36
    D. 37

Working with Shapes

Sides or parts of a shape can be compared to determine **symmetry**, or whether the shape is exactly the same on both sides when a dividing or mirror line is drawn through it. Lines that divide shapes into equal parts are known as lines of **symmetry**. Lines of symmetry (or any other lines) can be used to dissect shapes or change them into new figures. For example, a square can be cut in half to create two rectangles, or a parallelogram can be cut in half to make two triangles. Based on how the shapes are dissected, their component pieces may or may not be equivalent.

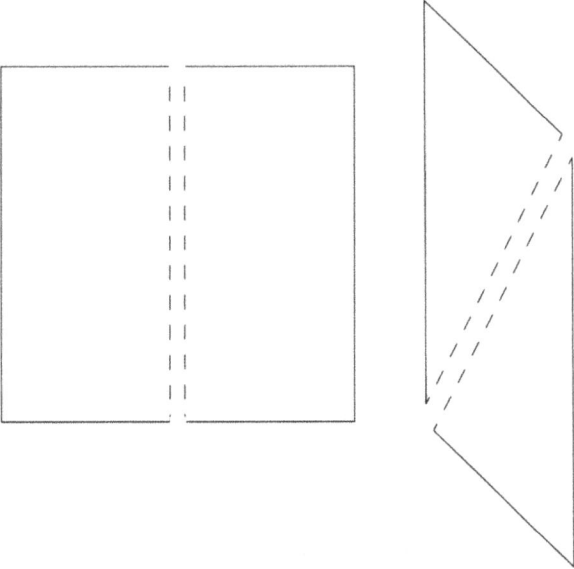

Figure 4.22. Lines of Symmetry

Shapes can also be manipulated or transformed. **Transformation** refers to moving a shape within a coordinate plane. **Reflection** flips the shape but does not change its size or shape; it creates a mirror image. **Rotation**, as its name implies, is the rotation of a shape by a certain degree. A **translation** is distinct from a reflection or rotation because the shape is not turned, flipped, or changed; it is only slid or moved across the plane.

Similar shapes have the same angle measurements and sides that are proportional. The **scale factor** is the ratio of corresponding sides of the figures. If the dimensions of a figure are **dilated** (made smaller or larger with proportional dimensions) by a scale factor of $\frac{a}{b}$, then the surface area of the new dilated solid is multiplied by $\frac{a^2}{b^2}$, and the volume of the new dilated solid is multiplied by $\frac{a^3}{b^3}$.

For example, in the solids shown in Figure 4.23., the scale factor is $\frac{16}{8} = 2$; therefore, the surface area of the second solid is equal to the surface area of the first solid multiplied by $2^2 = 4$, and the volume of the second solid is equal to the volume of the first solid's volume multiplied by $2^3 = 8$.

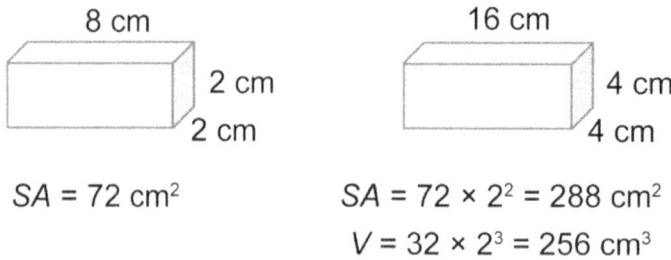

Figure 4.23. Dilated Solids

Practice Question

23) Cone *A* is similar to cone *B* with a scale factor of 3:4. If the volume of cone *A* is 54π, what is the volume of cone *B*?
- A. 72π
- B. 128π
- C. 162π
- D. 216π

Math in Research

Data Collection

In quantitative research, data is often collected in surveys, or questionnaires which often employ a Likert scale to understand people's habits or agreement with statements. Likert scales translate opinions into numerical values (i.e., very likely = 5; somewhat likely = 4; maybe = 3; somewhat unlikely = 2; very unlikely = 1; never = 0).

To be effective, surveys must be given to a representative **sample** within the total **population**. For example, to understand political leanings, a sample of people of various backgrounds, ages, and genders from various locations would be used. This would allow results to be **generalized** or applied to the broader population from the representative sample. If a representative sample is not used (e.g., if the survey is only given to White men in a suburb of Georgia), the results will be skewed and cannot be generalized to the entire American population.

Before generalizing data (which can only be done with higher-order statistical tests), researchers often run a preliminary test, called a **goodness-of-fit** test. Common goodness-of-fit tests are the Chi-square test and the Shapiro-Wilk test. These tests identify whether the data that one has obtained comes from a sample with a **normal distribution** (see next section). If the data is from a normal distribution, then higher-level **parametric** statistical procedures can be used. If the data is not from a normal distribution, then **nonparametric** statistical tests, which are less powerful, must be used.

Practice Question

24) As part of a class project, a student surveys seven of her peers to determine their favorite ice cream flavors. Because 6 out of 10 of her classmates prefer chocolate ice cream, she concludes that "Americans like chocolate ice cream best." What feedback might her teacher provide?
  A. Her sample did not have a normal distribution, so generalization to all Americans should be questioned.
  B. Her sample was not representative of the entire American population, so generalization is not possible.
  C. Her survey did not include Likert scale items, so it is not reflective of the total population.
  D. Her survey sought to answer only one research question, so a larger sample was needed.

Data Analysis

Statistics is the study of data. Analyzing data requires using **measures of central tendency** (mean, median, and mode) to identify trends or patterns.

The **mean** is the average; it is determined by adding all outcomes and then dividing by the total number of outcomes. For example, the average of the data set {16, 19, 19, 25, 27, 29, 75} is equal to $\frac{16 + 19 + 19 + 25 + 27 + 29 + 75}{7} = \frac{210}{7} = 30$.

The **median** is the number in the middle when the data set is arranged in order from least to greatest. For example, in the data set {16, 19, 19, **25**, 27, 29, 75}, the median is 25. When a data set contains an even number of values, finding the median requires averaging the two middle values. In the data set {75, 80, 82, 100}, the two numbers in the middle are 80 and 82. Consequently, the median will be the average of these two values: $\frac{80 + 82}{2} = 81$.

> **Helpful Hint**
>
> <u>Mo</u>de is <u>mo</u>st common. Median is in the middle (like a median in the road). Mean is average.

Finally, the **mode** is the most frequent outcome in a data set. In the set {16, 19, 19, 25, 27, 29, 75}, the mode is 19 because it occurs twice, which is more than any of the other numbers. If several values appear, an equal and most frequent number of times, both values are considered the mode.

Other useful indicators include range and outliers. The **range** is the difference between the highest and the lowest numbers in a data set. For example, the range of the set {16, 19, 19, 25, 27, 29, 75} is 75 − 16 = 59. **Outliers**, or data points that are much different from other data points, should be noted as they can skew the central tendency. In the data set {16, 19, 19, 25, 27, 29, 75}, the value 75 is far outside the other values and raises the value of the mean. Without the outlier, the mean is much closer to the other data points.

- $\frac{16 + 19 + 19 + 25 + 27 + 29 + 75}{7} = \frac{210}{7} = 30$
- $\frac{16 + 19 + 19 + 25 + 27 + 29}{6} = 22.5$

When a data distribution is symmetrical, the mean, median, and mode are the same; this is called a **normal distribution**. Generally, the median is a better indicator of a central tendency if outliers are present to skew the mean. If a distribution is **skewed left** (outliers tend to be smaller numbers), typically the mean is less than the median, and the median is the best indicator. If the distribution is **skewed right** (outliers tend to be larger numbers), typically the mean is greater than the median, and again, the median is the best indicator. So, the mean tends to be pulled toward the longer "tails" of the data.

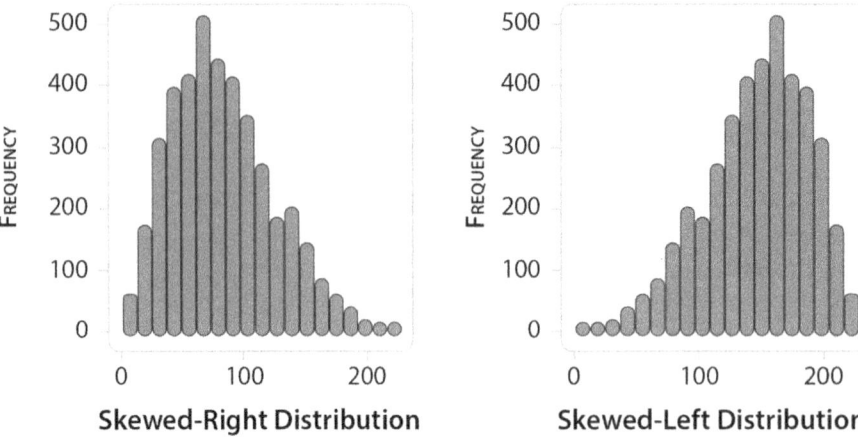

Figure 4.24. Skew

Sometimes the measures of central tendency are not the only or best way to analyze data. When data is **bivariate**, or includes two variables that may or may not be related, a bivariate analysis may be more appropriate. The simplest type of analysis is creating a scatterplot graph, where a **positive correlation** (increase in one variable is associated with an increase in the other variable) or **negative correlation** (an increase or decrease in one variable creates the opposite effect in the other).

When examining the scatterplot, one can determine whether the correlation (also sometimes called association) is **linear** or **non-linear**. If a straight line can be drawn through many of the dots, there is a linear association. If the pattern is more curved, it is a non-linear correlation.

Beyond measures of central tendency and correlations, data may also be analyzed in terms of ratios, proportions, and percent change.

As mentioned earlier, **ratio** is a comparison of two quantities. For example, if a class consists of 15 women and 10 men, the ratio of women to men is 15 to 10. This ratio can also be written as 15:10 or $\frac{15}{10}$. Ratios, like fractions, can be reduced by dividing by common factors

A **proportion** is a statement that two ratios are equal. For example, the proportion $\frac{5}{10} = \frac{7}{14}$ is true because both ratios are equal to $\frac{1}{2}$.

The **cross product** is found by multiplying the numerator of one fraction by the denominator of the other (*across* the equal sign).

$$\frac{a}{b} = \frac{c}{d} \rightarrow ad = bc$$

The fact that the cross products of proportions are equal can be used to solve proportions in which one of the values is missing. Use x to represent the missing value, and then cross multiply and solve.

$$\frac{5}{x} = \frac{7}{14}$$
$$5(14) = x(7)$$
$$70 = 7x$$
$$x = 10$$

A **percent** (or percentage) means *per hundred* and is expressed with the percent symbol (%). For example, 54% means 54 out of 100. Percentages are converted to decimals by moving the decimal point two places to the left.

$$54\% = 0.54$$

Percentages can be solved by setting up a proportion.

$$\frac{part}{whole} = \frac{\%}{100}$$

Percent change involves a change from an original amount. Often percent change problems appear as word problems that include discounts, growth, or markups.

In order to solve percent change problems, it is necessary to identify the percent change (as a decimal), the amount of change, and the original amount. (Keep in mind that one of these will be the value being solved for.) These values can then be substituted into the following equations:

- amount of change = original amount × percent change
- percent change = amount of change ÷ original amount
- original amount = amount of change ÷ percent change

Practice Questions

25) Ken has 6 grades in English class. Each grade is worth 100 points. Ken has a 92% average in English. If Ken's first five grades are 90, 100, 95, 83, and 87, what did Ken earn for the sixth grade?
   A. 80
   B. 92
   C. 97
   D. 100

26) What is the relationship between the mean and the median in a data set that is skewed right?
   A. The mean is greater than the median.
   B. The mean is less than the median.
   C. The mean and median are equal.
   D. The mean may be greater than, less than, or equal to the median.

Data Presentation

Data can be presented in a variety of ways. The most appropriate depends on the data being displayed. **Box plots** (also called box-and-whisker plots) show data using the median, range, and outliers of a data set. They provide a helpful visual guide, showing how data is distributed around the median. In Figure 4.27., 81 is the median and the range is 100 – 0, or 100.

Bar graphs use bars of different lengths to compare data. The independent variable on a bar graph is grouped into categories such as months, flavors, or locations, and the dependent variable will be a quantity. Thus, comparing the length of bars provides a visual guide to the relative amounts in each category. **Double bar graphs** show more than one data set on the same set of axes.

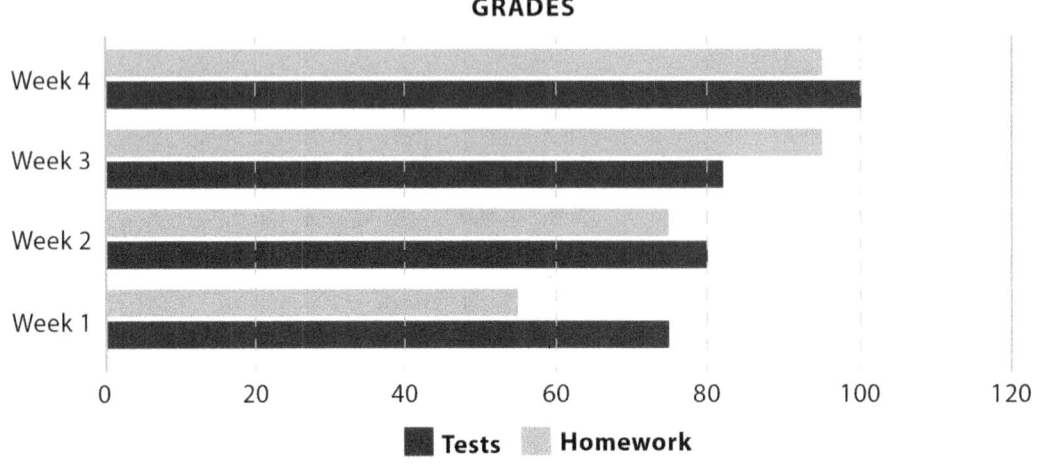

Figure 4.29. Double Bar Graph

Histograms similarly use bars to compare data, but the independent variable is a continuous variable that has been "binned," or divided into categories. For example, the time of day can be broken down into 8:00 a.m. to 12:00 p.m., 12:00 p.m. to 4:00 p.m., and so on. Usually (but not always) a gap is included between the bars of a bar graph but not a histogram.

Dot plots display the frequency of a value or event data graphically by using dots, and thus can be used to observe the distribution of a data set. Typically, a value or category is listed on the *x*-axis, and the number of times that value appears in the data set is represented by a line of vertical dots. Dot plots make it easy to see which values occur most often.

> **Check Your Understanding**
>
> What computer programs or digital tools can students use to create charts and graphs?

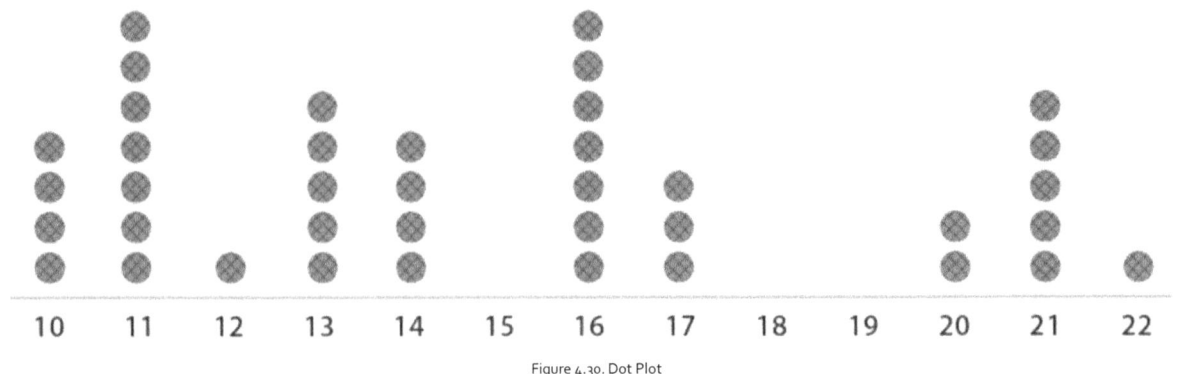

Figure 4.30. Dot Plot

Scatterplots use points to show relationships between two variables which can be plotted as coordinate points. One variable describes a position on the *x*-axis, and the other a point on the *y*-axis.

Scatterplots can suggest relationships between variables. For example, both variables might increase, or one may increase when the other decreases.

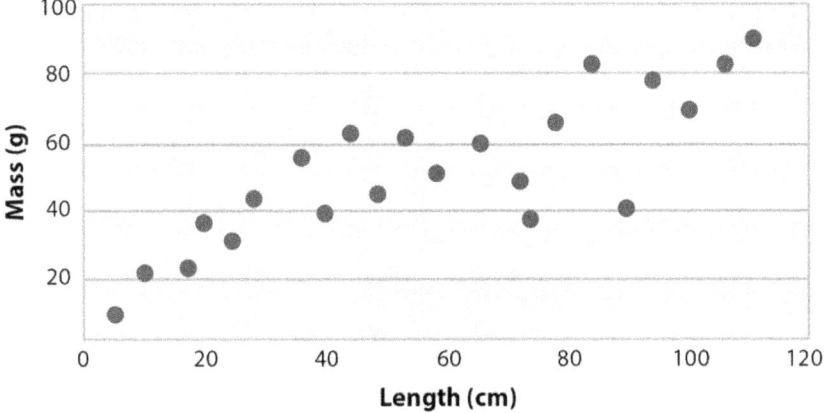

Figure 4.31. Scatterplot

Line graphs show changes in data by connecting points on a scatterplot using a line. These graphs will often measure time on the *x*-axis and are used to show trends in the data, such as temperature changes over a day or school attendance throughout the year. **Double line graphs** present two sets of data on the same set of axes.

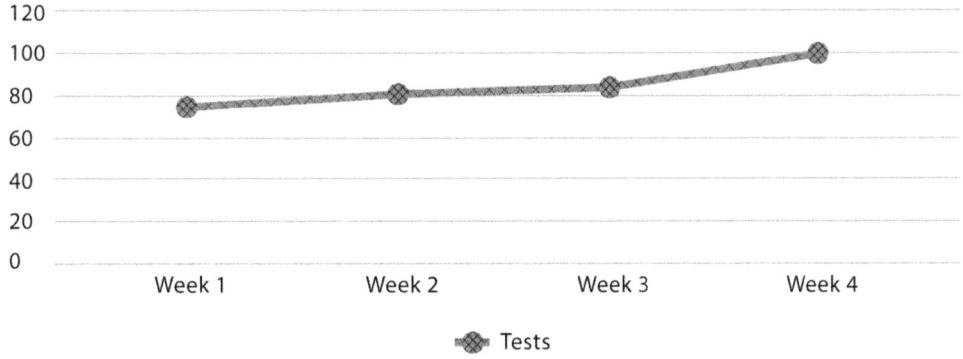

Figure 4.32. Line Graph

Circle graphs (also called pie charts) are used to show parts of a whole: the "pie" is the whole, and each "slice" represents a percentage or part of the whole.

Practice Question

27) The pie graph below shows how a state's government plans to spend its annual budget of $3 billion. How much more money does the state plan to spend on infrastructure than education?

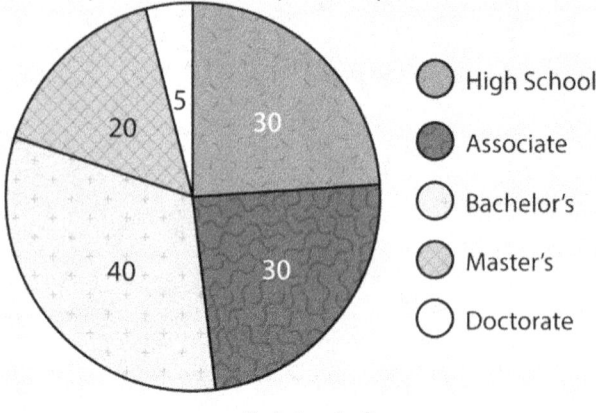

Pie chart question figure

A. $60,000,000
B. $120,000,000
C. $300,000,000
D. $600,000,000

Probability

Sometimes the goal of quantitative research and data analysis is to determine the chance of something occurring or to make a prediction.

Probability is the likelihood, or chance, that something will happen. Probability is expressed as a fraction with the numerator being the number of successful outcomes and the denominator being the total number of outcomes or as a decimal. For example, if there are 25 marbles in a bag and 4 marbles are red, the probability of randomly pulling a red marble out of the bag is or $\frac{4}{25}$ (also written as 0.16 or 16%).

Another example involves a spinner with 8 sections, with 3 that are choice A, 2 that are choice B, and 3 that are choice C. The probability of landing on choice A would be $\frac{3}{8}$ (also written as 0.375 or 37.5%).

Probabilities are always numbers between 0 and 1, inclusive. If there is no chance of something occurring, its probability is 0; if there's a 100% chance of something occurring, its probability is 1.

Replacement means putting something back the way it was before an event occurred. For example, the probability of drawing 4 red marbles out of 25 marbles twice, with replacement, would be $\frac{4}{25} \times \frac{4}{25} = \frac{16}{625}$. The same probability without replacement would be $\frac{4}{25} \times \frac{3}{24} = \frac{12}{600} = \frac{1}{50}$ since there would be one less red marble and one less of the total marbles. Note that probabilities are multiplied when the events are independent from each other.

For the probability of something happening at least one time, take the probably of the event not happening at all, and subtract this probability from 1. For example, the probability of rolling a two on at least one of two dice would be *1 minus the probability of not rolling a two on either die*, which would be $1 - \left(\frac{5}{6} \times \frac{5}{6}\right) = 1 - \frac{25}{36} = \frac{11}{36}$, or 0.31.

Practice Question

28) Some of a hotel's 400 rooms have an ocean view and the rest of the rooms do not. If the probability of getting a room with an ocean view is 35%, how many rooms do NOT have an ocean view?
    A. 140
    B. 200
    C. 260
    D. 300

Answer Key

1) A: The number 3 is not irrational because it can be written as the fraction $\frac{3}{1}$

2) C: The number $\frac{13}{14}$ is rational because it can be written as a fraction but not as a whole number (without the fraction). It is not imaginary because it does have an *i* component.

3) C: Divide 1.3208 by 5.2:
$$1.3208 \div 5.2 = 0.254$$
The number 5 is in the hundredths place (0.2**5**4)

4) C: Evaluate to find the expression with the greatest value:
$$-4(3)(-2) = 24$$
$$-16 - 17 + 31 = -2$$
$$18 - 15 + 27 = \mathbf{30}$$
$$-20 + 10 + 10 = 0$$

5) D: Solve inside the parenthesis first, and then add as follows: (216 ÷ 16) + (184 ÷ 16) = 13.5 + 11.5 = 25.

6) A: Use the order of operations:
$$(5^2 + 1)^2 + 3^3 = (25 + 1)^2 + 3^3 = (26)^2 + 3^3 = 676 + 27 = 703$$

7) B: Convert each term to an improper fraction and multiply/divide left to right:
$$1\frac{1}{2} = \frac{3}{2}$$
$$2\frac{2}{3} = \frac{8}{3}$$
$$1\frac{1}{4} = \frac{5}{4}$$
$$\left(1\frac{1}{2}\right)\left(2\frac{2}{3}\right) \div 1\frac{1}{4}$$
$$= \left(\frac{3}{2}\right)\left(\frac{8}{3}\right) \div \frac{5}{4}$$
$$= \frac{24}{6} \div \frac{5}{4}$$
$$= \frac{4}{1} \times \frac{4}{5} = \frac{16}{5} = 3\frac{1}{5}$$

8) A: Add the fractions and subtract the result from the amount of flour Allison started with:
$$2\frac{1}{2} + \frac{3}{4} = \frac{5}{2} + \frac{3}{4} = \frac{10}{4} + \frac{3}{4} = \frac{13}{4}$$
$$4 - \frac{13}{4} = \frac{16}{4} - \frac{13}{4} = \frac{3}{4}$$

9) D: Move the decimal until it is between the 3 and the 4, making a number between 1 and 10. Count the number of spots the decimal moved and make this value the exponent on the 10: 34,500,000. = 3.45 × 10⁷.

10) A: Substitute 5 for x: $2(5) - 5 = 10 - 5 = 5$

11) D: Use FOIL first, outer, inner, and last) to solve:
$$(3x + 2)(3x + 2) =$$
$$9x^2 + 6x + 6x + 4 = \mathbf{9x^2 + 12x + 4}$$

12) A: Isolate the variable x on one side of the equation:
$$5x - 4 = 3(8 + 3x)$$
$$5x - 4 = 24 + 9x$$
$$-4 - 24 = 9x - 5x$$
$$-28 = 4x$$
$$-\frac{28}{4} = \frac{4x}{4}$$
$$x = -7$$

13) A: Use the points to find the slope:
$$m = \frac{y_2 - y_1}{x_2 - x_1} = \frac{-3 - 9}{4 - (-2)} = -2$$

Use the point-slope equation to find the equation of the line:
$$(y - y1) = m(x - x1)$$
$$y - (-3) = -2(x - 4)$$
$$\mathbf{y = -2x + 5}$$

14) A: Complete the square. Start by moving c to the left side of the equation:
$$y = x^2 + 6x - 8$$
$$y (+ 8) = x^2 + 6x - 8 (+ 8)$$
$$y + 8 = x^2 + 6x$$

Take half of the coefficient of x and square it: $(6 \div 2)^2 = 9$. Add this quantity to both sides of the equation:
$$y + 8 (+ 9) = x^2 + 6x (+ 9)$$
$$y + 17 = x^2 + 6x + 9$$

Convert the right side of the equation to a perfect binomial squared:
$$y + 17 = (x + 3)^2$$

Rewrite the equation in vertex form:
$$\mathbf{y = (x + 3)^2 - 17}$$

15) B: The difference between the *x* value (2) and the difference between the *y* values (4) are both constant, so the function is linear. Find the slope to identify the right equation:

$$m = \frac{y_2 - y_1}{x_2 - x_1} = \frac{15 - 11}{5 - 3} = 2$$

y = 2*x* + 5 is a linear relationship because 11 = 2(3) + 5. The slope is 2 since there is a constant difference of 2 for the *x*-values and a difference of 4 for the *y*-values. Substitute the *x*- and *y*-values into the equation.

16) D: Plug in each set of values and determine if the inequality is true:
- $2(0) + 0 \le -10$ FALSE
- $2(10) + 2 \le -10$ FALSE
- $2(10) + 10 \le -10$ FALSE
- $2(-10) + (-10) \le -10$ **TRUE**

17) A: This question asks what equation can be used to calculate the amount of money Valerie will make in a week. The question says that she makes $740 per 40-hour work week. If she works any hours over 40, she gets paid an additional $27.75/hour. To calculate her total pay (*A*), subtract her total hours worked from 40:

$$t - 40$$

Then multiply that number by 27.75:

$$27.75(t - 40)$$

Then, add the base pay of $740 to get her total pay for the week:

$$A = 740 + 27.75(t - 40)$$

18) Answers:

A. $4.25 \text{ km} \left(\frac{1000 \text{ m}}{1 \text{ km}}\right) = 4250 \text{ m}$

B. $\frac{8 \text{ m}^2}{} \times \frac{1{,}000 \text{ mm}}{1 \text{ m}} \times \frac{1{,}000 \text{ mm}}{1 \text{ m}} = 8{,}000{,}000 \text{ mm}^2$

Since the units are *square* units (m^2), multiply by the conversion factor *twice*, so that both meters cancel (and $mm \times mm = mm^2$).

C. $12 \text{ ft} \left(\frac{12 \text{ in}}{1 \text{ ft}}\right) = 144 \text{ in}$

D. $23 \text{ m} \left(\frac{3.28 \text{ ft}}{1 \text{ m}}\right) = 75.44 \text{ ft}$

19) A: The sum of all the exterior angles of a regular *n*-gon is always 360°. Because there are 300 vertices in a 300-gon, the exterior angle at each vertex is $\frac{360}{300} = 1.2°$.

20) C: Add the length of each side to find the perimeter: 2 in. + 2 in. + 2 in. + 2 in. + 2 in. = 10 in.

21) C: All of the points lie on the circle, so each line segment is a radius. The sum of the 4 lines will be 4 times the radius:

$$r = \frac{75}{2} = 37.5$$

$$4r = \mathbf{150}$$

22) B: Use the third-side rule to find the possible values for the third side, and then calculate the possible perimeters:

$$13 - 5 < s < 13 + 5$$
$$8 < s < 18$$
$$13 + 5 + 8 < P < 13 + 5 + 18$$
$$\mathbf{26 < P < 36}$$

23) B: Set up a proportion, and cube the scale factor when calculating volume:

$$\frac{54\pi}{x} = \frac{3^3}{4^3}$$
$$x = \mathbf{128\pi}$$

24) B: Generalization is only possible with an adequate sample. Minimum sample size varies based on the statistical procedure to be used.

25) C: If Ken has six scores that average 92%, his total number of points earned is found by multiplying the average by the number of scores:

$$92 \times 6 = 552$$

To find how many points he earned on the sixth test, subtract the sum of the other scores from 552:

$$90 + 100 + 95 + 83 + 87 = 455$$
$$552 - 455 = 97$$

26) A: If the data is skewed right, the set includes extreme values that are to the right, or high. The median is unaffected by these high values, but the mean includes these high values and would therefore be greater.

27) A: Find the amount the state will spend on infrastructure and education, and then find the difference.

$$infrastructure = 0.2(3{,}000{,}000{,}000) = 600{,}000{,}000$$
$$education = 0.18(3{,}000{,}000{,}000) = 540{,}000{,}000$$
$$600{,}000{,}000 - 540{,}000{,}000 = \mathbf{\$60{,}000{,}000}$$

28) C: The probability of getting a room without an ocean view is equal to 1 minus the probability of getting a room with an ocean view:

$$P_{view} = 1 - P_{no\ ocean\ view}$$
$$P_{view} = 1 - 0.35 = 0.65$$

Use the equation for percentages to find the number of rooms without a view:

part = percentage × whole = (0.65)400 = **260 rooms**

5. Physical Education and Human Development

Basic Movement Skills

In early childhood, learning movement fundamentals requires movement concepts and fundamental motor skills. Teaching **movement concepts** helps children increase their understanding of body awareness and management.

The objective of **body awareness** is for students to explore the body's capabilities. In early childhood, students learn to identify and understand the locations of different body parts. They also practice the many shapes and positions they can form with their bodies. Teachers should help students gain an awareness of body movements and how the body can be used to communicate.

Spatial awareness is an understanding of where the body can move. Teachers should provide ample opportunities for students to explore the spatial qualities of movement. Examples include self-space, general space, pathways, range, and the direction of movement. Students should not only recognize these examples but also respect the space of others, travel through space in a purposeful manner, and adjust their range of movement depending on the task.

> **Helpful Hint**
>
> Developing body management skills means integrating agility, coordination, balance, and flexibility to create effective

The goal in teaching the **qualities of movement** is for students to understand how balance affects movement and the qualities of static and dynamic balance. Teachers should also help students generate and modify force to accomplish assigned tasks as well as differentiate among speeds so they can move more quickly or slowly. As students progress through the elementary grades, teachers should encourage them to accomplish movements within a certain amount of time and space.

Non-locomotor skills are movements that do not require moving through space. These include bending, stretching, twisting, turning, pushing, and pulling. **Object manipulation**, such as catching a ball, is also part of non-locomotor skills development. As students develop their movement skills, teachers should give children ample opportunities to explore them as well as combine them with locomotor skills so these can be applied to all physical education activities.

Locomotor skills are the numerous ways the body can move through space. They include walking, skipping, running, jumping, sliding, galloping, and leaping. Students should be given ample time to practice skills repeatedly after observing a proper demonstration.

When teaching students walking skills, teachers should demonstrate that each foot alternates and that there is always one foot touching the floor. Instruct students to point toes straight head, keep their eyes forward with their heads up, and with their weight transferred from the heel to the ball of the foot. Students can also practice walking at different speeds, on their toes, or with bent legs.

Students should also be instructed in **basic movement skills** beyond walking, such as how to step with the opposite foot when throwing a ball or completing the kick when using the foot to move a ball.

Sliding involves students moving sideways with a leading foot. Students should focus on keeping the weight on the balls of their feet, eyes focused on the direction of travel, with hips and shoulders pointing to the front. This **locomotor pattern** is commonly used in sports such as softball, basketball, and racquet sports. In the younger grades, the focus should be on introducing the basic movements so students develop proficiency in different sports as they get older.

As students begin to refine their movement skills, teachers should introduce **biomechanics**, or the science behind human movement. Biomechanics is impacted by myriad forces including gravity, which makes the human body return to the ground after jumping; friction, which causes a bowling ball to slow down as it moves toward the pins; and other laws of motion (see Chapter 3).

Practice Question

1) Which activity would provide the BEST opportunity for students to understand how friction is related to human movement?
   A. swinging
   B. sliding
   C. dribbling
   D. catching

Exercise Physiology

Health-related fitness includes the development of flexibility, cardiorespiratory endurance, muscular strength, and endurance:

- **Flexibility** refers to the body's range of motion of joints and can be developed through activities like stretching, yoga, and gymnastics.

- **Cardiorespiratory endurance** refers to the ongoing ability of the cardiorespiratory organs to get oxygen to the muscles during activity. This type of endurance is an important part of overall health; it is best developed through running, swimming, cycling, and other aerobic exercises.

- **Muscular strength** involves the amount of weight a muscle can move or the amount of force it can produce. Weight training and bodyweight exercises, such as push-ups and planks, help build muscular strength.

- General **endurance** refers to the body's ability to sustain a certain physical activity over time. Endurance typically improves as physical fitness increases with time.

> **Helpful Hint**
>
> Each class and grade level's fitness goal will be different, and modifications may be needed to match a lesson plan with the students' current fitness levels.

When designing lessons to promote fitness, teachers should keep in mind the **FITT (f**requency, **i**ntensity, **t**ime, **t**ype**) principle**. This acronym describes guidelines for a fitness plan, and it can be applied to the whole class or to individual students if necessary.

Frequency refers to how often students should exercise. For example, lifestyle exercises may be scheduled more frequently than endurance ones. The **intensity** of the activity describes how hard students need to work during each class. **Time** refers to how long students should participate in the activity. Students should participate in at least thirty to sixty minutes of age-appropriate physical activity daily, ten minutes of which should be moderate to vigorous activity. The **type** of activity describes the kinds of activities students practice or play. Teachers should create different lessons that incorporate a wide variety of lifestyle and recreational activities, active aerobics, flexibility, sports activities, and strength and muscular endurance exercises.

Physical activity can improve **body composition**, or the percentage of various parts of the body, such as skin, muscle, bone, fat, and water. Most measurements of body composition determine the percentage of body fat a person has. What is considered a normal range varies by age and sex. Broader lifestyle changes, such as healthy eating, getting enough sleep, and prioritizing mental health can also have a positive impact on body composition.

While improved body composition is one benefit of physical fitness, it is certainly not the only one. Fitness improves brain function and memory and reduces negative emotions like anxiety or depression. It also promotes healthy sleep patterns and increases energy while lowering blood pressure.

Physical activity also comes with risk, the largest of which is the potential for injury. These injuries are most commonly to the muscles (such as a pulled or strained muscle) or to the skeletal system (such as a broken bone). However, people with underlying health conditions may have other risks.

Teachers must consult with a school nurse or a health professional regarding the needs of students with health conditions like asthma or diabetes; teachers should also be aware of the effects of medication students take and the symptoms of health emergencies. Lessons and physical activities may need to be modified to accommodate students' needs.

During physical education lessons, **safety** for teachers and students must be taken into consideration. Teachers should check the area before any activity or game begins to ensure there are no dangerous objects or hazards. Participants should also understand a signal from the teacher that indicates the beginning and end of play. A warm-up period before starting any activity will prevent injuries. For the sake of safety, teachers should also consider omitting skills that might put students in harm's way.

While most exercise or movement might take place in a physical education class, there is a growing movement to **integrate movement** across the content areas. This might involve activities like a four corners debate where students move to various corners of the room to show their opinion on certain topics, or scavenger hunts where student groups move around the room or school to locate certain items.

Teachers will need to consider the various needs of students during any physical activity. Not only will students be at various levels of fitness and have various existing body compositions, but students may have disabilities that require special modifications or accommodations. Modifications might include adjusting the duration of activities or using sports equipment more appropriate for students' needs. For example, students with limited upper body strength could use foam balls instead of heavier baseballs or softballs.

Sometimes, whole group activities can be adapted to be more inclusive. This is known as **adaptive physical education**. Popular adaptive PE games often use balloons instead of balls for games like dodgeball or basketball, but many other strategies are also appropriate and may be listed on a student's individualized education plan (IEP).

Additionally, students will enter physical education programs with a wide range of past experiences, so familiarity with common American sports or games should not be assumed. Students from diverse backgrounds can also share different sports or games with the class, but the PE lessons should also aim to include sports and games from many different cultures and parts of the world.

Practice Question

2) Which activity would BEST promote cardiorespiratory endurance?
   A. bowling
   B. stretching
   C. walking
   D. push-ups

Health

Lessons on healthy living are integral to a well-rounded physical education and health curriculum. While it is important for students to practice motor development skills, a good physical education and health curriculum also shows students the benefits of a healthy lifestyle. Improved physical fitness and knowledge of proper nutrition will help students in other areas of life, including self-discipline, cooperation, stress reduction, goal setting, and better relationships with peers.

> **Helpful Hint**
>
> Planting a garden is a great hands-on activity for teaching early elementary students about food and nutrition.

At the elementary level, lessons on health help students learn about wellness and unhealthy behaviors. They gain the ability to explain the importance of physical activity, what contributes to disease in the body, and how nutrition, stress and substance use affect their growth and well-being.

Teaching students about the physical systems in the body is a great introduction to the theories of health and gives them the fundamental knowledge to better understand **nutrition** and fitness. In the early elementary grades, the focus should be on the elements of a **balanced diet**. Looking at the healthy eating plate and identifying nutrients helps students learn how their choices affect their bodies.

Figure 5.2. MyPlate Food Guide

Nutrition is tied to growth and body composition, but it is not the only factor. **Body type**, which is inherited and largely unchangeable, will also impact the shape of the human body. Similarly, human **growth spurts**, or sudden increases in height and weight, are also a natural part of growing up.

Disease prevention and control is another part of human health. Students should learn about practical ways to prevent disease, such as practicing **personal hygiene**, identifying symptoms of diseases and how they affect the body, and how to prevent diseases. Students may also learn about injury prevention and safety. Topics would include basic safety rules, reacting to emergencies, and understanding strategies for self-protection.

Beyond the physical body, students also need to understand that their **mental health** contributes to social and emotional well-being. Students should learn different strategies and skills to improve their relationships with others and themselves. Topics can include

- friends and family,
- effective communication,
- appropriate emotional responses, and
- assuming responsibility for their own decisions.

Older students will learn about stress, its effects on the body, and how to identify resources and constructive ways of dealing with it.

Learning about **substance abuse** helps older students understand the impact drugs can have on their lives. Lessons should help students understand how alcohol and other types of drugs (including some types of medications) affect the body when abused; students should learn about decision-making. More specifically, lessons can examine media, peer pressure, and other external factors (such as laws) that impact decision-making. Equally important are lessons on internal factors, like addiction.

Overall health is also impacted by mental processes. Of particular importance is the development of a positive **self-image**, or the way individuals perceive themselves. A healthy mind and body can contribute to a positive self-image, but students must be prompted to recognize that there is no such thing as a perfect body.

One aim of physical education programs is to develop people who will become committed to lifelong health. Goal setting can help students meet this aim by helping them establish good habits, such as getting at least thirty minutes of exercise per day, five days a week.

Practice Question

3) Which of the following methods is NOT an appropriate activity for teaching students about the benefits of nutrition?
   A. showing students a picture of the USDA food plate and creating a balanced meal using the guidelines
   B. showing students a picture of the food pyramid and creating a balanced meal using the guidelines
   C. showing students possible side effects when they eat too much sugar
   D. showing students the types of food that can help to decrease risk of disease

Physical Education and Social Development

The goal of any physical education program should be to engage all students in ways that will allow them to improve their physical fitness, learn to enjoy movement and recreation, and develop appropriate social skills. To help students obtain these goals, teachers should be aware of important social aspects related to physical education, which may vary based on the individual student.

Research suggests that opportunities to engage in physical activity can improve student confidence and even reduce certain delinquent behaviors. Athletic participation has been proven to foster a positive **school climate**, sense of belonging, and school pride. For maximum benefits, physical education should always be **developmentally appropriate**, or tailored to the developmental level of the participants.

In planning developmentally appropriate activities, teachers should consider the physical and social-emotional development of students, with a focus on inclusion. Activities that require a high degree of existing physical fitness or specific training are likely to be least appropriate for younger students and may lead to frustration. Similarly, games or activities that students have already mastered may quickly become stale.

Activities will likely include both those that involve **competition**, such as group sports like kickball, soccer, or basketball, and those that do not, such as stretching and dance. While there is some debate about the role of competition in physical education programs, many experts believe that the most important factor is how innately competitive sports and activities are facilitated. Students must be taught **sportsmanship**, or the belief that sport is, above all, a social interaction that should be enjoyed for its own sake.

There are drawbacks to competition in sports, such as stress and a possible loss of confidence. Students should be encouraged to focus on their own effort and their own improvement over time versus the outcome of a game reflected in a score. Furthermore, **cooperation** should be emphasized over competition whenever possible. Opportunities for students to work together with each other toward a goal and improve communication and teamwork skills should be nurtured as part of group activities.

As part of participation in physical education activities, teachers should also be aware of differences between cultures. Of particular relevance is the difference between **individualist versus collectivist cultures**. Individualist cultures, like the United States, often value individual achievement and competition. In contrast, collectivist cultures, common in many Asian, African, and Latin American nations, value group success. Teachers should consider both value systems when designing activities so that students have opportunities to learn in both familiar and new ways.

Students will also have various fitness levels and activity preferences as well as varied physical abilities. To accommodate all students, some classes employ a station or center approach where students can select from various activities as well as the use of adapted or modified activities (see "Exercise Physiology" section). Additionally, teachers should be aware that standards of dress for physical education, such as shorts and t-shirts, may not be aligned with cultural norms that prioritize modesty. Flexibility to accommodate the modesty needs of all students may be required.

Practice Question

4) Which activity is LEAST tailored to a collectivist culture?
   A. planning and performing a pair modern dance routine
   B. a parachute game where groups toss a ball back and forth
   C. square dancing
   D. tennis

Answer Key

1) B: When sliding, the body is slowed by friction against the slide.

2) C: Brisk walking for sustained periods can promote cardiorespiratory endurance and may be a good option for students with little existing cardiorespiratory endurance.

3) B: The food pyramid was replaced by the MyPlate guidelines to demonstrate healthy food choices.

4) D: Tennis is most often an individual sport, where two individuals engage in direct competition.

6. Visual and Performing Arts

Dance

Dance is typically defined as rhythmic body movements in sequence. Dance comes in many forms, sometimes called styles or genres. Style of dance is often associated with a certain culture, but all dance is similar in its existence as a medium for human **artistic expression**. All dances also contain what is often referred to as **elements of dance**: movements of the body using time, space, and energy. Dance elements are distinct from **dance techniques**, which are the particular skills required for a style or genre of dance (e.g., a plié in ballet).

A dance performance may be a **dance study** (a short performance made up of different **phrases**, or sequences of related movements) or a **dance work**, which is typically a longer performance with a clear beginning, middle or development, and end.

Some dances are **choreographed**, or planned phrases. Choreographed dance involves the intentional use of space, time/tempo, repetition, and energy. Other dances are improvised, such as getting up to dance at a friend's wedding. Students can plan or improvise dance in response to different types of **stimuli** designed to inspire feelings, thoughts, and actions. These stimuli may include

- music,
- literary or nonfiction texts,
- objects,
- print or video images,
- symbols,
- past experiences, and
- dances they have observed others perform.

When dancing, students employ both **locomotor** movements, or those where the body travels in space (e.g., skips and leaps) and **non-locomotor** movements, or those where the body does not travel in space (e.g., twists and bends).

Students will learn many technical dance skills, such as **coordination**, or the ability to control or execute movements; **balance**, or the ability to establish and maintain the body's equilibrium; **rhythm**, or the ability to move the body in sync with music; and **tempo**, or the ability to dance at the appropriate rate of speed. Dancers will also develop **kinesthetic awareness**, or an awareness of how different parts of the body are moving while in motion.

Some dance performances will be solos; others will be done in a group. Either way, dancers must maintain **spatial awareness**, or an understanding about the space around them. Dancers in groups must maintain appropriate **spatial relationships** with other dancers as they perform in a shared or **negative space**, which is the area between dancers. Negative space exists in contrast with **personal space**, or the area as far as the individual dancer can reach.

> **Did You Know?**
>
> Though *Swan Lake* is now regarded as one of the most famous ballets ever, its first performance in 1877 was judged harshly by critics, who called it "too noisy."

Students receiving dance instruction will also be tasked with interpreting dance they see their peers or professionals perform. In interpreting or analyzing dance performances, students should consider the following:

- genre or style
- movement patterns and characteristics
- the time period and/or location from which the dance originates
- what the dance reveals about the time and/or location represented

Analyzing dance in this way will help students develop **dance literacy**, or general knowledge of dance. Students should also become familiar with basic dance styles such as **ballroom dance**, which began in France in the 1500s and includes styles like the waltz, tango, and quickstep; **performance dance**, which includes ballet, modern, and contemporary dance; **jazz dance**, including tap, swing, the Charleston, and disco; **Latin dance** like salsa, flamenco, and lambada; other **global dances** like polka and belly dance; and **hip-hop dance** like breakdance, locking, and popping.

Students should also be aware of the intersection between dance and human culture, how dance has changed over time, and how certain dance styles have influenced other dance styles in a process of blending and borrowing.

Practice Question

1) A student is struggling to complete a full turn and sometimes stumbles or has to put his hands down. Which technical dance skill should this student practice?
  A. tempo
  B. rhythm
  C. spatial awareness
  D. balance

Music

Teaching music is important to help students enhance skills that they can transfer to other subject areas. Students who are exposed to music education tend to do better in language development (e.g., reading tests) than students who are not. Music education helps to develop the left side of the brain, which is critical to processing language. Music also engages numerous parts of the brain, including the cognitive, hedonic, planning, and sensory systems. Furthermore, research has shown links between spatial intelligence and music studies, which means that students learn to visualize the different elements that are working together and recognize patterns, which corresponds with the problem-solving skills needed in mathematics.

As a music teacher, it is also important to help students make connections between music across other disciplines and the real world. To do so, teachers must vary lessons. For example, listening to music can teach students about different musical genres and expose students to the history of these. Music can also be connected to literature: students may learn to conduct research for a music-related project and in the process draw upon knowledge learned in different classes. Lessons on music culture may also tie into social studies.

To make real-world connections, teachers help students recognize the impact of music in their everyday lives:

- Teachers expose students to music from popular culture, such as commercials, movies and television shows.
- Teachers can also help students understand the emotional aspects of music (e.g., by using songs to remember significant events).
- Providing and studying informational texts is another way for students to understand music in real-world contexts.

Teaching music requires that the teacher has a sound knowledge of music notation, music-making, and **music terminology:**

- Music **notation** is a method of writing down music so that anyone can play it.
    - It helps composers create music by clearly indicating how they want it to sound.
    - Anyone who can read music will be able to play or sing the song accurately.
    - Teachers can start helping students understand music notation by presenting it and breaking down the different elements of the modern system of notation.

Figure 6.1. Musical Notation

The main system of notation currently used is writing musical notes on a **stave**, which is composed of a five-line **staff** with four spaces in between:

- The music is read from left to right, and there is usually a **clef** in front of a staff of written music.
- The **clef** helps to show exactly which notes are played, such as the treble clef or the bass clef.
- The location of the note on the staff indicates the **pitch**, or the position of a sound within the range of sounds.
    - Sharps or flats may be in front of the note.
    - Notes that are very high or low can be placed on ledger lines above or below the stave.
- The **key signature** is found after the clef, which indicates which sharps or flats will be used regularly.
- The **time signature**, placed afterwards, divides the music into regular groupings of beats using bars or measures.
    - There are usually words that show the tempo, or the speed of music.
    - There may also be dynamic marks to indicate how loud or soft to play the music at certain points.

Understanding music terminology can help students develop a better understanding of the elements of music. Teachers must explain what pitch, rhythm, melody, texture, timbre, and dynamics are and how they apply to music. Teachers should help students develop these concepts by reading musical notation, listening to music, and carrying out practical exercises.

Pitch can be high or low; scales are created by organizing patterns of pitches with intervals in between. Types of **scales** include chromatic, gapped, pentatonic, and major/minor. Having students listen to many pitches and practice the different types of scales offers them a more practical approach to learning. Teachers typically start by using a number system to help younger students learn the notes and then move on to *solfeggio* (*do, re, me, fa, so, la, ti, do*) as they progress.

Rhythm governs time in music. It is a specific pattern in time—a tempo—much like a steady pulse. These are organized into **meter**, which arranges these pulses into groups. These then can be further divided into two, three, or four smaller units. To help students develop an understanding of rhythm, teachers begin by using familiar songs or nursery rhymes and have the students clap along. The students feel and count the beats in a song, learning to distinguish when notes should start and end. Students can then understand the rhythmic patterns of the song. Students can progress to recognizing rhythm just by listening to a song or creating it by playing a musical instrument.

A combination of pitch and rhythm is called a **melody:**

- Melody describes the size of the intervals of the contour (rising or falling)—the tune of a song.
- As such, it is the main focus of a song and a way for a composer to communicate with her audience.

Harmony relies on the melody and is the simultaneous use of pitches or chords—the notes that support melodies:

- To develop the concept of melody, teachers should have students listen to and consider how a melody rises and falls, or compare melodic contours; these actions develop melodic personality.
- Teachers can also introduce the names and sounds of notes first to help children develop a sense of melody and understand how to read music.

Having students learn a five-note scale and the different clefs can teach them how different pitches affect the melody. As students progress through the grades, teachers can even create lessons that help students see how different melodies can imply different emotions.

The **timbre**, or **tone**, is the musical characteristic that distinguishes between different instruments. When discussing timbre, students should be exposed to as many sounds as possible. Students can describe the sound by naming the instrument (once they have learned it), or using different terms:

- brassy
- bright
- raspy
- shrill
- dark
- buzzy

As students become more advanced, they can group different timbres according to instrument type, whether it be woodwind, brass, string, or percussion. Students should be taught to understand that the timbre is the same even if the same instrument is played at different pitches and volumes.

Dynamics refers to the loud or soft parts of a piece of music. They can change gradually or suddenly (crescendo or decrescendo), or have a large dynamic range if there are very soft and incredibly loud passages in the composition.

Combining melody, rhythm, and harmony is what makes up the **texture** in a composition, as these all determine the overall quality of the sound. Texture includes the number of layers and how these relate to one another. There are different types of musical textures:

- **Monophonic** is made of one voice or line with no accompaniment.
- **Polyphonic** includes many musical voices that imitate or counter one another, including the rhythm or melody (e.g., songs popular during the Renaissance or Baroque periods).
- **Homophonic** consists of a main melody which is accompanied by harmonic chords (e.g., a singer with a piano accompaniment).
- The texture would be considered **homorhythmic** if all parts have a similar rhythm.

> **Helpful Hint**
>
> Each instrument differs in high and low pitches. The instruments with the highest pitches tend to be in the woodwind family, with the piccolo being the highest. The lowest-pitched instruments tend to be in the brass or string family, with the double bass being the lowest.

Teachers should introduce one texture at a time so students have time to listen to and develop their understanding of how to accurately identify textures. Students can also preform different songs to get a feel for how different textures work.

At the elementary level, students may learn to play simple instruments as they develop their understanding of the elements of music. At the early elementary level (up to the third grade), students may not have developed the fine muscle control that would allow them to play more complicated instruments. Teachers should select items, such as Orff and other simple percussion instruments, that are easier to play and help students visualize pitch and rhythm while they develop their motor skills. Later, recorders are introduced when students are able to physically play them. This simple instrument helps students develop the skills, such as breathing techniques, that are necessary for more advanced instruments and allows them to gain experience reading sheet music, which is simplified with recorders since there is only one tone. Teachers can also use the recorder to teach a wide variety of songs and ensembles using one instrument.

In the upper elementary grades, students should have developed the motor skills to play the types of instruments used in band programs. Since students should have learned how to read basic sheet music and utilize the breathing techniques appropriate for woodwind instruments, teachers can help students advance by applying their knowledge of other elements of music, such as harmony and timbre.

As in dance, music is a way for human artistic expression, and music is entwined with human culture. Students should be exposed to multiple musical styles and genres, understand the context of each, and recognize what is being communicated about a given culture or group. Students should be further encouraged to pursue their own musical interests and develop their own music based on their interests and experiences.

Practice Question

2) Which of the following instruments has the LOWEST pitch?
   A. piccolo
   B. double bass
   C. trumpet
   D. trombone

Theatre

Drama is an expression that tells a story to an audience through the actions and dialogue of characters, which are brought to life by actors who play the roles on stage. Dramatic works, called **plays**, are written in poetic or lyrical verses, or in regular prose. Along with the dialogue between the characters, authors rely on **stage directions** to describe the sets and to give instructions to the actors about what they are to do.

In some plays, actors perform long speeches in which the characters explain their thinking about philosophical ideas or social issues. These **monologues** can be directed toward another character. A monologue delivered as if nobody were listening is called a **soliloquy** (as in Shakespeare's famous "To be or not to be" soliloquy from *Hamlet*).

Sometimes characters in drama (or fiction) have very unique attributes, such as a manner of speech, dress, or a catchphrase. Such devices make characters memorable to readers and are known as **character tags**.

Dramatic interpretations may be based on **scripted dramas** or **improvised** (i.e., spontaneous) scenes and monologues. Younger students may participate in **guided drama experiences**, where a leader supports student actors via side-coaching and prompting without stopping the action of the play.

Students should also be given opportunities to learn about the **technical elements** of theatre, such as the integration of **lighting**, and **sound** elements, such as music or sound effects. Other elements include props, which can be **representational materials**—actual objects like silk flowers or trees— or **non-representational materials**, which can be made into props via imagination (e.g., a beam in the cafeteria that becomes a magic tree).

Materials for students to use to create their own props, scenery, puppets, and costumes should be part of the supplies of the theatre classroom. These supplies need not be elaborate and can be recycled materials, such as plastic bottles and cans (useful for sound effects); old boxes (useful for scenery); and scraps of fabric or discarded clothing (useful for costumes).

Large group performances are not the only activities in which students will participate. They might be given opportunities to tell stories, sing songs, or perform **spoken word poetry**, an oral performance of poetry with a certain beat or rhythm.

> **Did You Know?**
>
> The Ancient Greeks were the first to put on theatrical performances, which date back to the sixth century BCE.

Students should also have opportunities to connect English language arts skills with theatre as they consider the plot, characterization, setting, character motivations, and dialogue in dramas they read and perform. As with dance and music, dramatic interpretations from various cultures should be explored and analyzed for how they express important themes and ideas.

Practice Question

3) In an improvised duet scene, a student runs away from a desk in the classroom, screaming "Snake! Snake!" What does this exemplify?
   A. guided drama experience
   B. character tags
   C. stage directions
   D. non-representational materials

Visual Arts

The **visual arts** include drawing, painting, sculpting, and photography. While the tools and techniques used in these art forms can be very different, they all rely on the same foundational elements and principles.

A good understanding of the elements and principles of art is necessary for the creation and analysis of art. Teachers should show children that artists use these elements and principles to make decisions when creating their own art, and that students should apply this knowledge to their own works.

Art is created through the use of line, shape, form, value, texture, space, and color. Together, these are known as the **elements of art**.

Line in art is called a moving dot: it can control the viewer's eye, indicate form and movement, describe edges, and point out a light source in a drawing. Artists use different line qualities and contours to suggest form. To indicate value or a light source, artists use cross-hatching lines in varying degrees.

> **Helpful Hint**
>
> To engage young children, have them create and analyze art that relates to topics that are familiar to them, such as family, friends, sports, holidays, and animals.

A closed contour is what creates **shape**, which is two-dimensional. A shape can create balance and affect the composition, establishing positive and negative spaces. Different types of shapes include regular (i.e., geometric) and organic (i.e., free-form) shapes. When students understand the basics of shapes, they can create complex forms by combining simple organic and regular shapes.

Form is like shape except that it is three-dimensional. Creating form requires an understanding of how light reflects upon an object, or its **value**. Teachers should help students understand where the highlight, the reflected light, the mid-tone, the core shadow, and the cast shadows are in order to create an illusion of form. Having students create a value scale and understand how it applies to objects they see is also helpful. Value also helps to create **texture**, which refers to how an object would feel if someone were to touch it. Students can develop their sense of texture through exposure to a wide variety of objects and by understanding how light reflects off rough, smooth, matte, and shiny surfaces.

Creating an illusion of **space** can help students in creating an artwork on a two-dimensional surface. Students should experiment with different techniques such as overlapping shapes, shape placement, sizes of shapes, and perspective to see how objects can appear closer or farther away.

The color wheel is primarily used to teach students the theories of **color**. There are different types of colors:

- **Primary colors** (red, yellow, and blue) cannot be made using other colors.

- **Secondary colors** are made by mixing primary colors.
    - yellow + blue = green
    - red + blue = purple
    - red + yellow = orange
- **Tertiary colors** are made by mixing one primary color with half the saturation of a second primary color (e.g., blue + 1/2 red = violet).

The color wheel also shows **complementary colors**, which appear opposite each other on the wheel. When paired together, complementary colors offer a stark contrast that is pleasing to the eye.

Figure 6.2. The RGB Color Wheel

The **principles of art** refer to the composition of the elements of art within a piece of work. These principles include

- balance,
- unity,
- contrast,
- movement,
- emphasis,
- pattern, and
- proportion.

In order to create **balance** in an artwork, colors, forms, shapes, or textures need to be combined in harmony. Harmony also helps to create **unity** in a piece of work by creating a sense of wholeness.

Artists generate **contrast** by using various elements of art (e.g., shapes, form, colors, or lines) to capture the viewer's attention and draw it toward a certain part of the work. **Movement** guides the viewer's eye through a composition, usually to highlight areas of contrast or emphasis. Repeating occurrences of a design element (e.g., shapes, forms, or textures in an art piece) are called **patterns**. Finally, **proportion** describes the way in which the sizes of objects appear. For example, objects that are farther away appear smaller and have less detail than objects that are closer.

Figure 6.3. Principles of Art

Art history should also be taught so that students can gain an understanding of how artists and art made contributions to culture and society and how art reflects what is important in a society at a certain time. In studying art history, students learn how artists interact with their contemporaneous cultures, respond to historical events and social change, and address other artistic movements. Art history lessons should encourage students to ask why an artist created a certain piece of art, how it was used, and what its purpose was.

As students study individual artists and their bodies of work, they should be encouraged to consider the mind of the artist as she created the work, and how the artwork relates to its time period. Teachers should provide as much relevant background as possible so that students can use that knowledge to

> **Helpful Hint**
>
> Students should be encouraged to think about works of art as stories about life. One way to do this is by asking students to consider and articulate the "story" they see in a work of art.

view and discuss the artwork. Even young children can benefit from exposure to the art and music of the different civilizations throughout human history.

Teachers can also use art history to help students explore world history and other cultures. Students can be taught about art from ancient civilizations such as ancient Egypt, the ancient Mayans, ancient Ethiopia, classical Greece and Rome, and more. They can also be introduced to modern art from various cultures around the world.

Teachers can also engage students with art history by having them create art from different cultures and time periods. Students can use supplies like pipe cleaners, wood craft sticks, cardboard, and construction paper to build their own versions of ancient pyramids and temples. To help build motor skills, children can use modeling clay to make their own sculptures during a lesson on classical civilization. Watercolors, tempera paints, and pastels are also great tools for young students who may be inspired by Claude Monet or Jackson Pollock to make their own impressionist- and modern-style artworks.

Practice Questions

4) A first-grade teacher wants to show students how complementary colors can be used when painting. Which of the following colors should she NOT use as an example?
    A. blue and orange
    B. red and blue
    C. purple and yellow
    D. red and green

5) A kindergarten teacher has his students paint a picture that includes animals of different sizes. Which principle of art is the teacher introducing to his students?
    A. pattern
    B. movement
    C. proportion
    D. unity

Answer Key

1) D: Balance refers to the ability to retain the body's equilibrium and avoid stumbling or falling.

2) B: The double bass is part of the string family and is the lowest pitched instrument in an orchestra.

3) D: The student is using imagination to turn the desk into a snake.

4) B: Red and blue are not directly opposite on the color wheel. The other choices are all complementary colors.

5) C: Having students draw animals of different sizes introduces them to proportion, or the way the size of elements in an artwork relate to each other.

Practice Test #1

Subtest I: Reading, Language, and Literature

Selected Response

1) A teacher asks, "What word am I trying to say: /p/ /i/ /n/?" and instructs students to say the word. Which strategy is the teacher using to build phoneme awareness?
   A. phoneme blending
   B. phoneme deletion
   C. phoneme segmentation
   D. phoneme substitution

2) A student is able to orally substitute the initial consonant /g/ for /b/ in the word *boat* to make the word *goat*. Which concept is the student demonstrating?
   A. phonemic awareness
   B. letter-sound correspondence
   C. phonological awareness
   D. manipulation of onsets and rimes

3) Which of the following letters is most likely to be introduced FIRST in progressive phonics instruction?
   A. a
   B. g
   C. y
   D. m

4) What is the purpose of sight word instruction?
   A. to help students learn letter-sound correspondences to improve accuracy
   B. to help students manipulate sounds in words to improve auditory skills
   C. to help students recognize words automatically to improve fluency
   D. to help students use word parts to improve reading comprehension

5) Most English roots originally come from which languages?
   A. German or French
   B. Spanish or French
   C. Latin or Greek
   D. Arabic or Phoenician

6) Read the sentences:

   1. The park naturalist visited the class to talk about the migration of monarch butterflies.

   2. The naturalist visited the class to talk about the migration of monarch butterflies from the park.

How do the two sentences differ?
- A. The word *park* acts as an adjective in the first sentence and is part of an adjective phrase in the second sentence.
- B. The word *park* is the subject of the first sentence, and the word *naturalist* is the subject of the second sentence.
- C. The word *park* is the subject of the first sentence and the predicate in the second sentence.
- D. The word *park* acts as an adjective in the first sentence and is part of an adverb phrase in the second sentence.

7) Read the sentence:
Despite the fact that the larger dog was ten times its size, the tiny dog continued to bark with ferocity.

The sentence above is an example of a
- A. simple sentence.
- B. compound sentence.
- C. complex sentence.
- D. compound-complex sentence.

Questions 8 – 9 refer to the poem below from *A Child's Garden of Verses* by Robert Louis Stevenson.

   "The Moon"

   The moon has a face like the clock in the hall;

   She shines on thieves on the garden wall;

   On streets and fields and harbor quays,

   And birdies asleep in the forks of the trees.

   The squalling cat and the squeaking mouse,

   The howling dog by the door of the house,

   The bat that lies in bed at noon,

   All love to be out by the light of the moon.

   But all of the things that belong to the day

   Cuddle to sleep to be out of her way;

   And flowers and children close their eyes

   Till up in the morning the sun shall rise.

8) Which type of figurative language is used to describe the moon's face?
   A. metaphor
   B. assonance
   C. alliteration
   D. simile

9) How does the reader know that the word *quays* is pronounced using /ē/ as opposed to /ā/?
   A. from the poet's use of simile
   B. from the poet's use of rhyme scheme
   C. from the poet's use of personification
   D. from the poet's use of point of view

10) Original Sentence:

    The scientist looked at the rocks to learn interesting things about the past.

Revision:

   The geologist examined the rocks to discover evidence of historical events.

The revised sentence reflects an improvement in which of the following elements of writing?

   A. conventions
   B. organization
   C. sentence fluency
   D. word choice

11) A student is giving a speech on school start times. The following quote is included in his presentation:

   Elementary school should start at 9 a.m. instead of 7:30 a.m. because children do their best thinking when they get enough sleep and have time to eat a healthy breakfast.

Which of the following is the BEST paraphrase of the speaker's message?

   A. Later school start times are better for learning because children get more rest and eat properly.
   B. School should start at 9 a.m. instead of 7:30 a.m. because children do their best thinking when they get enough sleep and have time to eat a healthy breakfast.
   C. Elementary school should start earlier than it does now.
   D. Many students are too tired during the school day to concentrate on learning.

12) Which of the following is an effective strategy for strengthening decoding skills?
   A. teaching character analysis
   B. teaching word families
   C. teaching active listening
   D. teaching fact and opinion

13) How could a teacher BEST model inferencing during reading?
   A. by thinking aloud
   B. by providing a graphic
   C. by drawing a plot pyramid
   D. by conducting a word investigation

Practice Test #1

14) Which of the following is true of qualitative measures of text complexity?
   A. They are readability scores based on word frequency and sentence length.
   B. They are analytical measurements determined by knowledge demands.
   C. They are statistical measurements determined by computer algorithms.
   D. They are determinations of reading level based on professional judgment.

Questions 15 – 18 refer to the following text excerpt from *Black Beauty* by Anna Sewell.

The name of the coachman was John Manly; he had a wife and one little child, and they lived in the coachman's cottage, very near the stables.

The next morning he took me into the yard and gave me a good grooming, and just as I was going into my box, with my coat soft and bright, the squire came in to look at me, and seemed pleased. "John," he said, "I meant to have tried the new horse this morning, but I have other business. You may as well take him around after breakfast; go by the common and the Highwood, and back by the watermill and the river; that will show his paces."

"I will, sir," said John. After breakfast he came and fitted me with a bridle. He was very particular in letting out and taking in the straps, to fit my head comfortably; then he brought a saddle, but it was not broad enough for my back; he saw it in a minute and went for another, which fitted nicely. He rode me first slowly, then a trot, then a canter, and when we were on the common he gave me a light touch with his whip, and we had a splendid gallop.

15) Which inference can the reader make based on the text?
   A. John Manly does not like his job.
   B. John Manly has respect for horses.
   C. John Manly is a coachman with a family.
   D. John Manly has bought a new horse.

16) Which point of view is used by the author?
   A. first-person
   B. second-person
   C. third-person objective
   D. third-person omniscient

17) Which of the following is the BEST summary of the excerpt?
   A. John Manly is a coachman who lives with his wife and a child in a cottage near a set of stables. He works in the stables grooming horses for the squire.
   B. After he has breakfast, John Manly has a splendid gallop by the watermill and along the river with a new horse from the stables.
   C. The horse is new to the stables, but the squire does not have time to check his paces, so he asks John Manly to do it, but John has to have breakfast first.
   D. The coachman, John Manly, grooms the horse and fits him comfortably with a bridle and saddle. Then, he takes the horse for a ride to test the horse's paces for the squire.

18) How can the reader BEST use the context of the excerpt to understand the meaning of the word *paces*?
   A. The reader can find the definition of the word in the paragraph that follows.
   B. The reader can figure out the word's meaning by analyzing its root and affix.
   C. The reader can use the connotation of the word to determine its meaning.
   D. The reader can analyze the setting for a hint to the meaning of the word.

19) A fourth-grade English language learner who speaks Spanish fluently writes "I have hunger" instead of "I am hungry." This is an example of which of the following?
   A. interlanguage effects
   B. bridging
   C. code-switching
   D. preproduction

20) Which of the underlined word groups is a verbal phrase?
<u>Living with her Aunt Sally</u> was something <u>that always intrigued Marie</u> <u>because her aunt</u> was <u>such a fun and interesting lady</u>.
   A. Living with her Aunt Sally
   B. that always intrigued Marie
   C. because her aunt
   D. such a fun and interesting lady

21) Which prewriting assignment would BEST prepare students for writing a quatrain poem?
   A. an investigation of the word *quatrain*
   B. listing pairs of rhyming words
   C. a mini-lesson on syllabication
   D. a concept map on the topic

22) Before reading a nonfiction text about sharks, Mrs. Rogers draws a KWL chart on a piece of chart paper and lists both what students already know about sharks, and what they want to know. What is Mrs. Rogers' purpose for using a KWL chart before reading?
   A. to introduce students to new vocabulary
   B. to prepare students to sequence text events
   C. to activate student background knowledge
   D. to provide an overview of the text information

23) Which assessment tool is MOST effective for tracking progress in oral reading fluency?
   A. portfolio
   B. reader's theater
   C. running record
   D. phonics screener

24) Which of the following can be classified as narrative writing?
   A. an opinion piece on a political candidate
   B. an essay on the causes and effects of erosion
   C. a poem that evokes the feeling of a spring thunderstorm
   D. a funny story about an adventure at the zoo

25) Read the following sentence:
Lucy thought the first movie was better then the second one.

What error has been made in the sentence above?
- A. The verbs are past tense.
- B. *Then* indicates time, not comparison.
- C. *One* is a dangling modifier.
- D. The subject is misplaced.

26) Which word in the sentence below is misspelled?

Geology is typically regarded as a tuough subject to master.
- A. geology
- B. typically
- C. tuough
- D. master

Constructed Response

For questions 27 and 28, you are to prepare a written response of approximately 100 – 200 words.

Read each assignment carefully before you begin to write. Think about how you will organize what you plan to write.

27) **Use the information below to complete the exercise that follows:**

A second-grade teacher has an English language learner in her classroom named Dolo. Dolo can easily copy down the spelling word list from the whiteboard into his notebook, can follow many classroom directions, and can say some English words and phrases, such as "thank you" and "hello."

Write a response in which you describe the student's second language development. Make sure to cite specific examples to support your conclusions.

28) **Read the excerpt below from *Five Weeks in a Balloon* by Jules Verne, and then complete the exercise that follows:**

There was a large audience assembled on the 14th of January, 1862, at the session of the Royal Geographical Society, No. 3 Waterloo Place, London. The president, Sir Francis M——, made an important communication to his colleagues, in an address that was frequently interrupted by applause.

This rare specimen of eloquence terminated with the following sonorous phrases bubbling over with patriotism:

"England has always marched at the head of nations" (for, the reader will observe, the nations always march at the head of each other), "by the intrepidity of her explorers in the line of geographical discovery." (General assent). "Dr. Samuel Ferguson, one of her most glorious sons, will not reflect discredit on his origin." ("No, indeed!" from all parts of the hall.)

"This attempt, should it succeed" ("It will succeed!"), "... "and, should it fail, it will, at least, remain on record as one of the most daring conceptions of human genius!" (tremendous cheering)

"Huzza! Huzza!" shouted the immense audience, completely electrified by these inspiring words.

"Huzza for the intrepid Ferguson!" cried one of the most excitable of the enthusiastic crowd.

The wildest cheering resounded on all sides; the name of Ferguson was in every mouth, and we may safely believe that it lost nothing in passing through English throats. Indeed, the hall fairly shook with it.

Write a response in which you do the following:

- Describe the point of view in the excerpt.
- Describe the impact of specific word choices on tone in the excerpt.
- Be sure to cite specific evidence from the text.

Subtest II: History and Social Science

Selected Response

1) Which of the following is NOT a true statement about the ancient Greek civilization?
   A. Men and women lived in different parts of a house.
   B. They built aqueducts to carry water to public toilets.
   C. Greek cities had an agora.
   D. Socrates was a famous Greek philosopher.

2) Luther and Barbara wanted to start a business in the engineering field. They were trying to decide between hiring one staff member and using the leftover money to purchase new inventory, or hiring two staff members to increase their marketing reach. These choices would be an example of which of the following?
   A. needs
   B. scarcity
   C. opportunity cost
   D. supply and demand

3) Which of the following would be the MOST useful for studying population patterns within the state of California over a period of time?
   A. a bar graph detailing population numbers over a period of thirty years
   B. a map with the number of people living in different parts of California in the year 2000
   C. a photograph showing how many people were at a state fair
   D. a bar graph detailing population percentages compared with other states

4) Which of the following is NOT a responsibility of the executive branch?
   A. approving laws
   B. making laws
   C. implementing laws
   D. enforcing laws

5) Which of the following constitutional amendments is NOT considered part of the Bill of Rights?
   A. the right to bear arms
   B. the right to address witnesses arranged by the government when on trial
   C. the right to equal protection under the law
   D. freedom of speech

6) Asking citizens to be civil minded and independent and making the people as a whole sovereign is characteristic of which of the following?
    A. republicanism
    B. government
    C. economics
    D. communism

7) Which of the following did NOT contribute to the outbreak of the American Revolution?
    A. the Boston Tea Party, in which colonists threw 298 chests of tea into the sea
    B. Britain banning further westward expansion with the Proclamation of 1763
    C. General Thomas Gage ordering troops to capture Thomas Jefferson and Samuel Adams
    D. Charles Townshend taxing glass, oil, lead, and paint

8) Which of the following established the concept of judicial review?
    A. the John Peter Zenger trial
    B. *Marbury v. Madison*
    C. the Dred Scott case
    D. the Scopes Monkey trial

9) Which of the following lands was acquired during the Louisiana Purchase?
    A. the land roughly bordered by the Rocky Mountains, the Mississippi River, and the Rio Grande River
    B. the land roughly bordered by the Rocky Mountains, the Mississippi river, and the northern border of modern-day Texas
    C. the land between the Rocky Mountains and the Mississippi River, and modern-day Georgia
    D. the land roughly bordered by the Rocky Mountains and the Mississippi river, including modern-day New Mexico

10) Which of the following historical figures was a major architect of the US Constitution?
    A. Thomas Jefferson
    B. George Washington
    C. James Madison
    D. Patrick Henry

11) Which of the following protects against forced self-incrimination in the United States?
    A. separation of powers
    B. the First Amendment
    C. the Fifth Amendment
    D. popular sovereignty

12) Which of the following were part of the New England colonies?
    A. New York, Connecticut, and Massachusetts
    B. Connecticut, Massachusetts, and New Hampshire
    C. New Hampshire, Massachusetts, and New Jersey
    D. New York, New Jersey, Pennsylvania, and Delaware

13) Which of the following lessons helps students develop an understanding of a market economy?
    A. Students explore economic competition in their area and identify local business competitors.
    B. Students explore making smart buying decisions by comparing prices of goods.
    C. Students work together to decide what is necessary to rebuild a community.
    D. Students explore how individuals generate income.

14) Students in fourth grade are studying a map of the Nile during ancient Egyptian times and answering questions related to landmarks and places. Which of the following social studies skills is being assessed in this exercise?
    A. understanding spatial relationships
    B. understanding historical timelines
    C. using topographical maps
    D. understanding physical geography

15) Which of the following describes a practice common to many Native American groups in California prior to European arrival?
    A. a carefully planned central government
    B. a rigid social hierarchy
    C. alliances with other groups
    D. adaptiveness to the local environment

16) Which mountain range had to be blasted through as part of the construction of the Transcontinental Railroad?
    A. Cascade Range
    B. Transverse Ranges
    C. Klamath Mountains
    D. the Sierra Nevada range

17) Why did the first Native Americans of California settle in isolated communities?
    A. They lacked a common language.
    B. They encountered geographic barriers.
    C. They wanted to avoid warfare.
    D. They found scarce natural resources.

18) Which of the following describes a practice common to many Native American groups in California prior to European arrival?
    A. a carefully planned central government
    B. a rigid social hierarchy
    C. alliances with other groups
    D. adaptiveness to the local environment

19) Why did California have significant political independence as part of Mexico?
    A. The Bear Flag revolt guaranteed self-government.
    B. The region was far away from the central government.
    C. The Californios had not yet elected a governor.
    D. The constitution allowed for territorial governance.

20) Which of the following was a result of the California Gold Rush?
    A. the founding of the Pony Express
    B. the construction of the Transcontinental Railroad
    C. widespread unemployment
    D. growing labor movements

21) Where is MOST of the surface fresh water of California located?
    A. along the coast
    B. in the south
    C. in the north
    D. under the desert

22) A worker at a strawberry farm uses some of her wages to purchase food for her family. This flow of money is part of which of the following?
    A. the circular flow model of economic exchanges
    B. the business cycle
    C. monetary and fiscal policy
    D. economic growth

23) Which of the following is NOT a major part of the economy of California?
    A. aerospace
    B. tourism
    C. agriculture
    D. diamonds

24) Which part of California's constitution allows for the public to call for the removal of a public official?
    A. initiative
    B. referendum
    C. recall
    D. petition

25) Where did the California trail system begin?
    A. Ohio
    B. Missouri
    C. Kansas
    D. Virginia

26) Dust Bowl migrants were often treated poorly by those already living in California primarily because they
    A. were seen as competition for scarce jobs.
    B. had contributed to an ecological disaster.
    C. participated in some labor movements.
    D. were featured in famous photographs and literature.

Constructed Response

For questions 27 and 28, you are to prepare a written response of approximately 100 – 200 words.

Read each assignment carefully before you begin to write. Think about how you will organize what you plan to write.

27) **Complete the exercise that follows:**
Colonial Spanish California and Mexican California were marked by both change and continuity.

Using your knowledge of California history, prepare a response in which you

- identity two ways that these societies reflected continuity;
- identify two ways that these societies reflected change; and
- describe how and why these changes came about.

28) **Complete the exercise that follows:**
Reconstruction did not succeed in helping formerly enslaved African Americans in the South gain full participation in society.

Using your knowledge of American history, prepare a response in which you

- identify two reasons for which Reconstruction did not achieve this outcome;
- identify one way in which Southern legislators responded to Reconstruction; and
- explain how this legislation limited the rights of African Americans in the South.

Subtest III: Science

Selected Response

1) Which pH level is classified as a base?

    A. 2
    B. 4
    C. 6
    D. 8

2) Which body system is responsible for the release of growth hormones?
    A. digestive system
    B. endocrine system
    C. nervous system
    D. circulatory system

3) Which example illustrates a physical change?
    A. Water becomes ice.
    B. Batter is baked into a cake.
    C. An iron fence rusts.
    D. A firecracker explodes.

4) Which example demonstrates refraction?
   A. rainbow
   B. echo
   C. mirror
   D. radio

5) Which term describes a relationship between two organisms where one organism benefits to the detriment of the other organism?
   A. mutualism
   B. parasitism
   C. commensalism
   D. predation

6) Which organelle makes proteins?
   A. mitochondria
   B. cytoplasm
   C. vacuole
   D. ribosomes

7) Which statement is true?
   A. Earth is much closer to the sun than it is to other stars.
   B. The moon is closer to Venus than it is to Earth.
   C. At certain times of the year, Jupiter is closer to the sun than Earth is.
   D. Mercury is the closest planet to Earth.

8) Which example has the LEAST amount of kinetic energy?
   A. a plane flying through the sky
   B. a plane sitting on the runway
   C. a ladybug flying towards a flower
   D. a meteorite falling to Earth

9) Which statement is true?
   A. Mass and weight are the same thing.
   B. Mass is affected by gravitational pull.
   C. Weight is affected by gravitational pull.
   D. Mass is related to the surface area of an object.

10) When the moon moves into the shadow of Earth, what is it called?
    A. a solar eclipse
    B. a lunar eclipse
    C. a black hole
    D. a supernova

11) Which example demonstrates body systems working together to maintain homeostasis?
    A. Jessica's tracheotomy opened a breathing obstruction.
    B. Max's muscles, tendons, and ligaments allow his joints to bend.
    C. Kevin's bones thicken from an excessive production of growth hormones.
    D. Stacy shivers from the cold.

12) Which simple machine is shown in the picture below?

A. inclined plane
B. pulley
C. screw
D. wedge

13) Which lesson can BEST introduce a geology unit about the layers of the earth?
A. a lesson on hydroponics
B. an discussion on geothermal energy
C. a lecture about solar energy
D. a class on hydropower

14) Which activity demonstrates a chemical change?
A. dissolving drink mix in water
B. slicing an apple
C. cooking an egg
D. melting an ice cube

15) Which activity could be used to demonstrate Newton's third law of motion?
A. hitting the 8-ball with the cue ball in billiards
B. rolling two balls of different masses down a ramp
C. dropping a ping-pong ball
D. swinging a pendulum

16) Which plant is an example of a dicot?
A. wheat
B. pine
C. bean
D. corn

17) The periodic table can be used for all of the following EXCEPT
A. grouping elements by properties.
B. looking up atomic mass.
C. determining if an element is a metal.
D. identifying the rareness of an element.

18) A river ecosystem experiences an extreme fluctuation in chemical composition due to pollution, and many organisms die, decreasing the total number of organisms. What can be said about this system?
    A. It is going through a life cycle change.
    B. It is NOT at dynamic equilibrium.
    C. It is NOT an open system.
    D. It is going through an accommodation.

19) If both parents are homozygous for type A blood, what will be true of their child?
    A. He will have type AB blood.
    B. She will have a 50% chance of having type A blood.
    C. He will have type O blood.
    D. She will have a 100% chance of having type A blood.

20) A teacher has students watch a video on the Greenwich Observatory in Greenwich, England. Which lesson is the teacher most likely introducing?
    A. lunar eclipses
    B. black holes
    C. latitude
    D. longitude

21) Use the passage below to answer the question that follows:
The largest inland desalination facility is located in El Paso, Texas. The plant helps local residents gain access to drinkable water because the groundwater in the vicinity is brackish. Brackish water from the Hueco Bolson aquifer is fed into the facility, which can produce as much as 27.5 million gallons of fresh, drinkable water each day!

Information provided in the passage would be most useful for a lesson on which of the following?

    A. alternative energy sources
    B. mitigation of greenhouse gas emissions
    C. natural resource use
    D. the water cycle

22) Which statement BEST supports plate tectonics theory?
    A. The Earth is comprised of several layers.
    B. Mountains are often found at plate boundaries.
    C. Earthquake magnitude can vary with each plate movement.
    D. Fossils suggest ancient lifeforms existed on both land and water.

23) Use the diagram below to answer the question that follows.

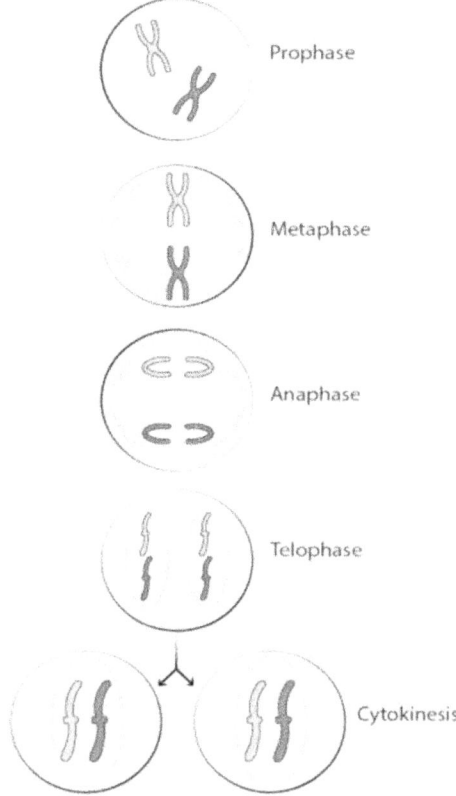

This diagram shows which of the following?
   A. gamete formation
   B. cell division
   C. sexual reproduction
   D. cloning

24) From where do radiosondes, also called weather balloons, collect data?
   A. stratosphere
   B. thermosphere
   C. troposphere
   D. mesosphere

25) In an experiment designed to test whether exercise leads to weight loss in a random sample of horses at a ranch, what is the independent variable?
   A. weight loss
   B. exercise
   C. horses at the ranch
   D. the random sample

26) What might cause results from an experiment to NOT be generalizable?
   A. if only a correlation is identified
   B. if the sample is too small
   C. if only one variable is tested
   D. if multiple questions are tested

Constructed Response

For questions 27 and 28, your responses will be evaluated based on the following criteria:

PURPOSE: the extent to which the response addresses the constructed-response assignment's charge in relation to relevant CSET subject matter requirements

SUBJECT MATTER KNOWLEDGE: the application of accurate subject matter knowledge as described in the relevant CSET subject matter requirements

SUPPORT: the appropriateness and quality of the supporting evidence in relation to relevant CSET subject matter requirements

27) **Complete the exercise that follows:**
   An amateur scientist is tracking changes in the forest habitat behind his home. He notes that deer, which were once plentiful in the forest, are now rare as the forest's size has shrunk, and the stream that once ran through the forest was filled in due to urban development. He also notes that smaller woodland creatures, like squirrels, have become more prevalent in the area as overall biodiversity has decreased. He concludes that the squirrels have pushed the deer and other primary consumers out of the ecosystem as competitors for food.

Using your knowledge of ecology

- describe the misconception underlying the amateur scientist's explanation for the shift in biodiversity;

- provide an alternative explanation for the change; and

- provide at least two additional factors impacting biodiversity that the amateur scientist should consider.

28) **Use the graph below to complete the exercise that follows:**

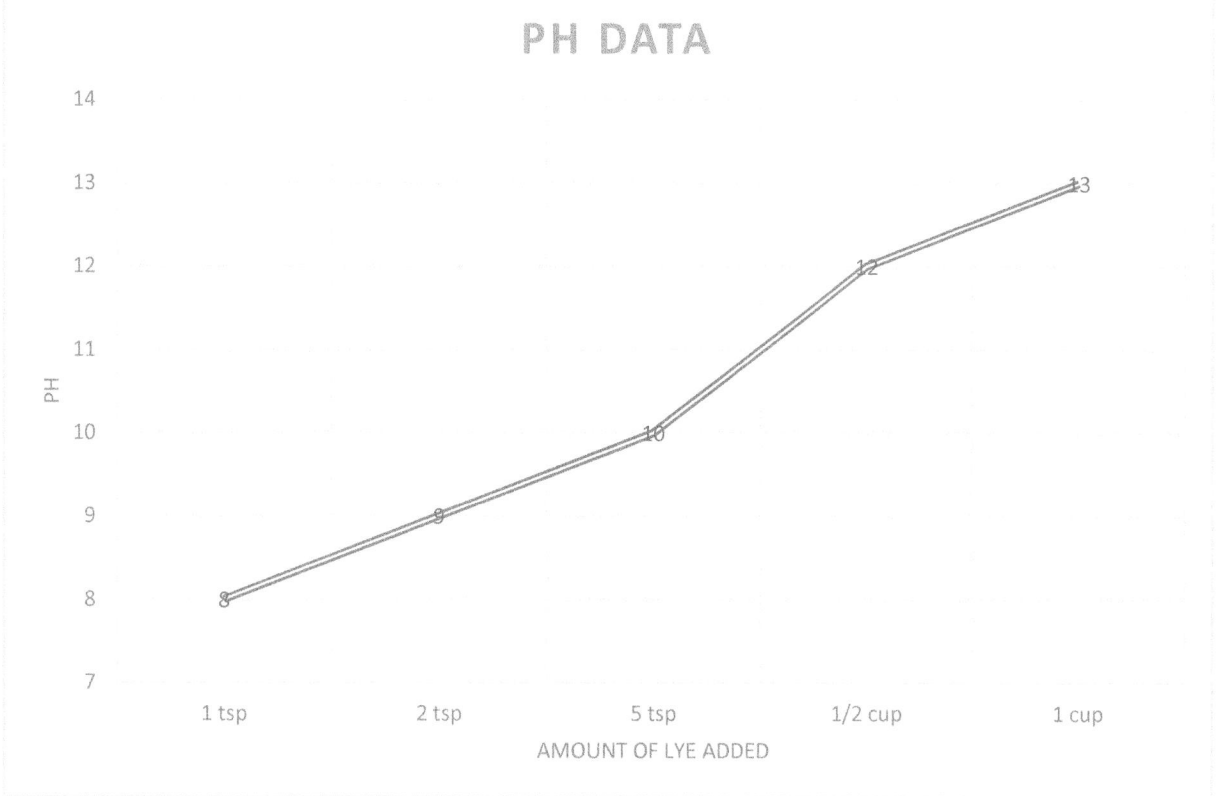

The graph represents the results of an experiment where various amounts of lye were added to identical 6-oz cups of water.

Using your knowledge of pH and the scientific method

- identify the independent and dependent variables;
- explain one strength and one weakness of this experimental design; and
- identify one conclusion from this experiment and how the data supports it.

Subtest IV: Mathematics

Selected Response

1) Which equation demonstrates the associative property of addition?
   A. 2 + (1 + 5) = (2 + 1) + 5
   B. 2(1 × 5) = (2 × 1)5
   C. 1 × 3 = 3 × 1
   D. 2(7 + 4) = 2 × 7 + 2 × 4

2) Using the information in the table, which equation demonstrates the linear relationship between x and y?

x	y
3	3
7	15
10	24

A. $y = 6x - 6$
B. $y = 5x - 6$
C. $y = 4x - 6$
D. $y = 3x - 6$

3) Using the table, which equation demonstrates the linear relationship between x and y?

x	y
3	−18
7	−34
10	−46

A. $y = -6x - 6$
B. $y = -5x - 6$
C. $y = -4x - 6$
D. $y = -3x - 6$

4) Robbie has a bag of treats that contains 5 pieces of gum, 7 pieces of taffy, and 8 pieces of chocolate. If Robbie reaches into the bag and randomly pulls out a treat, what is the probability that Robbie will get a piece of taffy?

A. 1
B. $\frac{1}{7}$
C. $\frac{5}{8}$
D. $\frac{7}{20}$

5) Kim and Chris are writing a book together. Kim writes twice as many pages as Chris. Altogether, there are 240 pages in the book. Which equation shows how many pages Chris writes?

A. $2 + 2p = 240$
B. $p + 2p = 240$
C. $2p - p = 240$
D. $p - 2p = 240$

6) An ice chest contains 25 sodas, some regular and some diet. The ratio of diet soda to regular soda is 1:4. How many regular sodas are there in the ice chest?
   A. 1
   B. 4
   C. 20
   D. 25

7) Which inequality is equivalent to $10 \leq k - 5$?
   A. $k \leq 15$
   B. $k \geq 15$
   C. $k \leq 5$
   D. $k \leq 10$

8) Which statement describes the images?

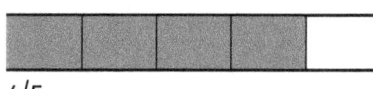
1/5

2/5

3/5

4/5

   A. When the numerator stays the same and the denominator increases, the fraction increases.
   B. When the numerator increases and the denominator stays the same, the fraction increases.
   C. When the numerator and the denominator increase, the fraction decreases.
   D. When the numerator stays the same and the denominator decreases, the fraction decreases.

9) Danny collects coins. The table shows how many of each type of coin Danny collects for four days. Which statement is true?

Danny's Coin Collection

	Pennies	Nickels	Dimes	Quarters
Day 1	1	4	3	0
Day 2	4	3	2	5
Day 3	5	2	2	4
Day 4	1	2	3	1

A. The mean number of nickels is greater than the mean number of quarters.
B. The mean number of quarters is greater than the mean number of pennies.
C. The range of dimes is greater than the range of quarters.
D. The median number of pennies is five.

10) A table is 150 centimeters long. How many millimeters long is the table?
A. 1.5 mm
B. 15 mm
C. 150 mm
D. 1500 mm

11) How many mm longer is line segment MN than line segment KL?

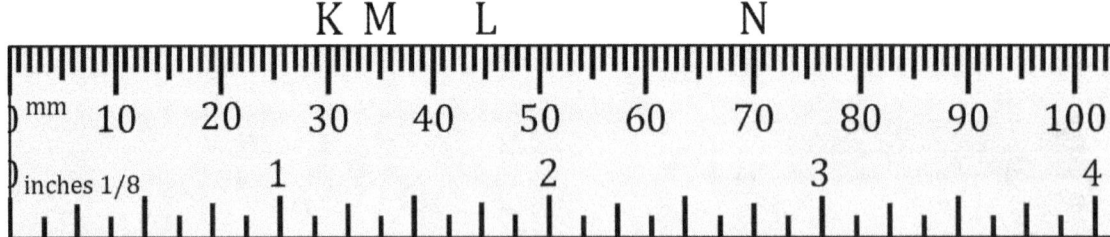

A. 15 mm
B. 20 mm
C. 2 mm
D. 55 mm

12) The formula for distance is $d = r \times t$. How long will it take a plane to fly 4,000 miles from Chicago to London if the plane flies at a constant rate of 500 mph?
A. 20 hours
B. 8 hours
C. 45 hours
D. 3.5 hours

13) What is the perimeter of the shape?

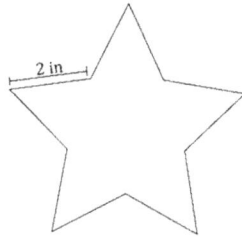

- A. 2 mm
- B. 4 mm
- C. 10 mm
- D. 20 mm

14) What is the area of the shape?

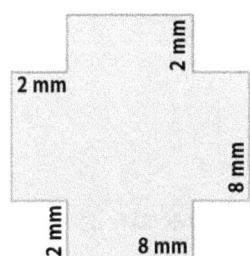

- A. 64 mm²
- B. 16 mm²
- C. 128 mm²
- D. 6 mm²

15) Which three-dimensional solid has 2 triangular faces and 3 rectangular faces?
- A. pyramid
- B. cube
- C. rectangular prism
- D. triangular prism

16) What is the equation of the following line?

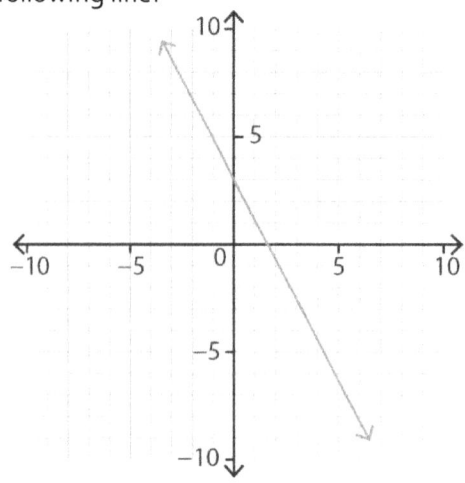

- A. $y = -4x + 3$
- B. $y = -2x - 3$
- C. $y = 2x + 3$
- D. $y = -2x + 3$

17) What is the equation of the line perpendicular to $-2y + 4 = 6x$ that has the same y-intercept?
- A. $y = -\frac{1}{3}x + 2$
- B. $y = \frac{1}{3}x + 2$
- C. $y = \frac{1}{3}x - 2$
- D. $y = 3x + 2$

18) What are the solutions to the equation $2x^2 - 5x + 2 = 0$?
- A. $x = 2, 4$
- B. $x = 2, 3$
- C. $x = \frac{9}{4}, 2$
- D. $x = \frac{1}{2}, 2$

19) Find $(f - g)(x)$ when $f(x) = x^2 + 6x$ and $g(x) = x - 2$.
- A. $x^2 + 5x + 2$
- B. $x^2 + 7x + 2$
- C. $x^2 + 4x$
- D. $5x + 2$

20) Which of the following expressions describes the area of the triangle below?

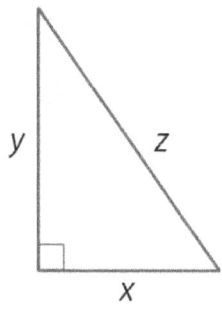

- A. $x + y + z$
- B. $\frac{xy}{2}$
- C. xyz
- D. $\frac{xyz}{2}$

21)

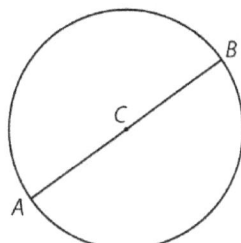

The circle above shows a walking path through a park. If the distance from A to B is 4 km, how far will someone travel when they walk along arc AB?

- A. 4 km
- B. 2π km
- C. 8 km
- D. 4π km

22) Bart surveyed his classmates to determine their favorite pizza toppings. The data was as follows:

Anchovy	1
Pineapple	2
Olives	4
Pepperoni	9
Bacon	2
Canadian bacon	1

Which topping is the mode?
- A. anchovy
- B. olives
- C. pepperoni
- D. pineapple

23) The figure below shows similar triangles *ABC* and *DEF*.

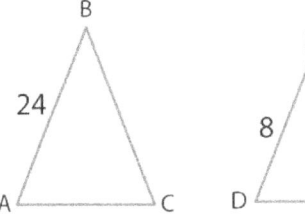

Which of the following statements is true?
- A. $DF = \frac{AC}{3}$
- B. $DF = AC - 16$
- C. $DF = 2AC$
- D. $DF = \frac{2}{3}AB$

24) The students on the track team are buying new uniforms. T-shirts (*t*) cost $12, pants (*p*) cost $15, and a pair of shoes (*s*) costs $45. The team has a budget of $2,500. Write a mathematical sentence that represents how many of each item they can buy.
- A. $t + p + s \leq 2500$
- B. $\frac{t}{12} + \frac{p}{15} + \frac{s}{45} \geq 2500$
- C. $12t + 15p + 45s \leq 2500$
- D. $12t + 15p + 45s \geq 2500$

25) Write the number 4,520,000 in scientific notation.
- A. 452×10^4
- B. 4.52×10^5
- C. 4.52×10^6
- D. 0.452×10^7

26) One day in January, the low temperature was −7°F. During the day the temperature rose 15 degrees. What was the high temperature for that day?
   A. −23°F
   B. −8°F
   C. 8°F
   D. 23°F

Constructed Response

27) Write a system of equations that models the following scenario. Make sure to choose appropriate variables, and then solve the system to find the exact number of apples and oranges purchased. Explain why a customer purchasing both apples and oranges could not purchase 30 pieces of fruit for $45:

   Apples are sold for $1.50 each and oranges are sold for $1.25 each at the grocery store. A customer purchases 27 pieces of fruit, totaling $36.50.

28) The local DMV has reported that 16-year-olds have not been passing the multiple-choice test required to obtain a temporary driving license as consistently as in previous years. This conclusion was based on the results from a random sample of twenty 16-year-olds who completed the 20-question, multiple-choice test on driving skills. The data set below lists the number of questions scored correctly from each of the 16-year-olds:

12	14	16	13	17	12	19	11	9	15
11	10	20	15	3	18	20	14	12	15

Complete the following:

- Display this data in a stem plot.
- Calculate the mean, median, and mode.
- Are there any outliers?

Subtest V: Physical Education

Selected Response

1) Which of the following is a non-locomotor skill?
   A. skipping
   B. bending
   C. throwing
   D. leaping

2) Which of the following sports or activities is not appropriate to teach in second grade?
   A. kickball
   B. football
   C. freeze tag
   D. simple obstacle courses

3) Which of the following goals is MOST important to develop in students participating in physical education programs?
   A. proficiencies in multiple sports and games
   B. enough cardiorespiratory endurance to run half a mile without stopping
   C. a lifelong commitment to participate in physical activity
   D. an ability to lead a team in a physical activity

4) Which activity is MOST aligned with an individualist cultural perspective?
   A. long jump
   B. relay racing
   C. basketball
   D. synchronized swimming

5) What does the FITT principle entail?
   A. flexibility, intensity, toning, and type
   B. frequency, intensity, time, and type
   C. freedom, innovation, technique, and tempo
   D. frequency, intention, time, and technique

6) How can teachers best strive to prevent injury during physical education lessons?
   A. following the rules of all games and sports without any accommodations or modifications
   B. offering opportunities for students to increase flexibility and range of movement
   C. giving students clear goals to accomplish during each activity
   D. providing a choice of activities at various stations or centers

7) To prepare students for a gymnastics unit that will involve the use of a balance beam, activities might include which of the following?
   A. object manipulation
   B. locomotor skills development
   C. hopping on one foot
   D. doing push-ups

8) Which physical education activity would BEST allow for an integrated unit on Newton's laws of motion?
   A. softball
   B. cross-country running
   C. hurdles
   D. high-intensity interval training

9) Which personal safety topic is MOST appropriate for a first-grade physical education class?
   A. avoiding drunk driving
   B. responsible social media use
   C. knowing parents' phone numbers
   D. the use of evasive self-defense movements

10) Which food group makes up the LARGEST part of the MyPlate recommendation?
    A. protein
    B. dairy
    C. grains
    D. vegetables

11) Which activity is MOST likely to help physical education participants develop socially?
    A. an obstacle course
    B. a school clean-up event
    C. distance running
    D. a kickball game

12) Which type of class structure is MOST likely to help students of all abilities participate in physical activity?
    A. teacher-directed drills
    B. student choice stations
    C. circuit training
    D. free play time

13) To increase student's endurance, they should perform exercises
    A. for the same duration each class.
    B. for an increased duration each class.
    C. at an increased intensity each class.
    D. with better technique each class.

14) What should children be taught about their weight and height?
    A. It will change as they go through growth spurts.
    B. Water intake can impact both metrics.
    C. It will decrease as their cardiorespiratory endurance increases.
    D. Protein intake will increase both metrics.

Constructed Response

15) For question 15, you are to prepare a written response of approximately 100 – 200 words.

Read the assignment carefully before you begin to write. Think about how you will organize what you plan to write.

Complete the exercise that follows:

Listed below are the steps in a game designed for children in the early elementary grades:

Monster Ball

> *1. Draw a large square in chalk on a cement surface (or tape off the gym floor).*
>
> *2. Place a large exercise ball in the center of the square.*
>
> *3. Divide the class into two teams on either side of the square with the ball in the center. Assign one team as the red team and one team as the blue team.*
>
> *4. Provide each team with buckets of smaller balls in their team's color.*

5. Advise that the objective of the game is to throw the smaller balls at the exercise ball, knocking it out of the square into the other team's side. Students pick up and re-use balls in their team's color and continue to throw until one team is the winner. Students may not touch the center ball or block balls with their bodies. Balls may be retrieved from inside the square but not thrown from inside the square.

Using your knowledge of physical education, discuss two ways in which this game could be modified to include learners of various abilities.

Subtest VI: Human Development

Selected Response

1) Which child's development is MOST atypical?
   A. a kindergarten student who can only sound out some CVC words
   B. a second-grade student who prefers playmates of the same age
   C. a fourth-grade student who cries when being dropped off at school
   D. a sixth-grade student who cries when another student insults her in front of peers

2) Which activity would likely allow a student with high spatial-visual intelligence to highlight his strengths?
   A. coordinating a schoolwide recycling event
   B. drawing a map of the school campus
   C. running the school store
   D. managing a school sports team

3) Who should provide guidance to a child working within her ZPD?
   A. a peer with a similar ZPD
   B. a more capable peer
   C. a peer with developed socialization skills
   D. a peer with a large, expressive vocabulary

4) Which utterance is LEAST suggestive of a child who is seeking autonomy?
   A. "I can do it."
   B. "Let me."
   C. "I am hungry."
   D. "I know how."

5) Which child has the MOST developed emotional regulation skills?
   A. a fifth grader who is able to form a best friend relationship
   B. a third grader who asks permission before taking something
   C. a kindergartner who automatically goes to a cool-down zone when angry
   D. a preschooler who can identify emotions associated with happy and sad faces

6) A young child who knows "The Alphabet Song" learns that the letters also make sounds. This is an example of which of the following?
   A. assimilation
   B. accommodation
   C. scaffolding
   D. undermining

7) Which of the following children is MOST clearly in need of further assessment for an apparent delay in physical development?
   A. a third grader who struggles to hold a pencil
   B. a first grader who runs more slowly than her older sister
   C. a fifth grader who cannot do a pull-up
   D. a kindergartner who can only catch with both hands

8) Which of Erikson's stages happens between the ages of five and twelve?
   A. initiative versus guilt
   B. industry versus inferiority
   C. autonomy versus shame and doubt
   D. trust versus mistrust

9) If a child is able to picture an idea in her mind, the child is demonstrating which of Bruner's stages?
   A. the enactive stage
   B. the symbolic stage
   C. the iconic stage
   D. the operational stage

10) Which situation is MOST suggestive that a child may need interventions?
    A. a two-year old who has not begun to babble
    B. a one-year old who is speaking in single words
    C. a two-year old who drops article like *a, an,* and *the*
    D. a one-year old who does not pronounce all words clearly

11) How is prosocial behavior connected with character development?
    A. Character development helps children learn to form relationships based on prosocial behaviors.
    B. Character development gives children the moral framework that drives prosocial behaviors.
    C. Prosocial behaviors help children recognize character development in others.
    D. Prosocial behaviors give children the reasoning behind character development.

12) Which of the following is one possible outcome of childhood physical abuse?
    A. aggressive behavior toward peers
    B. shifts in typical growth spurts
    C. premature birth of children
    D. early onset of puberty

13) At what age do children begin to understand the emotions of others?
    A. four months
    B. one
    C. two
    D. five

Constructed Response

For question 14, you are to prepare a written response of approximately 100 – 200 words.

Read the assignment carefully before you begin to write. Think about how you will organize what you plan to write.

14) Complete the exercise that follows:
Use your knowledge of human development to complete the following tasks:

- Describe the difference between receptive and expressive language.
- Discuss how each develops and the special considerations that must be taken into account for second-language learners.

Subtest VII: Visual and Performing Arts

Selected Response

1) Which of the following types of media is NOT appropriate for younger elementary students to use independently in an art class?

    A. tempera paints
    B. hot glue gun
    C. scissors and white glue
    D. crayons

2) Which of the following would be an appropriate activity for first graders during a simple lesson on rhythm?

    A. The teacher makes loud and soft sounds on a drum.
    B. The teacher plays a pattern on the drum, and students try to repeat it.
    C. Students listen to different percussion instruments.
    D. The teacher plays music at different speeds and students clap to indicate the tempo.

3) Which of the following reasons BEST describes why a teacher would introduce the recorder to students in an elementary class?

    A. It can help students learn proper breathing techniques.
    B. It allows teachers to teach a wide variety of songs and ensembles effectively.
    C. It is appropriate for students who may not have well-developed motor skills.
    D. It helps teachers show students pitch and rhythm.

4) Which of the following are NOT complementary colors on a color wheel?

    A. blue and orange
    B. red and blue
    C. purple and yellow
    D. red and green

5) Which of the following descriptions BEST describes timbre in music?

    A. Timbre refers to the different sounds of various instruments.
    B. Timbre refers to the loudness of an instrument.
    C. Timbre refers to the pitch of an instrument.
    D. Timbre refers to combining melody, harmony, and rhythm.

6) Which of the following is considered a hip-hop dance style?
    A. lambada
    B. popping
    C. jazz
    D. quickstep

7) A dance study is made up of a sequence of which of the following?
    A. stimuli
    B. tempos
    C. phrases
    D. balances

8) An improvised dance is the opposite of which of the following?
    A. a dance work
    B. a choreographed dance
    C. an observed dance
    D. a dance technique

9) During a dance rehearsal, students are continually bumping into each other. What do they need more practice with?
    A. keeping sufficient negative space
    B. identifying personal space
    C. kinesthetic awareness
    D. synchronization

10) Very young students who are not able to memorize lines could participate in theatre via which of the following?
    A. monologues
    B. spoken-word poetry
    C. guided drama experience
    D. scripted stage directions

11) Which of the following is a representational material for a dramatic production?
    A. a pole in the gym that is labeled "tree"
    B. a square on the floor that a character knows to run to
    C. a memorable phrase, like "see ya," that a character utters
    D. a real quilt used as a prop in a scene

12) A student with limited verbal skills could participate in a theatrical production by doing which of the following?
    A. developing a unique character tag
    B. providing sound effects on cue with percussion instruments
    C. performing a soliloquy to an empty room
    D. delivering a monologue that has been memorized ahead of time

13) Which piece of art is MOST likely to have texture?
   A. painting
   B. collage
   C. drawing
   D. lithograph

Constructed Response

For question 14, you are to prepare a written response of approximately 100 – 200 words.

Read the assignment carefully before you begin to write. Think about how you will organize what you plan to write.

14) **Complete the exercise that follows:**
Art can tell a story about real life.

Using your knowledge of visual art, write a response in which you

- identify a specific work of art that tells a story about real life;
- describe the "story" it tells; and
- explain how it could be used as a mentor piece for a student project.

Practice Test #1 Answer Key

Subtest I: Reading, Language, and Literature

Selected Response

1) A: The strategy of phoneme blending requires students to combine phonemes to make a word.

2) A: Phonemic awareness is an understanding of how phonemes can be orally manipulated to change the meanings of words.

3) D: The letter *m* is most likely to be introduced first because it contains its sound in its name and only forms one sound in words.

4) C: Sight word instruction is designed to help students recognize high-frequency words automatically, without decoding, so they can read with fluency.

5) C: Most English roots are Greek or Latin.

6) A: The word *park* acts as an adjective describing the noun *naturalist* in the first sentence and is part of an adjective phrase *from the park*, which modifies the noun *migration* in the second sentence.

7) C: The sentence is an example of a complex sentence with one dependent clause and one independent clause.

8) D: A simile is a comparison made using the words *like* or *as*.

9) B: The poet uses an *aabb* rhyme scheme throughout the poem, which lets the reader know that the word *quays* should be pronounced to rhyme with *trees*.

10) D: The revised sentence replaces vague and non-descriptive words with more specific words that provide the reader with a clearer idea of the author's message.

11) A: This sentence paraphrases the original sentence most accurately because it restates the speaker's main idea and reasoning in a revised and concise way.

12) B: Word family instruction is a decoding strategy that reinforces student understanding of word patterns.

13) A: Thinking aloud is when a teacher verbalizes thoughts and insights to model how to think logically and critically when applying a reading comprehension skill.

14) B: Analysis of the knowledge demands required by a text is a qualitative measure of text complexity.

15) B: The way that John Manly takes care to make the horse comfortable before riding leads the reader to infer that he has respect for horses.

16) A: First-person point of view is written from the direct experience of one character—in this case, the horse—as indicated by the pronouns *I* and *my*.

17) D: This is the best summary because it provides a brief explanation of the excerpt's main idea and key details. It only includes the most necessary information a reader needs to comprehend the story section.

18) A: The author provides a definition of the word *paces* in the next paragraph when he lists them as trot, canter, and gallop.

19) A: Interlanguage effects are systems of rules created by a language learner that may, as in this case, be erroneously based on the rules of the native language.

20) A: "Living with her Aunt Sally" is a gerund phrase where the phrase acts as both the noun and the subject of the sentence.

21) B: A quatrain poem contains one or more four-line stanzas with a rhyme scheme, so a list of rhyming words is a helpful prewriting assignment.

22) C: A KWL chart activates student background knowledge about a topic before reading.

23) C: A running record allows teachers to track oral reading progress over time.

24) D: A personal story with a plot arc is an example of narrative writing.

25) B: The word *than,* which is a conjunction used to make comparisons, should be used instead of *then,* which is an adverb that means *at that time.*

26) C: The word *tuough* should be spelled "t-o-u-g-h."

Constructed Response

27) SAMPLE ANSWER: Dolo is very likely in the preproduction stage of second language development, also known as the silent period. He likely has more words in his receptive vocabulary than in his expressive vocabulary, which is why he is able to follow simple classroom directions. Similarly, because he has heard common words and phrases like "thank you" and "hello" so frequently, he is likely able to copy or parrot these phrases from time to time, but this is not precisely productive language.

Copying the spelling words from the whiteboard into his notebook is also consistent with the preproduction stage as this activity does not indicate that he knows what the words mean or can pronounce them; however, it may suggest that his native language uses the Latin alphabet if he finds that forming the letters familiar.

28) SAMPLE ANSWER: In this excerpt from *Five Weeks in a Balloon*, a third-person point of view is employed, but with some nuance. For example, in the third paragraph, the narrator speaks directly to the reader ("for the reader will observe . . ."). This technique of breaking the fourth wall connects the reader and narrator but also allows the narrator to add humor, suggesting that every nation believes itself to be a leader among others.

The tone of the excerpt is somewhat humorous and lighthearted, with witty quips and some indication that the speaker is exaggerating. Phrases like "bubbling over with patriotism" and "wildest cheering" suggest that the atmosphere is a lively one but also, perhaps, that the speech is a little over the top.

Subtest II: History and Social Science

Selected Response

1) B: The ancient Romans—not the ancient Greeks—built aqueducts and developed public toilets.

2) C: Opportunity cost refers to the cost of the loss of one option when it is rejected for another. (In this case, if Luther and Barbara choose to hire one staff member, they lose the marketing potential another employee would make possible, whereas if they choose to hire two, they lose the leftover money.)

3) A: A bar graph that features the population over a number of years would help researchers analyze population patterns.

4) B: While the executive branch can approve laws, only Congress can make laws.

5) C: The Bill of Rights is composed of the first ten amendments; it is the Fourteenth Amendment that guarantees equal protection under the law.

6) A: Republicanism also stresses natural rights as central values.

7) C: While troops were ordered to capture Samuel Adams, they were not asked to capture Thomas Jefferson.

8) B: The *Marbury v. Madison* case established judicial review.

9) B: In 1803, Napoleon sold this section of land— the land roughly bordered by the Rocky Mountains, the Mississippi river, and the northern border of modern-day Texas, to finance his European wars.

10) C: Madison not only advocated for the ratification of the Constitution; he also helped write the Federalist Papers.

11) C: The Fifth Amendment allows people to abstain from giving testimony that may incriminate them.

12) B: Connecticut, Massachusetts, and New Hampshire were part of the New England colonies.

13) A: Competition in business is an aspect of the market economy.

14) A: Introducing maps allows students to acquire an understanding of the world around them. They can use this knowledge to create their own maps.

15) D: Native American groups in California adapted to the resources in the surrounding environment and used them to build homes, find food, and make tools.

16) D: The Sierra Nevada range had to be blasted through with dynamite. Chinese Californians did much of this dangerous work.

17) B: California's diverse landscape, including deserts and mountains, prevented easy travel from place to place, and this led Native American groups to settle in smaller, largely isolated triblets.

18) D: Native American groups in California adapted to the resources in the surrounding environment and used them to build homes, find food, and make tools.

19) B: California was the "frontier" of the center of the Spanish colonial Empire in Mexico City. When Mexico gained its independence from Spain, California was still far removed from the center of government.

20) A: The Pony Express was developed to carry mail and packages from California to the Midwest. It was needed because of the new large number of people living in California due to the Gold Rush.

21) C: Most of the surface fresh water of California is located in the north, which presents a problem because most of the population is in the southern half of the state.

22) A: The circular flow of economic exchanges describes how money flows from producers (like the strawberry farmers) to workers and then back to producers.

23) D: While California has mining, this mining is mainly for precious metals—not diamonds.

24) C: Recall allows the public to call for a public official to be removed from office, which is a unique aspect of the state's constitution.

25) B: The California trail system began in Missouri and spanned 5,665 miles and ten states; it was used for westward migration to California.

26) A: Dust Bowl migrants came in the wake of the Depression and were often perceived as competition for scarce jobs, particularly as many were willing to work for very low wages.

Constructed Response

27) SAMPLE ANSWER: In both Spanish and Mexican California, society was organized along a social hierarchy, with European elites atop and Native Californians at the bottom. Furthermore, in both societies, the use of the land for farming or ranching was central to the economy. This land use centered on the rancho, or a large tract of land on which an individual was granted grazing rights.

However, there was also change when Mexico won independence from Spain in 1821 and California came under a new political authority. While the mission system was key to life in Spanish California and a major force for bringing Native Californians under European control, this system was dismantled rather quickly as the new nation sought to limit the role of Spanish clerics. Furthermore, while Spanish California had been largely self-sufficient, relying on trade between ranchos, presidios, and missions, Mexican California began to participate in international trade. As the rancho system expanded and cattle ranching grew, rancheros traded beef with American merchants for manufactured goods.

28) SAMPLE ANSWER: Reconstruction did not achieve the initial aims of Radical Republicans in granting the rights of American citizenship to African Americans in the South, including those who were formerly enslaved. This was largely due to violence against African Americans who tried to exercise their rights by Southern hate groups and the general lack of cooperation of Southerners in realizing the goals of Reconstruction. Because the ultimate goal of Reconstruction was to bring the nation back together, the US government did not pursue strong military action or punitive measures against Southern resistors.

Instead, the weak response allowed Southern legislators to enact Black Codes, which were laws enacted as early as 1865 to control the work, earnings, and movement of newly freed African Americans. These laws greatly restricted the ability of African Americans in the Southern states to buy and own property, conduct business, and earn a decent living. These laws sought to keep newly freed citizens as an inexpensive source of labor and protect the economic interests of White Southerners at the expense of newly emancipated Black Southerners.

Subtest III: Science

Selected Response

1) D: Bases have a pH between 7 and 14.

2) B: The endocrine system releases hormones, including growth hormones.

3) A: When water changes form, it does not change the chemical composition of the substance. Once water becomes ice, the ice can easily turn back into water.

4) A: The light of the sun hits rain droplets and bends into a band of colors. The bending of waves is refraction.

5) B: Parasitism describes a relationship in which one organism benefits from another organism to the detriment of the host organism.

6) D: Ribosomes are responsible for the production of proteins.

7) A: The sun is the only star in our solar system. The sun is about ninety-three million miles from Earth; the next closest star is about twenty-five trillion miles away.

8) B: Something that is not moving has zero velocity; therefore, it has no kinetic energy.

9) C: Weight is affected by gravitational pull.

10) B: A lunar eclipse is when the moon moves into the shadow of Earth, which causes the moon to become darkened.

11) D: Homeostasis refers to body systems working together to ensure that temperature, pH, and oxygen levels are optimal for survival. Sensors in Stacy's nervous system trigger her muscular system to shiver in an attempt to warm her body.

12) A: An inclined plane is a flat surface raised to an angle so that loads can be easily lifted.

13) B: Geothermal energy is a renewable energy source that comes from the heat within the earth. A discussion about geothermal energy would be a good setting to introduce a geology unit on the layers of the earth.

14) C: Cooking an egg is a chemical change. The heat changes the composition of the egg in an irreversible way.

15) A: Newton's third law of motion states that for every action there is an equal and opposite reaction. When the cue ball hits the 8-ball, the cue ball stops, and the 8-ball moves.

16) C: Dicots, like beans, have two embryos in one seed.

17) D: While the periodic table organizes elements, it does not give information on an element's rarity.

18) B: When a system is at dynamic equilibrium, the physical and chemical reactions in the system balance each other out. In this case, the system is not at equilibrium because there are now fewer organisms than before.

19) D: Homozygous genes (AA or aa) mean that the child will inherit that trait. Heterozygous genes (e.g., Aa, Bb) leave a chance that the child will not inhere a trait.

20) D: The Greenwich Observatory is the site of the prime meridian, or zero degrees longitude.

21) C: This passage provides information on ways in which humans are using a natural resource (water) in a nuanced way.

22) B: This is evidence of plate tectonics theory, which maintains that plates move.

23) B: This diagram shows mitosis, or cell division.

24) A: The stratosphere, the second layer of Earth's atmosphere, is where weather balloons collect data.

25) B: Exercise is what the researcher is controlling and what the researcher believes will have an effect on the horses, so it is the independent variable.

26) B: Generalizability refers to whether the results can be generalized to an entire population. If a sample is too small, results cannot be generalized to the broader population.

Constructed Response

27) SAMPLE ANSWER: The amateur scientist has made a misconception by limiting his understanding of the change in the ecosystem in terms of only one factor: competition among consumers at similar trophic levels on the food chain. Although it is true that both deer and squirrel are herbivores, they have very different needs from their environment.

An alternative explanation would be that squirrels, as organisms with less overall biomass, have lower nutrient and water needs, which can be met in a smaller environment with fewer resources. Because humans have dramatically changed the forest environment, it is more likely that squirrels are simply better adapted to life next to humans in smaller spaces with fewer resources.

In considering overall biodiversity, the amateur scientist might also consider secondary succession, which is the change in an already created habitat—in this case, the removal of a main water source. Additionally, the amateur scientist might consider how the reduction in the deer population impacts other layers of the food web. For example, because deer feed on producers (plants), fewer deer may actually increase plant biodiversity as more plants are able to grow and reproduce without constant grazing.

28) SAMPLE ANSWER: The independent variable in this experiment is the amount of lye, and the dependent variable is the pH measurement of the resulting solution. The amount of lye impacts the pH level of the resulting solution.

One strength of the experiment is that confounding variables, which are extraneous variables that may lead to experimental error, have been limited by the use of the same quantity of water each time (6 oz); however, one weakness of the experiment is that the amount of lye added did not increase in regular intervals. For example, it doubles from 1 to 2 teaspoons and from ½ cup to 1 cup, but it does not double from 2 tsp to 5 tsp or from 5 tsp to ½ cup (1/2 cup is 24 teaspoons).

One conclusion that can be drawn from this data is that as the lye concentration in water increases, the resulting solution will become more basic as evidenced by an increase in pH. This conclusion is supported by the fact that with only a little lye (1 tsp), the pH only increases slightly because water has a pH of around 7 (though the carbon dioxide in the air dissolves in the water and lowers pH); however, as the proportion of lye to water increases where one cup, or 8 oz, are added, the resulting solution is almost as basic as the lye itself.

Subtest IV: Mathematics

Selected Response

1) A: The correct answer is $2 + (1 + 5) = (2 + 1) + 5$. When using the associative property, the answer will remain the same in an addition problem regardless of where the parentheses are placed.

2) D: The correct answer is $y = 3x - 6$. Solve for y by replacing x with 3:
$$y = 3(3) - 6$$
$$y = 9 - 6$$
$$y = 3$$
This is the correct answer because the table says that when $x = 3, y = 3$.

3) C: The correct answer is $y = -4x - 6$. Solve for y by replacing x with 3:
$$y = -4(3) - 6$$
$$y = -12 - 6$$
$$y = -18$$
The table says that when $x = 3, y = -18$.

4) D: The correct answer is 7/20. Probability is the number of favorable events divided by the number of possible events. In this case, Robbie pulls out one treat from a bag that contains 7 pieces of taffy; therefore, 7 is the number of favorable events. There are 20 total treats in the bag because $5 + 7 + 8 = 20$ and $7 \div 20 = 7/20$.

5) B: The correct answer is $p + 2p = 240$. If p is the number of pages Chris writes, the equation shows that Kim writes $2p$, or twice as many pages as Chris writes. If the number of pages Chris writes is added to the number of pages Kim writes, the total is 240 pages.

6) C: The correct answer is 20. To solve the problem, use ratios. There is 1 diet soda for every 4 regular sodas for a total of 5 sodas:
$$\frac{4}{5} = \frac{x}{25}$$

Now, cross multiply:
$$4 \times 25 = 100$$

And
$$5 \times x = 5x$$

This can be written as $100 = 5x$. Next, isolate the variable by dividing 5 from both sides to get:

$$100 \div 5 = 5x \div 5$$

$$20 = x$$

7) B: The correct answer is $k \geq 15$. The sign is flipped from what is shown in the problem, but k is equal to or greater than 15.

8) B: The images show the numerator increasing while the denominator stays the same; meanwhile, the fraction is increasing.

9) A: To calculate the mean, add all of the numbers in a set and divide by how many numbers are in the set. The mean number of nickels is $4 + 3 + 2 + 2 = 11$ divided by 4 (because there are 4 numbers in the set) $= 2.75$ nickels. The mean number of quarters is $0 + 5 + 4 + 1 = 10$ divided by $4 = 2.5$ quarters. $2.75 > 2.5$.

10) D: The correct answer is 1,500 mm. One centimeter = 10 millimeters and 150 × 10 = 1,500.

11) B: Line segment MN begins at 35 mm and ends at 70 mm. Since $70 - 35 = 35$ mm, line segment MN is 35 mm. Line segment KL begins at 30 mm and ends at 45 mm. Since $45 - 30 = 15$ mm, line segment KL is 15 mm. To find out how much longer MN is than KL, subtract these two lengths to get 35 mm − 15 mm = 20 mm.

12) B: Time is distance divided by rate; $4000 \, mi / 500 \, mph = 8 \, hours$

13) D: There are 10 sides and each side is 2 mm in length. To find the perimeter, add the length of each side to find the total. $P = 2 + 2 + 2 + 2 + 2 + 2 + 2 + 2 + 2 + 2 = 20 \, mm$.

14) C: Find the area of the square as if it did not have cut-outs; each side would be 12 mm long. $12 \, mm \times 12 \, mm = 144 \, mm2$ Next, subtract the area of the cut-outs from the total area of the square. The area of each cut-out is $2 \, mm \times 2 \, mm = 4 \, mm2$. There are cut-outs in each of the 4 corners; therefore, multiply by 4; $4 \times 4 = 16$. Subtract the total area of the four cut-outs from the total area of the square without the cut-outs; $144 - 16 = 128 \, mm2$.

15) D: A triangle prism has 2 triangular faces and 3 rectangular faces.

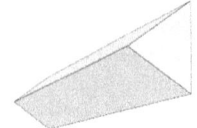

16) D: The y-intercept can be identified on the graph as $(0, 3)$; $thus, b = 3$.
To find the slope, choose any two points and plug the values into the slope equation. The two points chosen here are (2, −1) and (3, −3).

$$m = \frac{(-3) - (-1)}{3 - 2} = -\frac{2}{1} = -2$$

Replace m with −2 and b with 3 in $y = mx + b$.

The equation of the line is $y = -2x + 3$.

17) B: Rewrite the equation in slope-intercept form, $y = mx + b$.
$$-2y + 4 = 6x$$
$$-2y = 6x - 4$$
$$y = -3x + 2$$

The slope of this line is –3, and the y-intercept is (0, 2). The slope of a perpendicular line will be the opposite reciprocal, $\frac{1}{3}$. Using the same y-intercept, (0, 2), write the new equation in slope-intercept form:

$$y = \frac{1}{3}x + 2$$

18) D: Use the quadratic equation to find the solutions.
$$2x2 - 5x + 2 = 0$$
$$a = 2, b = -5, c = 2$$
$$x = \frac{-b \pm \sqrt{b^2 - 4ac}}{2a}$$
$$x = \frac{-(-5) \pm \sqrt{(-5)^2 - 4(2)(2)}}{2(2)} = \frac{5 \pm \sqrt{25 - 16}}{4} = \frac{5 \pm \sqrt{9}}{4} = \frac{5 \pm 3}{4}$$
$$x = \frac{5 + 3}{4} = \frac{8}{4} = 2$$
$$x = \frac{5 - 3}{4} = \frac{2}{4} = \frac{1}{2}$$

19) A: Subtract $g(x)$ from $f(x)$.
$$(x2 + 6x) - (x - 2)$$
$$x2 + 6x - x + 2$$
$$x2 + 5x + 2$$

20) B: Use the formula for the area of a triangle. In this triangle, y is the base and x is the height.
$$A = \frac{1}{2}bh = \frac{1}{2}xy = \frac{xy}{2}$$

21) B: Find the circle's radius:
$$4\ km \div 2 = 2\ km$$
Use the radius to find the circumference of the circle.
$$C = 2\pi r = 2\pi(2) = 4\pi$$
Arc AB is a semicircle, which means its length is half the circumference of the circle.
$$4\pi \div 2 = \mathbf{2\pi\ km}$$

22) C: The mode occurs the most often, so the mode is pepperoni.

23) A: Use the given lengths to find the scale ratio for the two triangles:
$$\frac{AB}{DE} = \frac{24}{8} = 3$$

The ratio of *DF* to *AC* will also be equal to 3 because they are corresponding parts of the two triangles. Set up an equation and solve for *DF*:

$$\frac{AC}{DF} = 3$$

$$DF = \frac{AC}{3}$$

24) C: Identify the quantities:

number of shirts = *t*

total cost of shirts = 12*t*

number of pants = *p*

total cost of pants = 15*p*

number of pairs of shoes = *s*

total cost of shoes = 45*s*

The cost of all the items must be less than $2,500: $12t + 15p + 45s \leq 2500$.

25) C: Move the decimal point 6 places to the left so that *a* is between 1 and 10:

4,520,000

$$= 4.52 \times 10^6$$

26) C: Add 15 degrees to –7 degrees: $-7°F + 15°F = 8°F$.

Constructed Response

27) SAMPLE ANSWER: For the first scenario, let *x* be the number of apples sold and *y* be the number of oranges sold. Because apples are sold at $1.50 each and oranges are sold at $1.25 each, the total amount sold is equal to $1.50x + $1.25y$. The first customer purchased $36.50 worth of fruit, so $1.50x + 1.25y = 36.5$. We also know that they purchased 27 pieces of fruit. The sum of the two variables *x* and *y* is equal to 27, which results in the equation $x + y = 27$. Putting this together, the system of equations is:

$$x + y = 27$$

$$1.5x + 1.25y = 36.5$$

This system can be solved by the substitution method. Solve for *x* in the first equation to obtain $x = 27 - y$. Then, plug this into the second equation to obtain $1.5(27 - y) + 1.25y = 36.5$. This simplifies into $40.5 - 1.5y + 1.25y = 36.5$, or $40.5 - 0.25y = 36.5$, which reduces to $-0.25y = -4$. Dividing both sides by -0.25 results in $y = 16$ because $x = 27 - y, x = 27 - 16 = 11$. Therefore, 11 apples and 16 oranges were sold.

The second scenario involves a similar system; however, the right-hand side values are different because it is assumed that there are 30 pieces of fruit sold for $45. The corresponding system is as follows:

$$x + y = 30$$

$$1.5x + 1.25y = 45$$

We can attempt to solve this using substitution as well. Solve for x in the first equation to obtain $x = 30 - y$. Then, plug this into the second equation to obtain $1.5(30 - y) + 1.25y = 45$. This simplifies into $45 - 1.5y + 1.25y = 45$, or $45 - 0.25y = 45$, which reduces to $-0.25y = 0$. Dividing both sides by -0.25 results in $y = 0$. Because $x = 30 - y, x = 30 - 0 = 30$. Therefore, 0 apples and 30 oranges were sold in this scenario; however, it is assumed that the customer purchased both apples and oranges, so this scenario is not possible.

28) SAMPLE ANSWER:

(a) A stem plot is similar to a histogram because it can help you visualize the data set. It is called a stem plot because it breaks up the data into a stem (the largest place-value digit) and the leaf (the remaining digits). In our data set, there are three stems—0, 1, and 2—because there are values in the 20s, 10s, and single digits. It might be easier to create the stem plot by first listing the values from smallest to largest. The "stems,"—the 0, 1, and 2—are listed on the left of the plot, and the "leaves" are listed in order on the right. Here is the corresponding stem plot:

Stem	Leaf
0	3 9
1	0 1 1 2 2 2 3 4 4 5 5 5 6 7 8 9
2	0 0

(b) The mean can be calculated by adding up all the values and dividing that sum by the total number of values. The sum of all 20 values is 276, so the mean is $\frac{276}{20} = 13.8$. For an even number of data values, the median is calculated by finding the mean of the two middle values. In order, the two middle values are both 14 and 14, so the median is 14. Finally, the mode is the value or values that appear the greatest number of times in the data set. Both 12 and 15 appear 3 times, so there are two modes: 12 and 15.

(c) In order to find any outliers, scan the data for any extreme values. It appears that the value of 3 is an outlier since it is extremely low in comparison to the rest of the values. This means that this person only answered 3 out of 20 questions correct.

Subtest V: Physical Education

Selected Response

1) B: Non-locomotor skills, like bending, are usually movements that tend not to require moving through space.

2) B: Second graders may not be coordinated enough to play football; furthermore, the sport poses numerous safety hazards.

3) C: In light of information on lifelong health outcomes, ensuring that students develop a lifelong commitment to participate in physical activity is a very important goal for any physical education program.

4) A: The long jump is a solo endeavor, so it is most aligned with individual achievement—not group achievement.

5) B: The FITT principle (frequency, intensity, time, and type) should guide exercise planning.

6) B: Increased flexibility and range of motion can be improved via stretching and yoga; this decreases the likelihood of injuries, such as pulled muscles and falls, as students have a better ability to move their bodies.

7) C: Hopping on one foot will help students develop balance.

8) A: Students could observe the way force on the ball (e.g., throwing it and hitting it) leads to the motion of the ball.

9) C: Students at this age are likely not developmentally ready for the other answer options, so teaching them to know their parents' phone numbers would be the most appropriate.

10) D: In a balanced diet, vegetables make up the largest portion of the plate per the USDA guidelines.

11) D: Team or group activities are more likely to help children develop socially than individual ones.

12) B: Student choice stations can be set up so that there are options for students of various fitness levels and physical abilities.

13) B: Slight increases in duration of exercise will help students build endurance.

14) A: Growth spurts are a natural part of childhood, and children should be prepared for them.

Constructed Response

15) SAMPLE ANSWER:

1. Some students might have physical disabilities that limit their ability to run after the thrown balls. Such students could be given their own bucket of small balls or they could work with a partner who would be in charge of collecting the balls, allowing the students with limited running or walking mobility to throw each ball and still get to participate to the fullest extent possible in the group activity.

2. Some students might be able to throw the balls with great force and accuracy, making the game end quickly; other students might not be able to throw the balls with much force at all, causing the game to go on for too long. As a modification, students could be assigned ball types (e.g., beach ball, foam ball, kickball, tennis ball) based on their skill levels. They could then be instructed that they may only use their own ball type for each throw.

Subtest VI: Human Development

Selected Response

1) C: By fourth grade, most typically developing children will have the social-emotional maturity to part with parents easily when taken to familiar places, like school.

2) B: Spatial-visual intelligence allows people to perceive and analyze the visual world with ease. Making a map would be a great activity to allow such a student to shine.

3) B: Per Vygotsky's zone of proximal development (ZPD), a peer who is more experienced and capable with the task at hand—the "more capable other"—should provide guidance in the child's ZPD. Eventually, the child will be able to perform the task herself.

4) C: This is not evidence of a desire for autonomy, only a desire to eat.

5) C: A student who can identify her own anger and then take action to regulate that anger exhibits developed emotional regulation skills.

6) A: The child is assimilating the new information into existing schema, so this is assimilation.

7) A: The ability to hold a pencil is a fine motor skill that should be developed well before third grade.

8) B: In the industry versus inferiority stage, children begin to develop self-esteem in part through peer interactions; however, if not encouraged, they may feel inferior or doubt their abilities.

9) C: In the iconic stage, learners can interpret the world via images or pictures but not necessarily words or symbols.

10) A: Babbling usually occurs between six and twelve months of age, so a two-year old who has not begun to babble may need interventions.

11) B: Character development is more about morality and understanding right and wrong. This serves as a framework that undergirds prosocial behaviors, such as caring for others and being patient.

12) A: Childhood abuse can lead the person who is abused to behave aggressively toward peers.

13) B: By one year of age, children can identify when a caregiver is happy, upset, or even afraid.

Constructed Response

14) SAMPLE ANSWER:

Receptive language refers to the language that humans take in and understand through hearing, and expressive language refers to the human ability to express oneself in words by talking.

Receptive language may develop more quickly than expressive language, especially in environments where children are exposed to lots of language. This often means that children can understand more than they can say themselves in early childhood. By listening to those around them, children will then begin to model these patterns of oral language on their own, moving from cooing to babbling during the first year of life. At about age one, they will often say their first word and then increase to two-word communications in toddlerhood and to more advanced telegraphic speech patterns, like "See car go!" by age two and a half.

For students who are second-language learners, the silent period, or preproduction phase, should not be confused with an overall lack of expressive language development. As with children who are developing skills in a first language, second-language learners may have more developed receptive language skills than expressive language skills at first and may need significant time before they are comfortable trying to express themselves in a second language.

Subtest VII: Visual and Performing Arts

Selected Response

1) B: Using a hot glue gun could potentially be a safety hazard for younger students.

2) B: Teaching patterns is an appropriate introduction to the concept of rhythm.

3) B: Using the recorder is a great way to teach songs and ensembles without teaching a new instrument every time.

4) B: These colors are not directly opposite on the color wheel and are therefore not considered complementary.

5) A: Also called tone, timbre is used to distinguish between instrumental sounds.

6) B: Hip-hop dance styles also include breakdance and locking.

7) C: A sequence of related dance movements is called a phrase.

8) B: Improvised dances occur spontaneously; choreographed dances are planned.

9) A: Negative space is the space between dancers, so these students need practice with keeping enough negative space.

10) C: In a guided drama experience, an adult gives directions or lines to the performers as the play is performed.

11) D: Representational materials are real or actual props; in contrast, non-representational materials are things that are deemed to have another identity (e.g., a paper towel roll that becomes a sword).

12) B: Providing sound effects on cue with percussion instruments does not require oral language skills.

13) B: Texture refers to how visual art would feel if touched. Because collage tends to be three dimensional and/or involve various materials, it is most likely to have texture.

Constructed Response

14) SAMPLE RESPONSE:

Diego Rivera's painting "The Flower Carrier" tells the story of hard work and love. The painting features an image of a man crawling on his knees with a large wicker basket of flowers tied to his back. Behind him, a woman—most likely his wife—is helping him steady the heavy basket, most likely so he can stand and the flowers can be taken to a market for sale. This is the story of work, labor, and the struggle to support oneself and one's family; however, it is also the story of love and cooperation. Without his wife's help, there is little hope of the man getting the beautiful flowers to the market.

This image could be used as a mentor piece for a project in which students create a piece that tells the "story" of someone who has helped them overcome a challenge. Just as in the famous painting by Rivera, students could be asked to include an image related to their challenge and a depiction of the person who helped them overcome it in action by offering assistance.

Online Resources

Trivium includes online resources with the purchase of this study guide to help you fully prepare for the exam.

Practice Test

In addition to the practice test included in this book, we also offer an online exam. Since many exams today are computer based, practicing your test-taking skills on the computer is a great way to prepare.

Review Questions

Need more practice? Our review questions use a variety of formats to help you memorize key terms and concepts.

Flash Cards

Trivium's flash cards allow you to review important terms easily on your computer or smartphone.

Cheat Sheets

Review the core skills you need to master the exam with easy-to-read Cheat Sheets.

From Stress to Success

Watch "From Stress to Success," a brief but insightful YouTube video that offers the tips, tricks, and secrets experts use to score higher on the exam.

Reviews

Leave a review, send us helpful feedback, or sign up for Trivium promotions—including free books!

Access these materials at:

cirrustestprep.com/cset-multiple-online-resources

www.ingramcontent.com/pod-product-compliance
Lightning Source LLC
Chambersburg PA
CBHW080727230426

43665CB00020B/2646